PRIMARY

GREAT **WORSHIP** FOR KIDS

HE IS LORD

STANDARD PUBLISHING
Cincinnati, Ohio

Writers

Karen Wingate, Unit 1
Sharon L. Morphew, Unit 2
Vicki Ziese, Unit 3
Bonnie Hudson, Unit 4
Sarah Lyons, Unit 5
Debbie Pickett, Unit 6

Artists

Dan Grossmann—Pages 8, 12, 13, 91 Activity Pages 4B, 5B, 6A, 8A, 10B, 11B, 12A, 14B, 15B, 19B, 20B, 24B
Brenda Mann—Activity Pages 1A, 3B, 6B, 7B, 9A, 9B, 13A, 13B, 18B, 22A, 26A, 26B
Shauna Mooney—Pages 11, 14, 15, Activity Pages 5A, 8B, 12B, 14A,16A, 19A, 25A, 25B
Debora Weber—Activity Pages 1B, 2B, 4A, 21A, all other inside art
Sandy Wimmer—Title Page, Pages 2, 3, 5–7, 9–11, 121, 175, Activity Pages 2A, 3A, 7A, 10A, 11A, 15A, 16B, 17A, 17B, 18A, 20A, 21B, 22B, 23A, 23B, 24A

Library of Congress Cataloging-in-Publication Data

Great worship for kids. Primary.
p. cm.
ISBN 0-87403-841-3 (v. 1)
1. Worship (Religious education)
BV1522.G67 1991
268'.432—dc20 91-8431
CIP

Table of Contents

What Is Great Worship for Kids? 5
How to Use This Material 6
Worship Bulletins 8
Worship Plan Sheet 9
Activities for Special Days 11

Unit One: Worship God for His Creation
1. God Created the World 17
2. God Created the Animals 21
3. God Created You and Me 25

Unit Two: Worship God for His Promises
4. God Keeps His Promises 29
5. God Shows Us His Promises 33
6. God Keeps His Promise to Be With Us 37
7. God Keeps His Promise to Give Us Everything We Need 41
8. God Keeps His Promise to Provide Our Needs 45

Unit Three: Worship God for His Care
9. God Cares for Us by Giving Us Families 49
10 God Cares for Us Night and Day 53
11. God Cares for Us Wherever We Go 57
12. God Cares for Us by Giving Us Food and Water 61
13. God Cares for Us by Giving Us Rules 65

Unit Four: Worship God for Jesus
14. Joyfully Worship God for Jesus 69
15. Thank God for Jesus 73
16. Tell Others About Jesus' Birth 77
17. Honor God for Sending Jesus (Christmas Session) 81
18. Jesus Was a Special Child 85

Unit Five: Worship God for Giving Us Friends
19. God Gives Us Friends 89
20. God Shows Us How to Be a Friend 93
21. God Shows Us How to Be a Friend to Leaders 97
22. God Is A Friend to Those Who Are Happy or Sad 101

Unit Six: Worship God for Being Our Friend
23. God Is Kind to Those No One Likes 105
24. God Is Our Friend Even When We Do Wrong 109
25. God Forgives Us When We Do Wrong 113
26. God Is Our Friend 117

Activity Pages 121
Worship Songs 175

What Is Great Worship for Kids?

Welcome to 26 weeks of great worship sessions for your Primaries. What makes the worship a great experience for your kids? What is *Great Worship for Kids*? To determine what great worship is, we must first determine what it is not.

Great Worship for Kids is **not** a second Sunday-school hour. The emphasis in Sunday school is on instruction. The emphasis in worship is on worship.

Great Worship for Kids is **not** a mini-adult worship service. Primaries do not think like adults. Great worship for kids enables them to worship on their level of understanding and development.

Great Worship for Kids is **not** a service designed simply to keep children occupied while adults are in worship. The children's worship is as important and meaningful as the adult worship.

What **is** *Great Worship for Kids*? It is a program in which your Primaries truly worship God with understanding and have the opportunity to actively participate in worship. Primaries take part both in preparation and in actual worship.

Each session provides six small-group activity choices. In the small groups, children prepare to lead the call to worship, Scripture, prayer, special music, devotional, offering, Lord's Supper, or personal praise. As Primaries learn about God – who He is and what He has done, they are given opportunity to respond in praise and thanksgiving. Thus, Primaries are led to worship God.

When children participate in this worship program, they
KNOW Biblical concepts and basic skills of worship.
FEEL positive attitudes toward worship.
DO actively participate in worship.

When children prepare and lead the worship time, they learn the worship is giving, not receiving. Worship is active, not passive. Worship is my responsibility, not the responsibility of the person in front of the church.

Worship cannot be forced on anyone. But when children know who God is and what He has done, they can respond in love, praise, and thanks. Their response is true worship.

How to Use This Material

How Is This Material Organized?

This book contains 26 sessions. The sessions are divided into six units of three, four, or five sessions each. The units explore reasons for worshiping God. Worship God: for His creation, for His promises, for His care, for Jesus, for giving us friends, for being our friend. The sessions are based on Scriptures taken from Standard Publishing's Primary Sunday-school curriculum.

The sessions are planned so that children work in small groups to prepare the elements of the worship time (call to worship, Scripture, special music, devotional, and so on). The elements the small groups have prepared are then incorporated into the worship time.

Each weekly session is designed to last 80-95 minutes. This includes the time between the end of Sunday school and the beginning of adult worship.

The sessions are organized into six segments.

Worship Focus
Transition Time (10-15 minutes)
Launching the Theme (10 minutes)
Building the Theme (30 minutes)
Sharing in Worship (20-25 minutes)
Closing Moments (10-15 minutes)

What Happens in Each Segment?

Worship Focus

This section gives a reason for worshiping God. Worship God because . . . He knows everything; He is kind; He is the only God; He is our friend. Every activity in the session centers on the worship focus.

Transition Time
(10-15 minutes)

Transition Time is the flexible time between Sunday school and children's worship. This is a casual time for relaxation and conversation. It includes a rest-room and drink break, as well as a game which allows the children to move around freely. This freedom is important after they have been sitting during the Sunday-school hour.

Involving the children in organized activity as soon as they arrive also avoids confusion and eliminates the moments you spend gathering children from the halls when you are ready to begin the worship time.

Launching the Theme
(10 minutes)

During *Launching the Theme*, the leader introduces the theme of the session to the pupils. The leader may tell a Bible story or modern-day story, use puppets, present an object lesson, present a skit, or ask children to role-play. Involving children during this section is a priority.

The leader also explains the small-group choices and allows children to choose in which group to participate. The leader guides the children to choose groups they are interested in. Depending upon the maturity level and group dynamics of the children, the leader may assign groups, rather than letting children choose.

Building the Theme
(30 minutes)

During this time, children work in their groups to prepare the elements of the worship time: call to worship, prayer, Scripture, special music, group singing, Lord's Supper, offering, personal praise, or devotional. During *Sharing in Worship*, the children present what they prepared in their groups.

Sharing in Worship
(20-25 minutes)

The large group gathers for the worship time. The leader directs this time and integrates the small-group activities into the worship time. Thus, the children participate in worship.

Closing Moments
(10-15 minutes)

Closing Moments is the flexible time between the end of Primary worship and the end of adult worship. This section lists a variety of activities, but each one can be dropped quickly and easily when the adult service is over.

What Other Materials Will I Need?

Activity Pages

Following the worship sessions is a section of fifty-two reproducible activity pages—two pages for each session. The pages are used in a variety of ways—an introductory game, a cut-out craft, words to a song, a cut and fold book, and so on.

Worship Songs

The final section of this book contains worship songs which are incorporated into the worship sessions. You may wish to pull out the song section and place it in a looseleaf notebook for easy reference.

Classroom Supplies

See the Suggested Supplies on this page for a list of supplies you should have available every week. At the beginning of each activity is a list of materials you will need. Read the session early in the week and make a list of any special items or supplies you will need to gather ahead of time.

How Many Leaders Do We Need?

A coordinating leader is responsible to plan *Transition Time, Launching the Theme, Sharing in Worship,* and *Closing Moments.* You will need as many other leaders as you have small groups during *Building the Theme.*

What If We Have Only One Leader?

Shorten *Launching the Theme,* and lengthen *Building the Theme.* Choose two or three small-group activities to complete with your group. The devotional includes a leader talk which can be completed without a group presentation, so you would not need to complete that activity. Some activities can be completed without adult guidance. Write or tape record the instructions for a self-explanatory activity. Choose older or more mature children to complete the activity. Choose an activity that you can lead the rest of the group in completing at the same time as the self-explanatory activity. If you have time, choose another activity to complete as a large group. During *Sharing in Worship,* omit sections if you did not offer the corresponding activity. The Lord's Supper, Offering, and Devotional may always be completed without the group presentations.

What If We Worship First And Have an Activity Time Second?

Use the activity in *Launching the Theme* to introduce the worship time. Then proceed with worship, using the leader talk provided with each section and the devotional talk to tie in the worship to the theme of the day. During the activity time, choose group activities from *Building the Theme* which reinforce the concepts discussed in worship. If you have time, children may share what they have learned in their small groups at the end of the session rather than completing the activity in *Closing Moments.*

What If One Small Group Finishes Early?

If you have not chosen to do the self-explanatory activity for that session, have the materials available. Children who finish early can complete that activity. A challenge activity is also included in each section. This activity is for gifted or older pupils and will take longer to complete. If you have children who are consistently finished early, assign them to this activity. You may also wish to use one of the reproducible activity pages in each session as an optional activity to be completed by pupils who finish early.

Suggested Supplies

index cards
Bibles
markers
pencils, pens
crayons
tape recorder
blank cassette tape
paper fasteners
yarn or string
chalkboard and chalk
stapler and staples
push pins
old magazines/newspapers
scissors
glue
cellophane tape
Plasti-Tak
paper hole punch
plain paper
writing paper
construction paper
newsprint paper
poster board
paper towels/tissues

Primary Worship

Worship Plan Sheet

Session _____ Date__________
Unit Title__________
Session Title__________
Worship Focus__________

Transition Time

Leader __________
Materials: __________
Preparation: __________
Procedure: __________

Launching the Theme

Leader __________
Materials: __________
Preparation: __________
Procedure: __________

Building the Theme

Group 1. __________ Leader __________
Materials: __________
Preparation: __________
Procedure: __________

Group 2. __________ Leader __________
Materials: __________
Preparation: __________
Procedure: __________

Group 3. __________ Leader __________
Materials: __________
Preparation: __________

Procedure: ______________________

Group 4. ______________ Leader ______________

Materials: ______________________

Preparation: ______________________

Procedure: ______________________

Group 5. ______________ Leader ______________

Materials: ______________________

Preparation: ______________________

Procedure: ______________________

Group 6. ______________ Leader ______________

Materials: ______________________

Preparation: ______________________

Procedure: ______________________

Sharing in Worship

Leader ______________

Closing Moments

Leader ______________

Materials: ______________________

Preparation: ______________________

Procedure: ______________________

Activities for Special Days

Rhyming Turkey

Purpose: Children will say thank-you prayers to God.
Materials: A copy of pages 13 and 14 for each child, crayons or markers, glue.
Distribute the copies of pages 13 and 14. Give the children the following instructions.
1. Color the pictures on the wheel, and the small pictures.
2. Cut out the small pictures. Match and then glue the pictures to make pairs of rhyming words on the wheel.
3. Color the turkey. Cut out the rectangle on the front of the turkey.
4. Cut out the wheel. Place it behind the turkey.
5. Match the dot on the turkey to the dot on the wheel.
6. Use a paper fastener to attach the wheel to the turkey.
7. Turn the wheel and say the rhyming words.
8. Use the rhyming words to say a thank-you prayer to God.

Christmas Tree

Purpose: Children will make an ornament to remind them to joyfully celebrate Jesus' birth.
Materials: A copy of page 15 made on construction paper for each pupil; pencils; scissors; glue; paper hole punch; yarn; crayons or markers, glitter, rickrack, narrow ribbon, construction-paper scraps, paint and paintbrushes, gold or silver star stickers, Christmas stickers, and so on to use to decorate the tree.
Distribute the copies of page 15. Give the children the following instructions.
1. On the four trees, write or draw four ways you will celebrate Jesus' birth.
2. Cut out the four tree patterns. Fold the patterns down the middle.
3. Spread glue on one side of one folded tree. Place another folded tree on the glue. Now glue the top side of this tree and place another folded tree on the glue. Do the same with the fourth tree. Then glue the open ends together. Your tree should stand up.
4. Punch a hole in the top of the tree. Tie yarn through the hole.
5. Decorate the tree. You can punch holes with a hole punch in the tree. You can punch holes out of construction paper with a hole punch and glue them on the tree for Christmas bulbs. You can can glue rickrack or ribbon on the tree for lights. You can add stars to your tree or sprinkle glitter on it.
6. Hang the tree in your room or on your Christmas tree to remind you to joyfully celebrate Jesus' birth.

Cornucopia

Purpose: Children will make a gift for a friend.
Materials: A copy of the pattern on page 12 for each child; construction paper; scissors; glue; a stapler; yarn or ribbon; a paper hole punch;

glitter, fabric scraps, ribbon, rickrack, or other items to use to decorate; popcorn, candy, or other treats to fill the cones.

Distribute copies of the cornucopia pattern Give the children the following instructions.

1. Glue your activity page to a piece of construction paper.
2. Cut out the pattern.
3. Write a sentence to a friend on the construction paper side of your pattern. Tell your friend why he or she is special.
3. Form the paper in the shape of a cone and ask a leader to staple the cone together.
4. Punch a hole near the top of your cone. Tie yarn or ribbon through the hole to make a hanger.
4. Decorate your cone.
5. Fill your cone with treats.
6. Give the cone to your special friend.

Valentine's Card

Purpose: Children will make a valentine's card for a friend.

Materials: A copy of page 16 made on white construction paper for each child; scissors; pencils; glue; crayons or markers; wallpaper scraps, fabric scraps, or construction paper scraps to decorate the card.

Distribute page 16. Give the children the following instructions.

1. Cut out the card. Then cut out the heart shape on the card.
2. Fold the card where it says Fold 1 and Fold 2.
3. Use a pencil to trace the heart shape onto the paper beneath the cut-out heart.
4. Unfold your paper. Glue scraps of wallpaper, fabric, or construction paper inside the heart shape to make a patchwork pattern. Be sure to fill the heart completely. You don't need to stay in the lines.
5. Fold your paper again. Open your card and write a note to a friend or member of your family. Tell them why they are special.

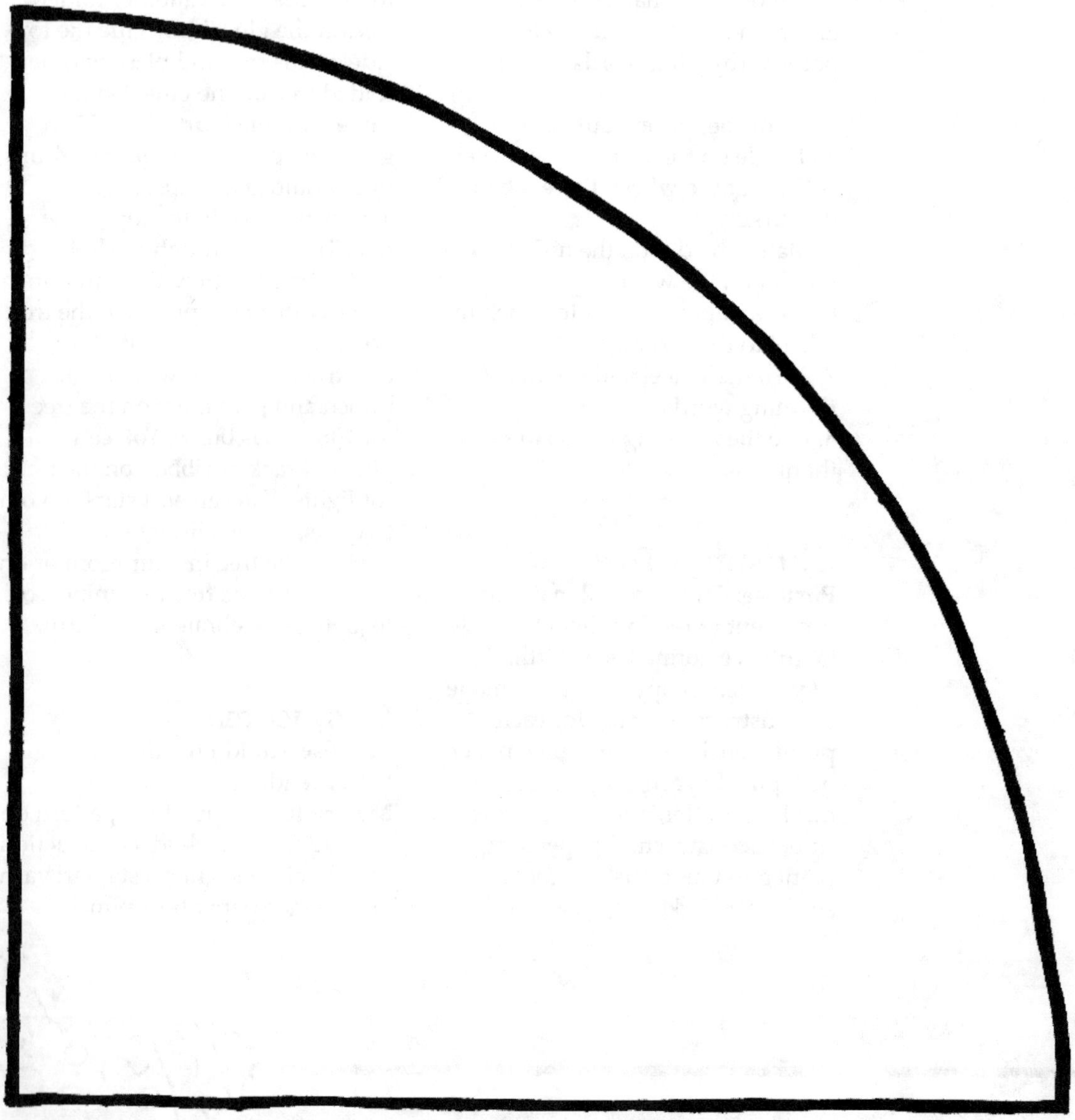

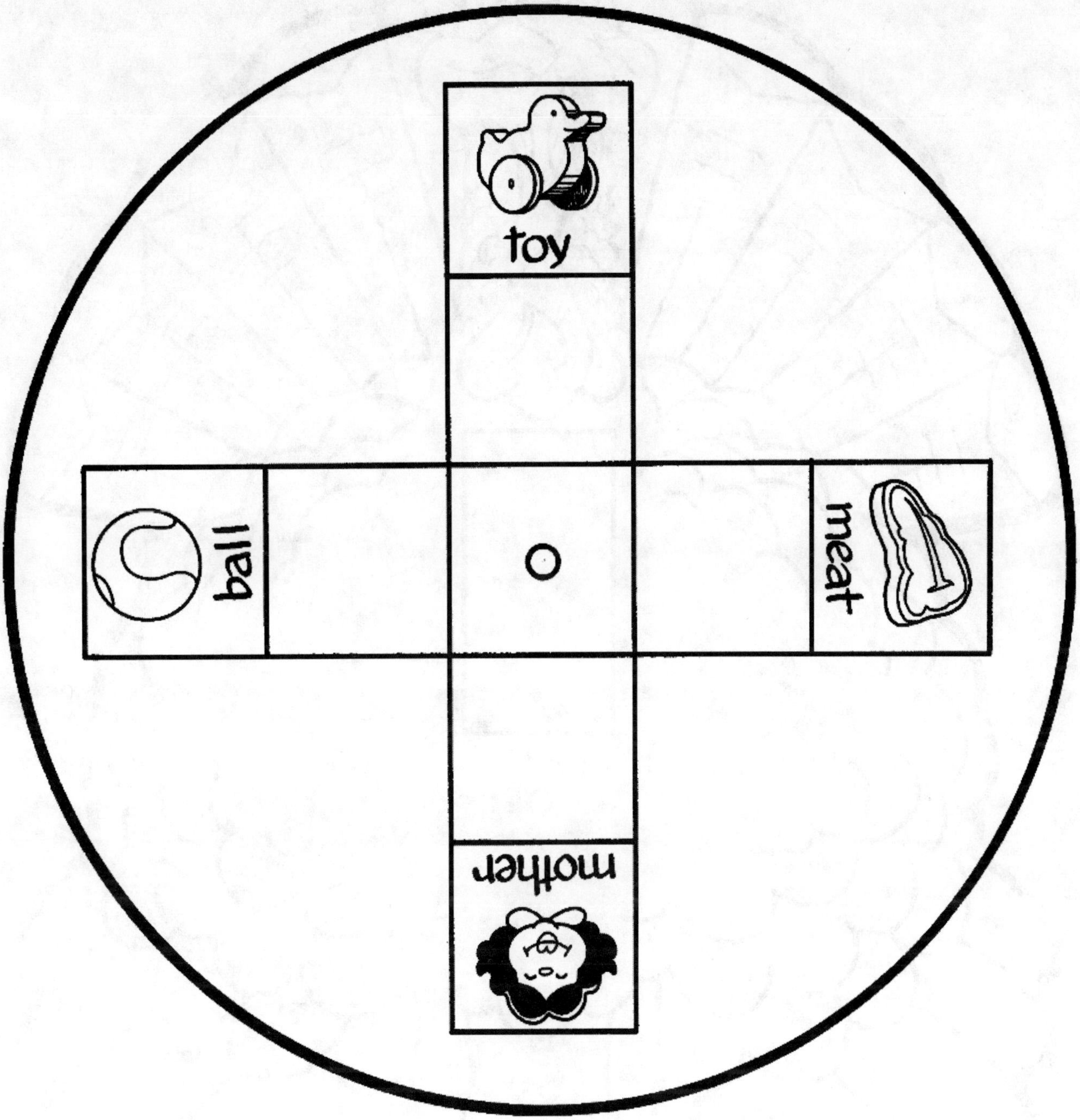
toy
ball
meat
mother

brother
eat
joy
all

God Created the World

Worship Focus

Worship God because He created the world.

Transition Time

(10-15 minutes)

Before today's session, find pictures of machines, such as cars, airplanes, space shuttles, or computers. Also find pictures of plants. Hide the pictures around the room. As the session begins, be sure to greet each child personally. As you speak to each child, tell him about the pictures hidden around the room. Encourage him or her to search for the pictures. If a child is reluctant to join in the search, go with him or pair him with an adult worker or another child. Praise each child as he or she finds a picture.

Launching the Theme

(10 minutes)

Gather the pictures and display them for the children. **Which picture shows the most complicated machine?** (Children answer. Display the picture of the space shuttle.) **A space shuttle has millions of parts. Scientists and engineers worked for many years to build a shuttle. They built and tested many different space shuttles before they found one that worked. And even though scientists have built a space shuttle, it still doesn't work all the time. Parts have to be fixed or changed or replaced. A space shuttle is a very complicated machine.**

(Display a picture of a plant.) **But even the simplest plant that God made is much more complicated than a space shuttle. A plant takes sunlight and changes it into food for itself. A plant takes carbon dioxide from the air and gives off oxygen. A plant produces a seed which will make an exact copy of itself. And a plant's machinery does not need to be fixed or changed or replaced.**

God made this wonderful machinery for plants, and He also made many, many kinds of plants. Flowers, trees, bushes, and grasses are beautiful to look at.

Not only are plants wonderfully complicated and beautiful to look at, plants are also good to look at. Scientists have discovered that the best color for our eyes is green! God even made the plants that cover most of our world in the color that is best for our eyes! Our God is amazing! Today we will worship God because He created the world.

Summarize the activities for *Building the Theme* and allow children to choose the groups in which they would like to participate. Have an equal number of pupils in each group.

Building the Theme

(30 minutes)

1. Call to Worship. This activity will be used during the next two sessions. Have a different group of children participate each week.

Provide pencils; tempera, finger, or watercolor paints; paintbrushes; old shirts or paint smocks; newspaper; and shelf paper. Prepare the work area by spreading newspapers under the table where you will work. Cut a piece of shelf paper a little longer than the length of the table and tape it to the table on both ends. Divide the shelf paper into four sections, and label the sections Day 1, Day 2, Day 3, and Day 4. Review what was created on the first four days of creation. Day 1: light, day and night; Day 2: air, sky; Day 3: land, seas, plants; Day 4: sun, moon, stars. Give each child a paint smock and a paintbrush. Assign each child or pair of children a day to illustrate. Ask the children to paint pictures of the things created on each day. They may wish to lightly sketch pictures with pencil and paint the sketches.

God created all these things from nothing. He is the only One who could do that. Why are you thankful for light? (It helps us see.) **Why are you thankful for air?** (We need to breathe it to live.) **Continue with the other things God created.**

During *Sharing in Worship*, children will display the mural. The child or children who painted each section will say, "God made ________ (objects painted). Thank You, God, for ________ (objects painted), because ________ (reason for being thankful)." For example, the first child could say, "God made light. Thank You, God for light because it helps us see." Practice the presentation with the children.

2. Scripture reading: This activity is for older or gifted children. You will need activity page 1A, crayons or markers, fourteen index cards, scissors, glue, tape, and poster board.

Only God could create the world from nothing. God said that every thing He created was good. Let's read verses from the Bible that tell about the good things God created. Read the verses from Genesis 1:1-19 *(ICB)* found at the end of this activity. You may wish to copy the verses on the chalkboard or a poster board before class, and display them for the children.

Distribute the activity pages to the children. Assign each child a picture or pictures to color and cut out. You will need four clocks (representing days), four happy faces (representing that God saw it was good), and one each of the other pictures (representing things God created). The children will glue each picture to an index card and put the pictures in order according to the verses. Then they will tape the cards in order to the poster board.

During *Sharing in worship,* each child will point to the card he or she made and say the sentence from Genesis 1:1-19 that corresponds with that picture. Have the children practice saying their sentences in order.

Option: Have the children repeat together at the appropriate times, "This was the first day," "This was the second day," and so on. You read the other sentences as children point to the pictures.

(Picture 1) God said, "Let there be light."

(Picture 2) God saw that the light was good.

(Picture 3) This was the first day.

(Picture 4) God made the air. God named the air *sky*.

(Picture 5) This was the second day.

(Picture 6) Then God said, "Let the dry land appear."

(Picture 7) God saw that it was good.

(Picture 8) Then God said, "Let the earth produce plants."

(Picture 9) God saw that all this was good.

(Picture 10) This was the third day.

(Pictures 11 and 12) God made two large lights. He also made the stars.

(Picture 13) God saw that all these things were good.

(Picture 14) This was the fourth day.

3. Offering. The children will worship God by caring for His creation. You will need newspaper, pencils, spoons, paper cups and saucers, potting soil, a pitcher of water, and house plant cuttings. (If you do not have any cuttings, ask parents or other church members to supply you with cuttings. Wandering Jew and spider plants are hardy house plants which will grow well for the children.) Spread the newspaper over the work area and lay out the supplies before the session.

Earlier we discovered some wonderful facts about plants. Our world could not exist without plants. How do plants help our world? (Children answer—keep the air clean, give us oxygen, make the world look beautiful, feed animals and insects.) **How can we worship God for giving us plants?** (Children answer—say a prayer, sing, or draw a picture to thank Him.) **One way we can worship God is by caring for plants.**

Give each child a cup and saucer, a spoon, a pencil, and a cutting. Give the children the following instructions, showing them each step as they pot the cutting: 1. Use a pencil to poke two or three holes in the bottom of your cup. 2. Fill your cup a little over half full of soil. 3. Make a small hole in the center of the soil with your thumb. 4. Place the end of the plant in the hole. 5. Fill the hole with dirt, tapping it down lightly with your fingers. 6. Place your cup on your saucer. 7. Add a small amount of water to your cup. If it begins running out the hole, you are adding too much.

How do we care for our plants so they don't die? We put them in a well lit place in our house and water them when the soil becomes dry.

During *Sharing in Worship,* each child will display his or her plant and tell where he or she will place it at home and how he or she will care for it.

4. Special Music. This group will learn the song, "The Seven Days of Creation" from page 177. The children will present it as special music.

You may choose to have piano, guitar, or autoharp accompaniment.Write the words to the song on a poster board or a chalkboard and display them for the children. Play or sing through the song once while the children listen. Then ask the children to sing with you. You may wish to assign each pair of children a different day. The children will take turns singing the line in the song which tells what God made on that particular day. For example, the entire group will sing "On the first day of creation the Lord God made for us." A pair of children will sing, "Light to light the earth." Then the group will join in with, "And the Lord saw that what He made was good."

If there is time after the children have learned the song, they may choose to cut out magazine pictures depicting creation and make a collage. The collage can be displayed as they sing.

5. Devotional. This group will provide a model of the sun and planets. You will need several colors of construction paper, scissors, glue, a large piece of cardboard, index cards, markers, and a picture of the sun and planets from an encyclopedia or science book.

God created our world perfectly. Our planet is the only one that has life on it. What does our planet have that the other planets do not have? (Water, air, plants, fish, birds, animals, humans.) **Today we will make a model to show the special, perfect way God created our planet.** Display the picture of the sun and planets for the children. Ask them to cover the cardboard with dark construction paper. Then ask them to decide where the sun and other planets should go on the cardboard. They will draw and color the planets on the construction paper. Then they will cut out the planets and glue them in the proper place. Have them copy the names of the planets and the sun on index cards and place the labels by the correct planets.

Option: You may wish to use a pencil to write the names of the planets and sun on index cards before class. The children can trace over the names with crayons or markers.

During *Sharing in Worship*, each child will point out and name the planet he or she made, and tell one thing the earth has that the planet does not have. For example, "This planet is Saturn. The earth has water, but Saturn does not have water."

6. Prayer. This group will prepare a tape about things God created. You will need poster board, construction paper, markers or crayons, a tape recorder, and a blank tape. Write the following interview questions on a poster board: What are you? Who made you? What did God say when He made you? How did you feel when God made you? What else was on the earth when God made you? What day of creation did God make you? What would our world be like without you? What would you like to say to God for creating you? Before the session, post the questions in a prominent place.

Only God could create the world from nothing. Imagine what it would have been like to see the world being created. What do you think creation sounded like? What do you think it looked like? How would you feel if you saw creation? Ask each child to choose something God made that they would like to pretend to be. Suggestions follow: Tree, flower, grass, ocean, stream, rock, dirt, mountain. Point out the interview questions and read them to the children. Ask them to draw a picture of the object they chose and think of answers to the questions while you interview.

Interview the children one at a time. Discuss answers before recording. Then turn on the tape recorder and ask the child the questions.

During *Sharing in Worship*, play the interview tape. Each child will display his or her picture as the interview is played.

Sharing In Worship
(20-25 minutes)

Omit any of the following sections if you did not offer the corresponding activity. The offering and devotional may be completed without the presentation of Groups 3 and 5.

Call to Worship (Group 1)**: God has made many beautiful things for us to enjoy. Today we will worship Him for the world He has created.** Ask Group 1 to present their mural.

Scripture Reading (Group 2): **God's Word, the Bible, tells us how God made the world God wanted the people in the world to have a written record of exactly how the world was made. Our Scripture readers will tell about the first four days of creation.** Ask Group 2 to present their story board.

Lord's Supper: Each week we have a special time during our worship. It is called the Lord's Supper. Jesus asked His friends to do this to remember Him until He comes again. This is a time when we think about Jesus and how much He loves us. You might want to give an explanation of who takes the Lord's Supper and why.

Offering (Group 3)**: There are many ways to worship God for making us and the world we live in. One way to worship Him is to take care of the world. The children in Group 3 discovered a way to care for God's world.** Ask Group 3 to present their plants. **Another way we worship God for making us is by giving Him our money. Let's worship God by giving now.** Pray and ask two children from Group 3 to collect the offering.

Special Music (Group 4): Ask Group 4 to sing "The Seven Days of Creation." The large group may join them on the repeating phrases.

Devotional (Group 5)**: Think of all the things God has made! It would be a pretty dull world without them. Can you imagine what our world would be like without any sun or water or flowers? Close your eyes for a moment. Try to shut out any sounds around you. Think about what it must have been like before God created anything. There is absolutely nothing around you. That's hard to imagine, isn't it?**

God took special care in creating each part of our world. And He did it in an orderly manner. What would have happened to the plants if He had created them first? There would be no water or light to help them grow. And each time He finished a day of creation, He said Himself that it was good. It was good. It was perfect.

Only God could create a perfect world. Some people will try to tell you our world

happened by chance. They say there was an explosion, and the world suddenly appeared. But the chances of such a perfect world evolving from a chance explosion is nearly impossible. The children from Group 5 discovered some facts about how special our world is. (Ask children from Group 5 to present their model.) **God had planned a beautiful orderly world when he created the earth. He placed the earth exactly the right distance from the sun, so that it wouldn't be too hot or too cold for life. He put a special gas around the earth to protect it from the sun's rays. This gas is called ozone. Without ozone to protect us from the sun, we could not live. God even tilted the earth a little bit, so that the whole planet could have day or night. If the earth weren't tilted, one side would be hot and sunny all the time, and the other side would be cold and dark.**

Let's think of some ways we can worship God for His fantastic creation. We can thank Him when we pray. We can admire His work. We can take time to enjoy a beautiful flower or pretty sunset and say "Thank You, God" as we enjoy it. We can take care of His world and not destroy it. We can pick up litter, be careful what we throw away as garbage, and we can plant trees and plants to keep our world beautiful. When we take care of God's world, we are telling Him that we appreciate the beautiful world He has given to us.

Personal Praise (Group 6): **Imagine what it would have been like to see and hear creation. The children from Group 6 will help us pretend that we were at creation.** (Play the interview tape as children display their pictures.)

Prayer: **We have talked about many reasons to worship God for His creation today. Think of one thing you would like to thank God for making. We'll go around the circle and name the things we are thankful for.** (Ask the child on your left to begin. Close with prayer when each child has named one thing.)

Closing Moments
(10-15 minutes)

Make sure the room is clean and everything is put away. Give each child a copy of activity page 1B and a pencil. The children are to find things God created by writing the first letter of each picture on the line below the picture. See if the group can figure out the words without any help. First graders may find this a bit challenging so be available to help or, if they are compatible, pair up first graders with second graders. The answers are: light, earth, sky, land, seas, trees, grass, flowers.

Suggested Resources

Gish, Duane T., *The Amazing Story of Creation from Science and the Bible* (Institute for Creation Research), 1990.

National Geographic

Your Big Backyard

Unit One
Worship God for His Creation

Session 2

God Created the Animals

Worship Focus

Worship God because He created the animals.

Transition Time
(10-15 minutes)

Send children in groups to the rest room or drinking fountain. Greet children as they arrive and involve them in the following game.

Animal Charades. Before the session, print animal names on separate slips of paper. Suggestions follow: monkey, elephant, dog, cat, kangaroo, crab, rabbit, shark. Each child will draw a slip of paper and act like the animal he or she drew. Children may use motions, but not words. The other children will guess what animal is being portrayed by saying, "God made (name of animal)."

Launching the Theme
(10 minutes)

You will need pictures of a spider in a web and a woodpecker.

Last week we looked at the world God created out of nothing. He made light and dark, earth and sky, land and water, sun and moon, and all the living plants. On the fifth and sixth days of creation God made all the animals. He made everything from the tiny flea to the giant elephant. He made birds to fly in the sky and fish to swim in the ocean. He made your pet dog and the wild mountain lion. Only an all-powerful God could create so many animals from nothing!

God made each animal special and able to survive in the place it lives. Display the picture of the spider in the web. **Have any of you seen one of these in your yard?** Pupils respond. **God made the spider able to produce silky strands in order to build a web. The spider makes one kind of smooth strand to build the main part of his web, and he uses a sticky strand in the middle of his web where he will trap insects. The spider makes a flower design with the strands in his web. How does the spider know to use sticky strands in the middle of the web? How does he know to make a flower design? The spider knows because God made the spider special.** Display the picture of the woodpecker. **How many of you have seen or heard a woodpecker? God made the woodpecker perfectly. He gave him a hard beak to peck holes in tree trunks. And he gave the woodpecker special cushions in his head to keep him from getting hurt when he pounds his beak on the tree. God gave the woodpecker a <u>long</u> tongue that he can use to find small bugs and insects in the holes in the tree. And since the woodpecker's tongue is so long, God gave him a special place to keep it. The woodpecker's tongue stays curled up under one nostril when he isn't using it.**

It is amazing how God designed each animal perfectly! Today we will worship God for creating the animals.

Explain the six small group activities to the children. Ask that those who worked on the mural last week go to another activity. Suggest that older children might be interested in the Animal Facts activity.

Building the Theme
(30 minutes)

1. Call to Worship. The children will continue creating a mural for the days of creation. Day number five and part of day six will be added to the mural this week. You will need a large sheet of newsprint, colored chalk, hair spray or clear fixative spray, and damp paper towels for clean up. Before the session, cover the work area with a large sheet of newsprint. Tape the newsprint to the table at both ends. Divide the newsprint into two sections. Label the sections Day 5 and Day 6. Read Genesis 1:21, 25 with the children. **What are some sea creatures that God created? What are some birds? What are some wild animals? What are some farm animals? What are some reptiles?** Make a list of the children's answers. Ask them to choose an animal from the list to draw on the mural using colored chalk. Birds and fish will be drawn in the section labeled Day 5. All other animals will be drawn in the section labeled Day 6. When the mural is completed, spray it with hair spray or clear fixative spray. Attach it on the wall next to the first section of the mural which was completed last week. Ask the children to clean their hands using damp paper towels. **Why are you thankful for birds?**

For fish? For wild animals? For farm animals? For reptiles?

During *Sharing in Worship*, each child will point to the picture he or she drew and say, "God made (creature he or she drew). I am thankful for (animal he or she drew) because (reason he or she is thankful)." Practice the presentation with the children.

2. Scripture. You will need a poster board, squares of paper, a glue stick, and crayons or markers. Before the session, print Genesis 1:21, 25 on the poster board. "So God created the great creatures of the sea and every living and moving thing with which the water teems according to their kinds, and every winged bird according to its kind. And God saw that it was good. God made the wild animals according to their kinds, the livestock according to their kinds, and all the creatures that move along the ground according to their kinds. And God saw that it was good."

Display the poster board for the children and read the verses aloud to them. Ask them to think of pictures for some of the words of the verses. Make a list of their picture ideas. Suggestions follow: water for *sea*; bird for *bird*; a happy face for *good*; a lion for *wild animals*; a cow for *livestock*; a snake for *creatures that move along the ground*. Assign each child a picture or pictures to draw on the squares of paper. Glue the pictures over the words on the poster board and practice reading the rebus Scripture together.

During *Sharing in Worship*, the children will display the rebus poster and read the Scripture once for the large group. Then they will ask the large group to join them in reading the Scripture a second time.

3. Prayer. This group will create animals out of clay or dough. Provide clay or dough for each child in the group, or have children work in pairs. Their task will be to create a new animal and name it. If the children need suggestions, ask them to choose favorite parts of animals they already know and combine them.

What can God's creations do that our creations can't do? (Encourage the children to be specific—walk, jump, hop, bark, growl, chew, hear, see, and so on.) Make a list of the children's answers on chalkboard or poster board.

During *Sharing in Worship*, each child or pair will display the animal and explain it. Then they will say a sentence prayer to God, naming one thing their animal can't do that God's creation can do. For example, "Dear God, My animal can't hop. Only You can make animals hop."

4. Special Music. This group will be writing new words to the tune, "The Farmer in the Dell." You will need poster board, a marker, and the song "God Made the Animals" from page 179. Before the session, write the following words on the poster board:

"God made the birds.
And God made the fish.
God made the animals.
Oh, we will worship God."

Read Genesis 1:21, 25 for the children. Then display the poster board. **We will sing a song to worship God for creating animals. This song is to the tune "The Farmer in the Dell."** Sing the song once for the children. Then ask them to sing through the tune on "da" while you sing the words again. The third time, ask them to sing the words with you. Practice the song several times.

What is your favorite bird that God created? Your favorite fish? Your favorite animal? Create new stanzas for the song, substituting the children's answers for the words *birds*, *fish*, and *animals*. An example follows.

"God made the doves.
And God made the sharks.
God made the kangaroos.
Oh, we will worship God."

Practice singing the song with the new stanzas. The children may draw pictures of the animals on the poster board if there is time. During *Sharing in Worship*, the children will display the poster board and sing the song.

5. Devotional This group will learn some interesting facts about animals. This activity is for older or advanced children. You will need copies of Activity page 2B, pencils, a tape player and cassette tape (optional), pictures of a lynx and salmon, poster board and markers.

Distribute the activity sheets and pencils. **What is an environment?** (The place where you live. The objects and weather and people that surround you.) **God made each animal perfect for its environment. Some animals live in cold environments, and God gave those animals thick skin or fur. Some animals live in very hot environments. God gave those animals the ability to go a long time without water. Today we are going to learn about two animals that God made perfect for their environments. Look at the questions on your activity page. I am going to read about the lynx and the salmon. Listen for the answers to the questions as I read.** Display the pictures of the lynx and salmon as you read the following paragraphs to the children. You may wish to record the paragraphs on a cassette tape before the session.

"A lynx is a large cat. A lynx hunts at night. He looks for food without making a sound. He has a stumpy tail, long bushy hair across his cheeks and throat, and large yellow eyes. He lives in Canada where it is very cold. His inch-thick fur keeps him warm in the winter. He has very furry feet. His furry feet help him walk on top of the snow without sinking.

"Baby salmon are born in rivers. When they are only a few months old, they start to swim downstream to the ocean. The trip to the ocean takes several years and is very long and hard. Salmon live for two or three years in the ocean. Then they swim back to the river where they were born. When they reach the river, they lay eggs for new baby salmon to be born."

Ask the children to choose the correct answers on their activity pages. The answers are: 1. a large cat, 2. at night, 3. his furry feet, 4. rivers, 5. 2 or 3 years, 6. back to the river.

If children have time, ask them to prepare a poster, using the pictures of the salmon and lynx. The poster should include ways God made the salmon and lynx perfect for their environment.

During *Sharing in Worship*, play or read the paragraphs about the lynx and salmon for the large group. If children made a poster, display it for the large group. Then ask children from the small group to read the questions from the activity page and allow the large group to choose the answers. Assign questions to children ahead of time and allow the children to practice reading the questions.

6. Personal Praise This group will write and illustrate books about their favorite animals. You will need copies of activity page 2A for the children, construction paper, glue or tape, crayons or markers, and pencils.

Distribute copies of activity page 2A and construction paper to the children. Ask them to glue or tape the activity page to the construction paper and fold it in half crosswise, so that the activity page is on the inside. **What is your favorite animal? Print the name of your favorite animal on the front of your book.** Allow children time to do so. Help children with spelling as needed. **Now open your book. What is one special thing about your animal? Print or draw a special thing about your animal on page one of your book.** Be sure children write on the left-hand side of their papers. Give suggestions as needed. **What will you say to God to thank Him for your animal? Print or draw your thank-You prayer to God on page two.** As time allows, ask children to decorate and color their book cover and borders.

During *Sharing in Worship*, each child will read or explain his or her animal book to the large group.

Sharing In Worship
(20-25 minutes)

Omit any of the following sections if you did not offer the corresponding group activity. The devotional may be completed without the presentation of Group 5.

Call to Worship (Group 1): **God made every kind of animal on days five and six of creation. Listen as Group 1 tells us about some of the special animals God made.** Group 1 presents.

Music: Lead the children in "The Seven Days of Creation" from page 177.

Scripture (Group 2): **Group 2 is going to read for us exactly what the Bible says about what God created.** Group 2 reads. Ask the large group to read with them a second time.

Prayer (Group 3): **Only God can create living things. Group 3 discovered some differences between what we create and what God creates.** Group 3 explains their new animals and prays.

Lord's Supper: Communion is a special time when we remember that Jesus took the punishment that we deserve for all the wrong things we have done. Read 1 Corinthians 11:23b-26 from the *International Children's Bible.* Pray and serve the Lord's Supper.

Offering: We worship God by giving money to help our church grow and to help others learn about Jesus. Pray, thanking God for the money the children have brought. Then ask two children to collect the offering.

Special Music (Group 4): Group 4 sings "God Made the Animals."

Devotional (Group 5): **So far this morning, we have talked about many kinds of animals. What are some of the animals we have mentioned?** Have the children name off different animals as quickly as they can. After about one or two minutes, stop the brainstorming and continue with the devotion. **We have listed many different animals. Yet there are many more that we haven't even mentioned! I am so glad God didn't make just one or two kinds of fish, two kinds of birds, and several different animals. Our world would be pretty dull. But He created thousands of different species of animals, each special and different from any other kind of animal. Only a God who is powerful and can do anything could fill our earth with so many special animals. One of our groups found out some interesting facts about two animals.** Have Group 5 tell the others about the lynx and the salmon now. If you did not offer this activity, read the paragraphs about the lynx and salmon printed in the instructions for Group 5. **God made many different animals. He also made each very special. He gave each animal special characteristics or tools to help it live where God wanted it to live. A lynx needs a lot of fur around his feet to keep him safe from the snow and ice. But if he lived in a hot area of the world, he wouldn't need all that fur. God made him just right to be able to live in a cold place.**

Man has made many

wonderful things: the airplane, the spaceship, the television. But man can't make living things. We made some wonderful new animals today. Group 3 told us about the animals they made. But they can't make their animals move on their own or make noise or eat or breathe. God made the animals so they can eat and breathe and move and have babies. Our God is a powerful, special God, isn't He?

Personal Praise (Group 6): **The children in Group 6 praised our powerful, special God for their favorite animals.** The children from Group 6 read and explain their animal stories. When they are finished, close with a short prayer, thanking God for making animals.

Closing Moments

(10-15 minutes)

Ask the children to help you clean the room by returning all supplies to the cabinets, putting all chairs back in order, erasing the chalkboard, putting all scraps in the trash can, and gathering all personal belongings.

Play the following game. Print the letters of the alphabet on the chalkboard. Ask the children to think of an animal name for each letter of the alphabet. For example, aardvark, bee, chicken, dog, and so on.

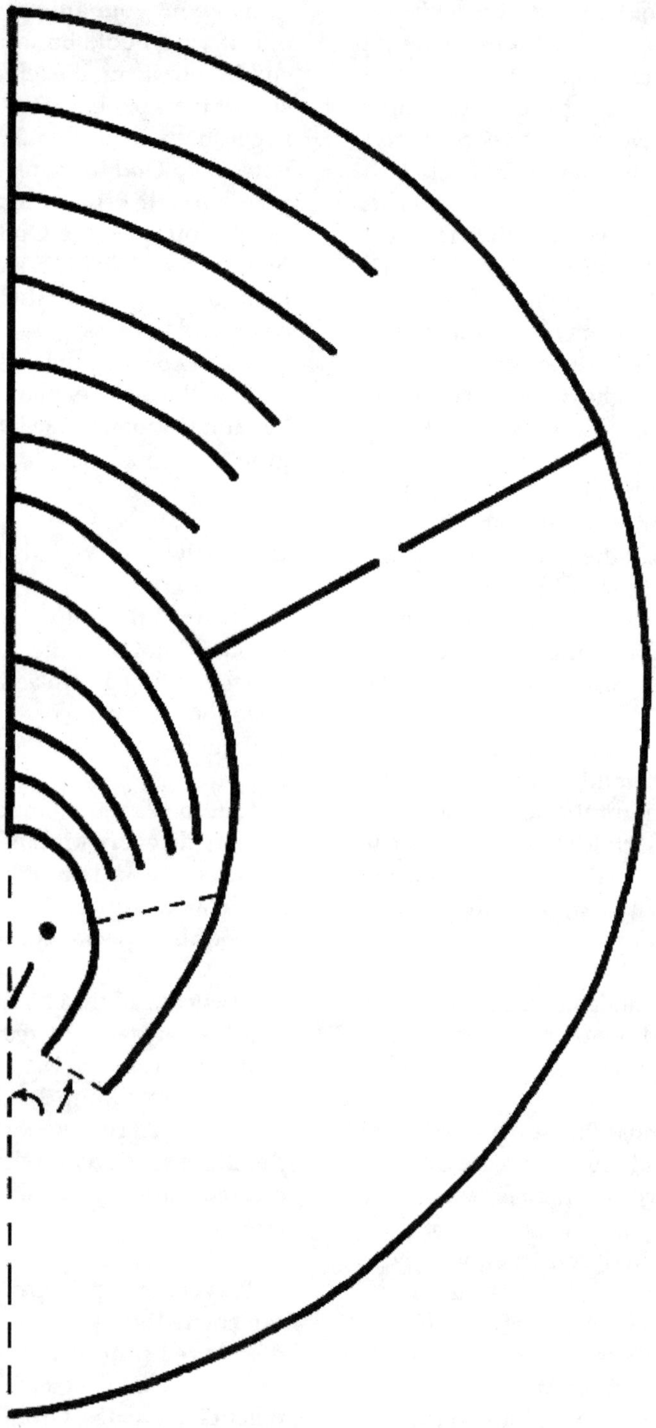

Suggested Resources

Gish, Duane T., *The Amazing Story of Creation from Science and the Bible.* (Institute for Creation Research), 1990.

National Geographic

Your Big Backyard

God Created People

Worship Focus

Worship God because He created people.

Transition Time

(10-15 minutes)

Send the children in small groups to the rest room and drinking fountain. As children arrive, involve them in the following activity.

Five Senses Grab Bag. Before the session, gather objects that can be identified by sight, sound, touch, taste, or smell. Suggestions follow: sight—pictures of places, animals, products, or people; sound—scissors, crackling paper, piano, bouncing ball; taste—lemon, sugar, salt; smell—apple, flower, chocolate; touch—dirt, sand, rice, macaroni. Place all the objects in a paper bag. Provide a blindfold.

Children will take turns identifying the objects using only one of their senses. When they taste, they must hold their noses. They must be blindfolded for all objects except the sight objects.

Launching the Theme

(10 minutes)

You will need a picture of an animal and a picture of a person.

What if I asked you to hear the apple, or see the salt, or smell the scissors, or taste the sand? God gave us five different senses so we could experience the world around us as much as possible. He made our bodies in an amazing way.

Last week, we talked about the many kinds of special animals that God made. Display the picture of the animal. **This week, we're going to talk about the most special creation of God—people.** (Display the picture of the person.) **In some ways, animals and people are very much alike. What are some ways we are like animals?** (We both breathe, eat, have hearts, stomachs, muscles, and so on.) **But God made people different and more special than the animals. Do you know how people are different from animals?** (Allow children to respond.) **People can think and feel. We can laugh and cry. We can love and care about other people. And people can know God and talk to Him. Animals can't do those things. Let's praise God today for making us so special.**

Divide the children into groups for *Building the Theme*. Before class, write the name of each activity on an index card. Write the names of the activities in six different colors.. Cut out equal numbers of strips of construction paper using the same colors you used on the cards. Distribute the strips to the children and ask them to go to the activity which corresponds with the color of their strip.

Building the Theme

(30 minutes)

1. Call to Worship. This group will complete the Creation mural begun in Session one. Provide a large sheet of newsprint paper; markers; pencils; scissors; glue; and fabric scraps, felt, yarn, ribbon, or buttons. Before the session, tape the newsprint paper to the table in the work area. Label the newsprint **Day 6.**

Read Genesis 1:26, 27 with the children. Distribute the materials, and ask them to create pictures of people. They may draw pictures of themselves, their friends, or their families. They may sketch the picture in pencil, and then glue the fabric on the sketch.

What are some special things that people can do that no other part of God's creation can do? Children respond. Suggestions follow: think, invent, plan, love, cry, pray to God, love God.

During *Sharing in Worship*, the children will display the mural. Each child will point to his or her pictures and name one special thing about people. Then he or she will say, "Thank You, God, for making people special." For example, People can pray to You, God. Thank You, God, for making people."

2. Scripture. This group will learn a verse to present to the large group. You will need activity page 3A, crayons or markers, and pencils.

Distribute the activity page to the children. Read the verse at the top of the page together with them. "I praise you because you made me in an amazing and wonderful way. What you have done is wonderful. I know this very well. (Psalm 139:14). **God made each one of us amazing and wonderful! What is one**

amazing, wonderful thing you like about yourself? (Allow children to share. Give suggestions as needed so that each child names one thing.) Ask the children to complete the activity page by drawing a picture of themselves, printing the thing they like about themselves, and printing a thank-You prayer to God. When the children have completed the page, practice reading Psalm 139:14 together several times.

During *Sharing in Worship*, the children will read Psalm 139:14 together. Then the children will display the activity pages and name the amazing, wonderful things that they like about themselves.

3. Music. This group will write new words to the song "God Is So Good" to praise God for making people. You will need the song "God Made Me" from page 179, a poster board or chalkboard, and markers or chalk. You may wish to record the song accompaniment on a cassette tape before class. Write the words to the first stanza on the chalkboard or poster board and display them for the pupils.

God made Adam and Eve on the sixth day of creation. But the Bible tells us that God has made you too. Because we are made in God's likeness, we are very precious to Him. One way we know that God loves us is because He made us. Today we will write new words to a song that thanks God for making us. Sing the song with the children several times. Then ask them to write new stanzas for the song, replacing the words "eyes," "hair," and "toes" with other parts of them that God made. Suggestions follow: mouth, ears, tongue, elbows, thumbs, ribs, heart, stomach, knees, legs, heels. Write the new stanzas on the poster board. Practice singing the song many times. Pupils may illustrate the song on the poster board if time allows.

During *Sharing in Worship*, children will display the poster board and sing the song for the large group.

4. Personal Praise. This group will make puppets of themselves to praise God for making them special. You will need paper plates (one for each child); yellow, brown, black, and red yarn; glue; craft sticks; and markers.

Do all people look alike? (No.) **No two people are exactly the same. God made each one of us a little bit different. We look different on the outside. We have different hair and eye color and different faces and different heights. But we're also different on the inside. We feel different ways about things, and we're good at different things. God made each of us very special. We are going to praise God today for making us special.** Distribute the materials to the children, and ask them to make a paper-plate puppet of themselves. They can draw with markers and use yarn for hair. Ask them to glue a craft stick to the back of their puppet. **What is one special thing about yourself? What will you say to thank God for that thing?**

During *Sharing in Worship*, the children will display their puppets and say a special thing about themselves. Then they will say, "Thank You, God, for making me special."

5. Devotional. This group will praise God for our five senses. You will need paper cups, water, salt, sugar, lemon juice, grape or fruit-flavored gum, two crayons (taped together), a clock with a loud tick. Before the session, put a small amount of salty water, sugar water, or lemon juice in each cup.

At the beginning of the session, we played a game using our five senses. Can you name our five senses for me? (Sight, smell, taste, hearing, touch.) **We are going to do some experiments using our five amazing senses!**

Give each child a cup. Ask half of the children to pinch their noses closed while they taste the liquid. The other half will taste without holding their noses. **How does the liquid taste? Do you need to smell to taste these things?** (No.) **God made our tongues able to taste sweet, salty, and sour things.** Give each child a piece of gum with the label removed. Ask half of the children to pinch their noses while they chew. The other half will chew without holding their noses. **What flavor is the gum? Do you need to smell to taste this?** (Yes.) **How does you food taste when you have a bad cold? It doesn't taste as good, does it? Our sense of smell helps us taste better.**

Ask children to close their eyes while you lightly touch the points of the crayons to their necks. **How many crayons did you feel?** (One.) Now touch the crayons to the children's fingers. **How many crayons did you feel?** (Two.) **Why did you feel a difference?** (Children respond.) **God made our fingers able to feel things better than our necks. Why?** (We touch many things with our fingers. We need to be able to feel more with them.)

Ask the children to close their eyes. Stand a few feet away from them and hold the ticking clock. **I want you to tell me when I move closer to you and when I move further away.** Slowly move towards the children, then away. **You heard the sound better when the clock was closer. How does sound reach our ears?** (The sound makes the air move (vibrate). When the moving air reaches our ears, it makes our eardrums move. When our eardrums move, they send tiny messages to our brain to tell us we hear a clock ticking.)

Choose an object across the room to look at. Cover one eye with your hand. Now hold up

your finger in front of the object to block it. Hold your finger in the same place and cover the other eye. What happened to your object? (Pupils answer.) **You can see it now. Why?** (Allow children to respond.) **Each eye takes a picture of the object. The brain puts both pictures together to help us know how big and far away the object is.**

During *Sharing in Worship*, the children will present these experiments for the large group. Assign children to prepare and present parts of the presentation. Depending upon the age and maturity of your children, you may wish to lead the discussion yourself with children assisting in distributing the materials.

6. **Prayer.** This group will compose a prayer to praise God for making the world. You will need a poster board and markers.

What did God make on the first day of creation? On the second day? Continue with the six days of creation. **Everything God made is special and important. What would our world be like if God had not made the sky or water or birds?** (Let children discuss.) **What would happen to us if there was no sun? What would our world look like without plants or trees? Can you imagine an entire world that looks like the Sahara desert—nothing but sand?** (Let children answer.) **God had a special purpose for each part of his creation. It needed to be there to make the perfect world He had planned. Today we will write a prayer to God to worship Him for making the world.**

Assign each child a day of creation. If you have more than six children, assign more than one child to each day. If you have less than six children, assign children more than one day. Ask them to think of a one or two sentence prayer, thanking God for what He made on that day of creation. Print the prayers on the poster board in order. If time allows, ask children to draw pictures of things God created on the poster board.

During *Sharing in Worship*, children will display the poster board and say their prayers to God. Practice saying the prayers in order during the small-group time.

Sharing In Worship
(20-25 minutes)

Omit any of the following sections if you did not offer the corresponding activity. The devotional may be completed without the presentation of Group 5.

Call to Worship (Group 1): Read Genesis 1:26, 27. Then ask Group 1 to present their mural.

Songs: Sing "The Seven Days of Creation" (#1) and "God Made the Animals" (#2).

Scripture (Group 2): **What are good words to describe how God made us? The Bible says God made us amazing and wonderful! Group 2 discovered some amazing, wonderful things about themselves.** Ask Group 2 to read their Scripture and present their activity pages.

Special Music (Group 3): Group 3 will present their song.

Lord's Supper: God doesn't want us to forget that He loves us, so He gave us the Lord's Supper to help us remember. The bread reminds us that Jesus' body was broken when he died. The cup reminds us that Jesus gave His life for us by giving His blood to take the punishment for the wrong things we have done. He loved us a lot! Pray and serve the Lord's Supper.

Offering: Remind children that sharing their offering is another way to worship God and to thank him for His love. Ask volunteers to pass the offering container.

Personal Praise (Group 4): **God made each person different on the outside and on the inside. Group 4 discovered some special and different things about themselves.** Ask Group 4 to present their puppets.

Devotional (Group 5): **For the last two weeks, we have been talking about how we can worship God because He made everything in our world. God saved the best for last. His best creation is us! We are very special to God because the Bible says we are made in His image. That means we are more like God than any other part of creation, and we are very special to Him. No other part of creation can think or talk or learn like people can. And only people can worship God and tell about Him.**

Have you ever thanked God for making you exactly the way you are? Maybe there are times that you don't like yourself or you wish you were someone else. God likes you just the way you are because He made you. And He made you different from everyone else in the world. Look at your hands. Isn't it amazing that your fingers move just the way your brain tells them to? You breathe without even thinking about it most of the time. God has made you in an amazing and wonderful way! The children in Group 5 discovered some amazing, wonderful things about our bodies. Ask Group 5 to present their experiments. If you did not offer Group 5, present the experiments to the entire group now. See Group 5 for materials and instructions.

God is the only one who could create you and all the rest of this magnificent world. We can worship God because of the wonderful things He has done. Who remembers what it means to worship God? (Let one or two children respond.) **To worship means to tell God how wonderful He is and how much we love and appreciate Him. We're going to worship God now**

through our prayer time by thanking Him for all the wonderful things He has made including you and me.

Prayer (Group 6): Ask the children to stand and form a circle. Ask the children from Group 6 to share their prayers. Close with prayer, thanking God for His amazing creation!

Closing Moments

(10-15 minutes)

After the room has been cleaned up and everything put away, give each child activity page 3B and a pencil. Ask the children to write in the small circles. the number of the day each object was created.

Suggested Resources

International Children's Bible

International Children's Handbook

National Geographic

Unit Two
Worship God for His Promises

Session 4

God Keeps His Promises

Worship Focus

Worship God because He keeps His promises.

Transition Time
(10-15 minutes)

As children assemble, allow them to go to the rest room and drinking fountain. Prepare the room for the following game.

Animal Alphabet Hop. You will need twenty large paper plates and a marker. Before the session, print the first letter of the name of an animal that could have been on the ark on each paper plate. Arrange the paper plates on the floor in two sets of ten. If you have a large class, make more sets of plates. Place the plates close enough to each other for a child to hop from plate to plate.

Divide the children into two teams. At your starting signal, the first child in each team stands by the first paper plate and names an animal that starts with that letter. Then he or she hops to the next paper plate and names another animal. When the child has named an animal for each paper plate, he or she tags the next person in line who then begins naming animals and hopping. The new player should not repeat names used by the player before him or her. Teams may help hoppers by calling out animal names for each letter. The team whose players finish first, wins.

Launching the Theme
(10 minutes)

Provide an animal sticker for each child. Use as many different kinds of animals as you have small groups. Place a blanket or a sheet over a table to represent Noah's ark. Gather the children under the blanket. If your class is too large to sit under a table, use building blocks to form an ark for your class to sit in.

Here we are all together in the ark. Listen. I hear a cow and an elephant. Now I hear a tiger. What animals can you hear? Why are we with all these animals in this ark? (Discuss.) **Listen, I hear something falling on the roof. What do you think that sound could be?** (Rain.) **Why is it raining so hard? How long is it going to rain?** (Discuss.)

Will Noah and his family and all the animals be safe? How do you know? (God promised Noah they would be safe.) **What is a promise?** (Something you say you will do.) **God always keeps His promises. He always does what He says He will do. Did God keep His promise to Noah? How?** (Yes. He saved Noah and his family from the flood.) **What does God promise us?** (To be with us, to help us do right, to hear our prayers, to give us what we need.) **Will God keep His promises to us? Of course He will! God always keeps His promises.**

Ask the children to find other children who have matching animal stickers. Assign each group to an activity.

Building the Theme
(30 minutes)

1. Call to Worship. The children in this group will read a poem about God's promises. You will need copies of activity page 4A.

One way we can worship God is by praising Him with a special poem. Why are we praising God today? (He keeps His promises.) Distribute copies of activity page 4A. **This poem tells about how God kept His promise to Noah. We are going to practice reading it together and then we will present it to the class during the worship time.** Divide into two groups. Group one will read together verse one. Group two will read together verse two. And both groups will read together verse three. Let each group practice reading their verse several times together. Decide how the verses should be read with expression or motions. For example, children could hold up two fingers for "two by two" and three fingers for sons all "three." Children could say "whine" and "fuss" in a whining and fussy voice. Children could start very softly on the last verse and build to a very loud voice by the last line. Group 2 will display animals and people mentioned in the poem during the reading. You may wish to practice the presentation with them at this time.

During *Sharing in Worship*, the pupils will read the poem for the large group, using the expression and motions they practiced.

2. Call to Worship. The children in this group will create Noah, his family, and animals to assist Group 1 in presenting the Call to Worship. You will need copies of activity page 4A, small paper cups, colored construction paper, scissors, glue, markers, crayons, pencils, felt scraps, buttons, chenille wire, and yarn.

Today we are worshiping God because He keeps His promises. One way we can worship God is through a poem. Distribute activity page 4A to the children. Read the poem with the children. **To whom did God keep a promise in this poem?** (Noah—God saved him, his family, and the animals from the flood.) **Group 1 is going to read this poem for the large group. We are going to make some people and animals to display as they read the poem.**

Distribute the materials to the children. Assign them a character or animal from the poem to create. Suggestions follow: two lions, two bears, two kangaroos, two cows, two pigs, two goats, Noah and his wife, Noah's three sons and their wives. Pupils can draw faces on their cups and use construction paper for ears or yarn for hair or beards. They can use chenille wire for arms or whiskers. They can use buttons for eyes.

When the pupils have completed their characters, read the poem aloud as they display their animals or people at the appropriate time during the poem. You may wish to practice the presentation with Group 1 at this time.

During *Sharing in Worship*, Group 2 will display their animals and people while Group 1 reads the poem.

3. Special Music. This group will learn a song about God's promises. You will need the song "God's Promise Is a Promise" from page 180, poster board, and markers. Before the session, print the words to the song on the poster board. You may wish to tape record the accompaniment to the song on a cassette tape.

What promise did God make to Noah? (To save him from the flood.) **Did God keep that promise?** (Yes.) **What promises does God make to us?** (To be with us, to take care of us, to give us what we need.) **Will God keep His promises to us? How can we be sure of this?** Display the poster board and play or sing "God's Promise Is a Promise" for the children. Then use the echo method to help the children learn the song. (You sing a line, and they repeat it.) Practice the song until the children are comfortable singing it. If time allows, children may illustrate the song on the poster board.

During *Sharing in Worship*, the children will display the poster board and sing the song. Then they will sing the song again, asking the large group to join them.

4. Scripture. This group will prepare a poster of a verse about God's promises. You will need a poster board, seven sheets of construction paper, markers, and Plasti-Tak or tape.

Today we worship God because He always keeps His promises. Print the words to Isaiah 38:7 on a chalkboard. "The Lord will do what he says." **What are some promises God makes to us?** (To be with us, to take care of us, to give us what we need, to help us do right, to hear our prayers, to take us to Heaven when we die.)

Distribute the seven pieces of construction paper. The children will fold the paper in half horizontally and write one word of Isaiah 38:7 horizontally on the folded sheet. On the inside of the folded paper, they will illustrate a promise God makes to us. For example, they could draw a child praying for "God hears our prayers," a home or food for "God gives us what we need," a child alone in the dark for "God will always be with us." Put tape or Plasti-Tak on the back of the papers, so children can attach them to the poster during *Sharing in Worship*. Pupils that finish their pictures early can draw a border for the verse on the poster board.

During *Sharing in Worship*, the children will present their pictures in the order of the verse words. Each child will show the picture and tell the promise God makes, then attach the paper to the poster board. After each child's picture is shown, the group will say, "The Lord will do what he says." Practice the presentation several times during the small-group time.

5. Devotional. The children in this group will create a wall montage of Bible people to whom God kept His promises. You will crayons, markers, construction paper, scissors, glue, and Plasti-Tak. Before the session, cut letters out of construction paper for the title **God Keeps His Promises**. Attach the letters to the wall with Plasti-Tak.

What promise did God make to Noah? (To save him, his family, and the animals from the flood.) **Did God keep His promise?** (Yes.) **God always keeps His promises. Can you think of other Bible people to whom God made promises?** (Allow children to respond.) Read the following Scriptures to the children—1Kings 17:4-6—ravens brought bread and meat to Elijah; 1 Kings 3:12; 4:29—God gave Solomon wisdom; Genesis 6:17, 18; 7:23—God saved Noah and his family from the flood. After each Scripture is read, ask **To whom did God make a promise? What was the promise? Did God keep His promise?** Divide the children into three groups. Assign each group a Scripture. Ask each group to draw a picture of their person and draw a picture of something about the promise God made to them. Suggestions follow: Elijah—bread, meat, a brook, a bird; Solomon—a book, a brain; Noah—an ark, water, animals. When the children have completed their pictures, use Plasti-Tak to attach them to the wall around the title you prepared before the session.

During *Sharing in Worship*, children will point to the pictures they drew, tell who the Bible person is, and tell what promise God kept to the person. Practice the presentation during the small-group time.

6. Prayer. This group will compose prayers thanking God for keeping His promises. You will need copies of Activity Page 4B, scissors, pencils, and glue.

What promise did God keep to Noah? (To save him and his family from the flood.) **What promises does God make to us?** (To be with us, to listen to our prayers, to help us do right, to take care of us.) Distribute copies of Activity Page 4B. **These children need to remember a promise God made to them. Listen as I tell you about each picture. Then choose a promise at the bottom of the page that we can remember. Look at the top picture. Justin is afraid of being alone in the dark. When are you afraid? What promise can we remember when we are afraid?** (I will protect those who know me.) **Look at the bottom picture. Sarah is sad because her best friend is leaving town and moving away. When are you sad? What promise can we remember when we are sad?** (I will never leave you.) Ask the children to cut out the promises and glue them below the pictures. Ask each child to choose a time when he or she is afraid or sad to tell the large group.

During *Sharing in Worship*, each child will name the time he or she is afraid or sad. Then the group thank God for the two promises from the activity page by saying, "Thank You, God. You promise, "I will protect those who know me. I will never leave you."

Sharing in Worship
(20-25 minutes)

Omit any of the following sections if you did not offer the corresponding activity. The devotional can be given without the presentation of Group 5.

Call to Worship (Groups 1 and 2): Group 1 will recite their poem while Group 2 displays their animals and people. **God kept His promise to Noah, and He will keep His promises to us. God always keeps His promises.**

Song: Sing "God Is So Good" from page 181.

Lord's Supper: God's most important promise was His promise to send His Son, Jesus. The Lord's Supper helps us to remember how God kept His promise. Pray and serve the Lord's Supper.

Offering: We worship God because He keeps His promises. One way we worship God is by giving an offering to Him. Choose two children to collect the offering.

Special Music (Group 3): **We can learn poems about God's promises. We can read about God's promises. And we can sing about God's promises. Group 3 will teach us a song called "God's Promise Is a Promise."** Group 3 will sing the song once. Then they will sing the song again, asking the large group to sing with them.

Scripture (Group 4): **God has made many promises to us. And God will keep every one of those promises. Group 4 will share a verse that says God will keep His promises.** Ask children from Group 4 to present their poster.

Devotional (Group 5): **I want you to raise your hand if you have told your mom or dad that you would pick up your all your toys in your room. When you told your mom or dad you would do something, that was a promise. Now put your hand down if you did not pick up all your toys. Did you keep your promise?** (Let children answer.) **Many people don't keep their promises. But Who always keeps His promises?** (Let children answer.) **That's right. God always Keeps His promises. The children in Group 5 found three Bible people who God made promises to. Let's see how God kept those promises.** Ask children from Group 5 to tell about Noah, Solomon, and Elijah. If you did not offer this activity, read the Scriptures listed in the activity now and ask the corresponding questions.

In the Bible, we can read about many more promises that God made to many, many people. But we can not find one time when God did not keep a promise. God kept His promises to the people in the Bible. God will keep His promises to us!

Closing Prayer (Group 6): **Let's thank God now for keeping His promises to us.** Ask children from Group 6 to share times they are sad or afraid and thank God for keeping His promises.

Closing Moments
(10-15 minutes)

Animal Relays. Have the children find their partner by finding the child who has a matching animal sticker. (See *Launching the Theme.*) Now have the children form a double line. The children are to imitate the animal on their sticker as they race to get to the ark (a table or wall to use as a goal). As soon as one child touches the goal, the next child in line may start. The first team to reach the ark safely wins. **Hurry, it's starting to rain. Run quickly to the ark so you will be safe.** Once the animals are all safely in the ark say, **Here we are, all safe in the ark. God promised to keep us safe. And God always keeps His promises.**

Unit Two
Worship God for His Promises

Session 5

God Shows Us He Keeps His Promises

Worship Focus

Worship God because He shows us He keeps His promises.

Transition Time
(10-15 minutes)

Allow time for a rest room and drink break. As children arrive, involve them in the following game.

Red, Red Rainbow. Before the session, arrange the chairs in a circle. Ask children to sit in the circle. Choose one child to be "It." "It" will walk around the circle tapping gently on the children's heads. As "It" is tapping he or she will say, "Red, Red, Red, Red, Rainbow." The child who is tapped when the word "Rainbow" is said will get up and chase "It" back to his or her spot in the circle. The child who did not reach the empty space first will be "It" for the next round. The next round will be "Orange, Orange Rainbow," then yellow, green, blue, and purple.

Launching the Theme
(10 minutes)

You will need a blanket or sheet, several colors of construction paper, and markers. Before the session, place a blanket or sheet over a table to represent Noah's ark. Make name tags for the children in as many different colors as you have small groups. Assign each small group a color that corresponds to one of the name tag colors. Gather the children under the blanket. If your class is too large to sit under a table, use building blocks to form an ark for your class to sit in.

Well, here we are all together again in the ark. The rain is coming down harder than ever. How long has it been raining? (Forty days and forty nights.) **Why were Noah and his family and all the animals kept safe in the ark?** (God promised to keep them safe.)

Listen, the rain has finally stopped. Let's all climb out of the ark. (Everyone should crawl out of the pretend ark.) **Oh, it feels so good to be outside again. Everything is so fresh and clean. Will God ever flood the whole world again?** (Discuss.) **How do we know that God won't flood the earth again?** (Guide the students to respond with the fact that God gave us a sign—the rainbow.) **When we see a rainbow, we can remember God's promises.**

Distribute the colored name tags to the children. Ask them to print their names on the name tags. Send children to the small-group activity that corresponds with the color of their name tags.

Building the Theme
(30 minutes)

1. Call to Worship. This group will present a verse for the Call to Worship. You will need different colors of construction paper, pencils, crayons or markers, scissors, and glue or tape. Before the session, cut the construction paper into strips 1" to 1 1/2" wide. You will need seven strips for each child in the group.

What is worship? (Telling God how special He is.) **God is special and different from us. One way God is different is that He always does what He says. What are some things that you say you will do for your mother? Your father? Your brother or sister? Your teacher? Your friend?** (Give pupils suggestions if needed—I will pick up my toys; I will go to bed without fussing; I will not lie; I will do my homework; I will always be your friend.) **Have you done what you said every single time?** (No.) **We can't always do what we say. But God always does what He says.** Read Isaiah 38:7 with the children. "The Lord will do what he says." Ask them to say the verse with you several times. Distribute the strips to the children. Ask them to write one word of Isaiah 38:7 on each strip and tape or glue the strips together to make a paper chain. Ask each child to choose one thing that He has told someone he will do to share with the large group during the worship time.

During *Sharing in Worship*, each child will tell the thing he or she promised to do, and say that he or she may not always be able to keep that promise. After each child shares, the whole group will say, "But the Lord will do what he says." For example:

Child: I told my teacher I would do my homework. I may not always do my homework.

Group: But the Lord will do what he says.

2. Special Music. This group will sing the song "God's Promise Is a Promise" using puppets for the worship time. You will need the song "God's Promise Is a Promise" from page 180, copies of activity page 5B, construction paper, scissors, craft sticks, and glue.

Play or sing "God's Promise Is a Promise" for the children. Then ask them to sing along with you. Distribute activity page 5B. Ask the children to glue the page to construction paper and cut out the figures. Then ask them to glue the puppets to craft sticks. Use a table turned on its side for a puppet stage. Ask the pupils to sing the song using the puppets. Practice the song many times.

During *Sharing in Worship*, children will sing the song using the puppets.

3. Scripture. The children in this group will make praise bookmarks to mark verses about God's promises. This activity is for older or gifted children. You will need copies of activity page 5A, crayons or markers, scissors, and glue.

We will praise God today for keeping His promises. God has made many promises to us. Where can we find those promises? (In the Bible.) **Today we will read verses about God's promises and make bookmarks to help us praise God for keeping those promises.** Read the following verses from the *International Children's Bible* with the children—John 3:16; Philippians 4:19; 1 John 5:15. After each verse is read, ask **What does God promise us in this verse?** (John—Jesus will save us, we will live forever; Philippians—God will give us everything we need; 1 John—God will listen to us.) Distribute the activity pages to the children. Read the verse on the bookmarks out loud together. **Today our mouths will praise God for keeping His promises.** Ask the children to decorate the bookmarks with crayons or markers and cut them out. They will then fold on the dotted lines and glue or tape the bookmarks together. When they are completed, the bookmarks should fit over the top edge of book pages. Divide the children into three groups. Assign each group a Scripture to read. The group will mark the Scripture pages in their Bibles using the bookmark.s

During *Sharing in Worship*, the groups will read their Scriptures. After each Scripture is read, the whole group will say, "My mouth will speak in praise of the Lord."

4. Personal Praise. This group will create rainbows to praise God for His promises. Provide large paper plates, scissors, 1" squares of tissue paper (red, orange, yellow, green, blue, purple), unsharpened pencils, glue, a paper hole punch, and yarn or string. Before class, make the rainbow shapes by doing the following. Cut the paper plates in half to form a half circle, cut out the center, and draw six guidelines to separate the colors.

What did God use to show His promise to Noah? That's right. He put a rainbow in the sky. We are going to make rainbows to help us remember the promises God makes. Does God always keep His promise? Of course, He does! Show the children how to take a piece of tissue paper and press it around the end of a pencil. They will press this into a small amount of glue and then press the tissue paper onto the paper plate to form a rainbow. When the rainbows are completed, punch holes in the top and string yarn through the holes for hanging.

What is a favorite promise that God makes to you? (Pupils respond.) **What will you say to God to worship Him for that promise?** Ask each child to say a worship sentence thanking God for a promise. Suggestions follow: Thank You, God, for promising to always be with me. God, I'm glad you promise to take care of me. God, You promise to keep me safe. You are the only One who can do that.

During *Sharing in Worship*, children will display their rainbows and say their worship sentences to God.

5. Devotional. The children in this group will create a wall montage, illustrating how God shows us His promises. Provide crayons, markers, construction paper, scissors, glue, and Plasti-Tak. Before the session, cut out the letters for the title **God Shows Us His Promises.** Use Plasti-Tak to attach the title to the wall.

How did God show Noah He would keep His promise never to destroy the earth again with a flood? (With a rainbow.) **God has given us some things to show us He will keep His promises. What has God given us to show He will keep His promise to take care of us?** (Parents or guardians, shelter, food, clothes.) **What has God given us to show He will let us live forever?** (He sent Jesus to die, and Jesus came back alive.) **What has God given us to show us He will never destroy the whole world again?** (The seasons never stop; day and night never stop.) Make a list of the children's answers on a chalkboard or poster board. Assign each child one thing to illustrate. When the children have completed their pictures, use Plasti-Tak to attach them to the wall around the title.

During *Sharing in Worship*, each child will point to his or her illustration and explain how that thing shows a promise of God. For example, for a picture of Jesus, the child could say, "God promises we will live forever. God shows us we can live forever because Jesus came back alive." For a picture of parents, a child could say, "God promises to take care of us. God shows us He takes care of us by giving us parents."

6. Prayer. Pupils will present situations and prayers about God's promises. You will need three pieces of poster board and markers or crayons. Before the session, write one of the following promises in large letters on each piece of poster board: God forgives the wrong things we do. God says we will live forever. God is always with us.

What are some of God's promises? How has God kept those promises? (Pupils respond.) **Listen to these stories and look at the promises. I want you to tell me which promise the child in each story needs to remember.**

Jessica's grandma is very sick. Jessica is afraid her grandma will die. She would miss her grandma very much. What promise should Jessica remember? (God says we will live forever.)

Chris isn't supposed to play with his older brother Jeff's radio-controlled car. One day Chris sneaked into Jeff's room to play with his car, and he wrecked it. Chris told Jeff he was sorry, but Jeff is so mad he says he will never forgive Chris. Chris feels terrible. What promise should Chris remember? (God forgives the wrong things we do.)

Sarah spends two hours alone at home every day after school because her mom and dad don't get home until suppertime. Sarah gets tired of playing games or watching TV, and sometimes she's afraid to be by herself. What promise should Sarah remember? (God is always with us.)

Divide the children into three groups. Give each group a poster board. Ask them to illustrate the story about the promise on the poster board and write a prayer, thanking God for keeping that promise.

During *Sharing in Worship*, you will read the situations. After each situation is read, the children will display the corresponding poster board and say their prayer to God.

Sharing in Worship
(20-25 minutes)

Omit any of the following sections if you did not offer the corresponding activity. The devotional may be completed without the presentation of Group 5.

Call to Worship (Group 1): **We say we will do many things, but we don't always do what we say. God always does what He says He will do.** Group 1 presents their Scripture and paper chains about God's promises.

Special Music (Group 2): Group 2 sings "God's Promise Is a Promise" using puppets.

Scripture (Group 3): **We can worship God by telling about His promises and singing about His promises. We can also worship Him by reading His promises in the Bible.** Group 3 will read the Scriptures they have marked.

Lord's Supper: God give us things to remind us of His promises. Jesus has given us things to remind us of His love. The Lord's Supper reminds us of Jesus' death on the cross for our sins. Let's remember Jesus now.

Offering: We worship God because He shows His promises. One way we can worship God is by showing our love to Him by giving an offering to Him. Choose two children to collect the offering.

Personal Praise (Group 4): **Think of all the promises God has made to you? What is your favorite promise? The children in Group 4 praised God for their favorite promises.** Group 4 presents their rainbows and praise sentences now.

Devotional (Group 5): **Who is your favorite football player? What team does He play on?** (Allow children to respond.) **When that player wanted to play on that team, he signed a contract. This contract is an agreement between the football player and the team. This agreement is like a sign to the team. It means that the football player promised to only play on that team. God made an agreement with us. He promised to never flood the whole earth again. The sign of this agreement was the rainbow. God also promised that day and night would not stop. God promised that the seasons of the year would not stop. The children in Group 5 found even more ways God shows us He keeps His promises.** Group 5 presents their promise wall. If you did not offer this activity, lead the following discussion. **God has given us some things to show us He will keep His promises. What has God given us to show He will keep His promise to take care of us?** (Parents or guardians, shelter, food, clothes.) **What has God given us to show He will let us live forever?** (He sent Jesus to die, and Jesus came back alive.) **What has God given us to show us He will never destroy the whole world again?** (The seasons never stop; day and night never stop.) After the presentation or discussion, continue with the devotional thoughts.

Every time we see the sun and the moon, the winter snow, the spring rain, or the autumn leaves, we can remember God keeps His promises. When we look at our parents, or eat our meals, or buy new clothes, we can remember God keeps His promises. And every time we see a rainbow in the sky, we can remember God keeps His promises.

Prayer (Group 6): **Group 6 learned about some children who need to remember God's promises.** Read the stories as the children display the poster boards and say their prayers.

Closing Moments

(10-15 minutes)

Rainbow Races. Have the children stand close together in a huddle with their colored name tags. Then on the count of three all the children try to find the missing colors of the rainbow. For example the child with a red name tag would try to find the children with the orange, yellow, green, blue, and purple name tags. As each rainbow is formed have these children sit together in a circle. **We worship God because He gave us a sign of His promises—the rainbow.**

Unit Two
Worship God for His Promises

Session 6

God Keeps His Promise to Be With Us

Worship Focus

Worship God because He keeps His promise to be with us and guide us.

Transition Time
(10-15 minutes)

As children assemble for the worship time, allow them to go to the rest room and to get a drink of water. While the children are out, prepare your room for the following game.

Traveling to Canaan. Use tape or chalk to make two parallel lines on the floor as far apart as possible (about 20 feet or more). Choose a child to be "Canaan." He or she stands with his or her heels on one line and his or her back to the other children. The other children line up behind the other line with their toes on the line. They are "Abraham" traveling to the land of Canaan.

At a signal, "Canaan" counts to five and then turns quickly around. While he or she is counting, each child moves toward "Canaan" as quickly as possible by putting one foot in front of the other in a heel-to-toe fashion. When "Canaan" reaches the count of five, the other children must freeze in their spots. If "Canaan" catches anyone moving, that child must return to the starting line and begin again. The winner is the first person to make it across the line into the land of Canaan. He or she then becomes "Canaan" and the first "Canaan" joins the others.

Launching the Theme
(10 minutes)

You will need several pieces of luggage or other items you would take on a trip. Before the session, print the numbers of the small-group activities you are offering on slips of paper. Label each paper **Activity Map**. Make as many maps for each group as you want children in the group.

Display the luggage for the children. **Are we all ready? Abraham is getting ready to leave on a trip. Let's pretend we are going with him. What do you think Abraham will take with him on his trip?** (Some responses could be his wife Sarah, nephew Lot, servants, animals, tents, food, clothes.) **Do you know why Abraham is going on a trip?** (God told him to leave his country.) **Does Abraham know where he is going?** (No.) **How would you feel if you had to move to a new place without knowing where you were going?** (Scared, worried.) **Do you think Abraham was scared?** (Probably not.) **Why wasn't he scared?** (God promised to take care of him and lead him to a new home.) **Did God keep His promise to Abraham?** (Yes. God gave Abraham a new home.) **Does God promise to take care of us when we travel? Yes, He does. He promises to always be with us and to guide us wherever we are.**

Describe the small-group activities to the children and distribute the activity maps to them. Ask them to go to the activity whose number corresponds to the number on their paper.

Building the Theme
(30 minutes)

1. Call to Worship. This group will create a wall montage, praising God for times He is with them and guides them. You will need construction paper, crayons or markers, scissors, and tape or Plasti-Tak. Use the title **God Keeps His Promises** that you used last week.

What promises did God make to Abraham when God asked Him to leave his home and his land? (God promised to be with Him and to show him where to go.) **Did God keep His promises?** (Yes. He gave Abraham a new home.) **God also promises to be with us and to guide us. When are some times that God is with us? Where are some places that God is with us?** (Allow children to respond.) Make a list of the children's suggestions. Examples follow: in the classroom, during a test, when I'm mad, at the playground, when I'm asleep, when I'm alone. Distribute the construction paper and crayons or markers. Ask the children to illustrate a time God is with us. Use tape or Plasti-Tak to attach the children's pictures to the wall around the title.

During *Sharing in Worship*, each child will point to his or her picture and tell the time God is with us.

2. Scripture. This group will make badges to remind them of a Scripture verse about God's promises. You will need large white name tags (self-sticking type), scissors, colored markers or crayons.

What did God promise to Abraham? (To be with him and to guide him) **Does God make that promise to us too? Let's look in the Bible to find out.** Ask the children to find ????? in their Bibles. Read the verse to them from the *International Children's Bible*. "I will be with you." Ask the children to say the verse with you several times.

Distribute the name tags to the children. Ask them to print "I will be with you" on each name tag. They will make enough badges for all the children in the large group. You may wish to print the verses on the name tags before class. Ask the children to decorate the badges, using markers or crayons.

During *Sharing in Worship*, children will distribute the badges to the group. Then they will say the verse from memory. They will say the verse a second time, asking the large group to join them.

3. Special Music. The children in this group will present a song about God's promises. You will need "The Lord Will Do What He Says" from page 181. Before the session, print the words to the two stanzas on a poster board. Leave room on the poster board for the children to write a third stanza.

What did God promise to Abraham? (God promised to be with him and to guide him.) **Did God keep His promises?** (Yes.) **God always does what He says He will do. Does anyone remember the Bible verse about God doing what He says.** (Pupils respond.) **The Lord will do what he says. Today we will sing a song of praise to God for doing what He says.** Display the poster board with the words of the song for the children. Ask the children to listen as you play or sing both stanzas of "The Lord Will Do What He Says." Then sing the stanzas again, asking the children to sing on "da." The third time, ask the children to sing the words of the song with you. **What can we say to God to worship Him for keeping His promise to be with us and guide us.** (Children respond.) **Let's write new words to the song, using our worship phrases.** Ask the children to dictate the worship words to you as you write them on poster board. Then sing the new stanza together several times. A suggestion follows:

"Thank You, God, that you're with us.
We sing a song to praise You.
We worship You for Your promise.
So let's all praise the Lord."

During *Sharing in Worship*, display the poster board as the children sing the song for the large group.

4. Prayer. This group will prepare an acrostic to lead the prayer time. This activity is for older or gifted children. You will need a poster board and markers or crayons. Before the session, print the name ABRAHAM in capital letters vertically on the poster board.

What promises did God make to Abraham? (To be with him and to guide him.) **Using the letters in the word *Abraham*, think of a word or phrase that describes one of the promises God made to Abraham. You may need to look in your Bibles to help you find these promises. The promises are found in Genesis 12:1-3 and 13:14-17.** You may need to guide the children with their answers or help to rephrase some of their words. Following is a sample acrostic.

A new land
B less him
R emember him
A great nation
H ome
A ll people blessed through him
M any grandchildren and great grandchildren

Ask the children to take turns printing the acrostic phrases on the poster board. **Let's use the acrostic to say prayers to God, thanking Him for keeping His promises.** Assign each child a phrase or phrases from the acrostic. Ask them to think of a sentence prayer to worship God for keeping that promise. For example, God, you promised Abraham you would make him into a great nation. Thank you for keeping your promise. You always keep your promises.

During *Sharing in Worship*, the children will display the acrostic and say their prayers. Practice presenting the prayers in order during the small-group time.

5. Devotional. This group will fill dictate a story about God keeping His promises. You will need copies of activity page 6B, a poster board or large tablet, and a marker.

What promises did God make to Abraham? (To be with him and guide him.) **Did God keep His promises?** (Yes. God always keeps His promises.) **God also promises to be with us and guide us. We are going to make up a story about a time when God kept His promise to be with someone.** Distribute copies of activity page 6B and ask the children to look at the pictures and tell what is happening. Ask questions to help them. **What is happening in the first picture? How does the girl feel? What is her name? Where is she moving? What is happening in the middle picture? How does**

the girl feel? How does the girl feel in the third picture? What promise could she remember? What could she say to God? How might God keep His promise? List the children's observations on a piece of paper. Then ask them to dictate a story about how God kept His promise to the girl. Print the story on the poster board. If they have time, children may wish to illustrate the story on the poster board. A sample story follows:

Rachel's family moved to a new city. She had to say good-bye to her best friend, Anna. Rachel was excited to live in a bigger house. She had her own room. But she was afraid. Maybe she wouldn't find another good friend. Rachel knew God promised to be with her always. She prayed, "God, please help me find a good friend. Help me find a friend like Anna." The next day, Rachel went outside. There was a girl with red hair in the next yard. The girl smiled at Rachel. The girl said, "Hi, my name is Andrea. Do you want to play kick ball?" Rachel smiled back. She had found a friend.

Ask a good reader to read the story for the large group during the worship time. Ask two other children to hold the poster board. During *Sharing in Worship*, the child will read the story as the other children display the poster board.

6. Personal Praise. This group will prepare praise posters to God for keeping His promises. You will need copies of Activity Page 6A, construction paper, scissors, glue, and markers or crayons.

What promise did God make to Abraham? (To be with him and guide him.) **God also promises us that He will be with us and guide us. When are some times that God is with you?** (Allow children to respond—when I'm afraid, alone, scared, happy, at school, with my family, at church, and so on.) Distribute copies of activity page 6A and the other supplies. **We are going to make praise posters to worship God for keeping His promises to be with us and guide us. Cut all the words out of the center of your activity page. Choose the words that you would like to say to God to thank Him for keeping His promises. You can use the words from the center of the activity page, or you can print your own words. Glue the poster border onto construction paper and print or glue your praise words in the center of the border. Draw a picture about the time God is with you.**

During *Sharing in Worship*, the children will display their posters and read their words of praise.

Sharing in Worship
(20-25 minutes)

Omit any of the following sections if you did not offer the corresponding activity. The devotional may be done without the presentation of Group 5.

Call to Worship (Group 1): We go many places. Wherever we are, God is with us. Many different things happen to us. No matter what happens to us, God is with us. Ask Group 1 to present their promise wall.

Scripture (Group 2): Group 2 made something to remind us that God will always be with us. Ask Group 2 to distribute the badges and say their Scripture.

Lord's Supper: When Abraham went to a new place, he probably remembered his friends at his old home. When Jesus was going away from His friends, He had a Last Supper so His friends would remember Him. We remember Jesus when we have the Lord's Supper. **Pray and serve the Lord's Supper.**

Offering: We worship God because He keeps His promises. One way we can worship God is by giving our offerings so others can learn about God's promises. **Choose two children to collect the offering.**

Special Music (Group 3): **Group 3 will sing a song about God's promises that they helped write. Then they will teach it to us.** Ask Group 3 to sing "The Lord Will Do What He Says." Then sing it several times with the whole class until they have learned it.

Prayer (Group 4): One way to praise God is to thank Him for keeping His promises to Bible people. Group 4 discovered some more promises God made to Abraham. Ask Group 4 to present their acrostic and prayers.

Devotional (Group 5): I want you all to stand and form a line behind me. We are going to take a little trip. You are probably wondering where we are going. As you are talking, lead the children around the room. Well, I really don't know where we are going. When God told Abraham to leave his home and move on, Abraham didn't know where he was going either. But God promised that He would be with Abraham and guide him. And God did. God led Abraham to a new home.

God doesn't need to lead most of us to a new home, but God can guide us in other ways. When we need to decide whether to do right or wrong, God guides us. When we decide whether to lie to our mom or tell the truth, God guides us. When we decide whether to yell at our little brother or be kind, God guides us. Can you think of other times God guides us? (Allow pupils to share.)

God is always with us, and He will always keep His promise to be with us and guide us. The children in Group 5 wrote a story about God keeping His promises. Ask the children from Group 5 to present their story. If you did not offer this activity, read aloud the sample story printed in that activity.

Personal Praise (Group 6): What will you say to God to thank Him for keeping His promises? The children in Group 6 made some posters to praise God for His promise to be with us. Ask Group 6 to present their posters.

Closing Prayer: Choose two boys and two girls to pray a few sentence prayers. Then close out the prayer time. Thank You, for keeping your promises to Abraham. And thank You for always being with us and guiding us. Help us all to remember that You are always with us. In Jesus' name, amen.

Closing Moments
(10-15 minutes)

You will need six index cards, six pieces of construction paper, six slips of paper, and a marker. Before the session, print the following Scripture on each index card. "You can be sure that I will be with you always. I will continue with you until the end of the world." Matthew 28:20b, *ICB.* Number the pieces of construction paper 1-6. Number the slips of paper 1-6. Post the construction paper in six different areas of the room. Place an index card below each piece of construction paper.

Divide the children into six groups. Give each group a numbered slip of paper. **Look at the number on your paper. Find the piece of construction paper that has the same number and go there. You will find a promise.** (Allow children to do so.) **Will God keep this promise?** (Yes.) **God always does what He says.**

God Keeps His Promise to Give Us Everything We Need

Worship Focus

Worship God because He keeps His promise to give us everything we need.

Transition Time

(10-15 minutes)

As children assemble for second-hour worship, allow them to go the the rest room and to get a drink of water. While the children are out prepare your room for Mother, May Father, May I.

Mother, May I, Father, May I. Clear a space large enough to play this game. Or if you have nice weather you can play this game outside. Choose a child to be the mother or the father. He or she stands at one end of the room. The other children stand in a straight line next to each other. To begin, the mother or the father will instruct the first child in line to move forward several steps. For example: 3 hops, 2 skips, 1 giant step, etc. That child will then ask "Mother, may I?" or "Father, may I?" The mother or father will then respond with "Yes, you may." The child then moves forward. If that child fails to ask "Mother, may I?" or "Father, may I?" he or she is not allowed to move forward. The next child in line is given a chance to move forward in the same way. Continue playing until all the children have had a turn to move forward or until one child reaches the mother or father.

Launching the Theme

(10 minutes)

The Announcement. Before class ask another person to come to your door with an important piece of mail. Prepare a boy baby announcement with the pertinent information concerning Isaac's birth. Give this to the delivery person to bring to your classroom. Also prepare name tags by putting a different family member sticker on small pieces of construction paper. For example three or four name tags would have stickers of babies; three or four name tags would have stickers of fathers, three or four name tags would have stickers of older children; and three or four name tags would have stickers of mothers. Stickers of grandparents, teenagers, or preschool children also could be used.

I hear a knock on the door. Delivery person knocks on door. **I wonder who that could be.** Open door to delivery person who says, "I have a special delivery for the Primary class." **We have a special letter. Let me read it to you.** Open letter and show the announcement to the children. **This is a baby announcement. A baby has been born to Abraham and Sarah. The baby's name is Isaac. What wonderful news! A new baby is so exciting. I know Abraham and Sarah were very glad when baby Isaac was born because they had wanted a baby boy for a long time. God had promised to give Abraham and Sarah a baby boy and God kept His promises. God will keep His promises to us too. God gives us everything we need. And one of the things we need is our families.**

Describe the small-group activities for *Building the Theme* to the children. Then have the children go to the activity that corresponds to their name tags.

Building the Theme

(30 minutes)

1. Call to Worship. This group will prepare a choral reading with a Bible verse as the repeating refrain. You will need copies of activity page 7A and crayons or markers.

The call to worship is an important part of our worship session. It helps everyone to stop thinking about other things and to start thinking about worshiping God. Today we are worshiping God for keeping His promises. What are some promises God has made to you? How has He kept those promises?

Distribute activity page 7A. Ask the children to draw pictures of times God kept His promises to them.

During *Sharing in Worship*, the children will display their pictures. Each child will say how God kept a promise to him or her. After each child shares, the large group will say, "God kept His promise, because the Lord will do what He says." Practice the presentation during the small-group time.

2. Special Music. The children in this group will write new words to a song to sing as special music during the worship time. You will need "God Is So Good" from page 181, a piece of poster board, and a marker.

Before the session, print the words to the song on the poster board. Leave room on the poster board for the children to write new stanzas.

"God is so good.
God is so good.
God is so good.
He's so good to me."

"God keeps His word.
God keeps His word.
God keeps His word.
He's so good to me."

"We worship God.
We worship God.
We worship God.
He's so good to us."

Display the poster board for the children. Sing the song once for the children. Then ask them to sing with you.

God promised Abraham and Sarah they would have a baby boy. God kept His promise. God promises to give us everything we need. And we all need families and people to care for us. Who are some people in your family that you are thankful for? (Allow children to respond.)

Ask the children to write new stanzas for the song, listing people in their families. An example follows:

"God gave us Moms.
God gave us Dads.
God gave us sisters.
He's so good to us."

During *Sharing in Worship*, children will display their poster board and sing the song. Then they will sing the song again, asking the children in the large group to join them.

3. Prayer. The children in this group will create a wall montage to lead the prayer thoughts during the worship time. You will need crayons, markers, construction paper, scissors, glue, adhesive tape, and Plasti-Tak.

What is the theme for today's worship lesson? (Worship God because He keeps His promise to give us everything we need.) **To whom did God keep a promise in today's Bible lesson?** (Abraham and Sarah.) **How did God keep keep His promise?** (By giving them a baby boy.) **God promises to give us everything we need. Does God keep His promise?** (Yes.) **What does God give us that we need?** (Allow children to respond—families, food, a home, friends, and so on.) Ask each child to choose one thing God gives us to draw a picture of. Use tape or Plasti-Tak to attach the pictures to the wall around the title **God Keeps His Promises** used the last three weeks. If you did not offer this activity previously, cut out the letters for the title before the session and attach them to the wall.

What can we say to God to thank Him for giving us these things? Ask each child to say a sentence prayer, thanking God for the thing he or she drew.

During *Sharing in Worship*, each child will point to his or her picture and say the sentence prayer, thanking God for giving us the things we need.

4. Scripture. This group will edit a version of today's Bible story to read during the worship time. This activity is for older or gifted children. You will need copies of activity page 7B, pencils, and Bibles.

Read the following verses with the children: Genesis 17:15-19; 18:10-12; 21:1-6. Distribute activity page 7B.

Look at the story on your activity page. This is our Bible story. But there are a few things wrong with it. Read the story and circle the right words to finish the story. Assist the children as needed.

A corrected version of the story follows:

"God made a promise to Abraham. God said, 'You will have a son.' Abraham laughed, 'I am 100 years old. My wife is 90 years old. We are too old to have children.' But God said, 'I promise. Sarah will have a son. You will name him Isaac.'

"When Sarah heard the news, she laughed. But God kept His promise. Sarah gave birth to a baby boy. They named him Isaac. Abraham and Sarah were very happy to have a baby."

During *Sharing in Worship*, the children will read the Scriptures. Then they will read the corrected version of the story. Assign each pupil a different Scripture or section of the story.

5. Devotion. This group will present the devotion during the worship time with a tape-recorded question and answer game. You will need a cassette player and a blank cassette tape.

God promised to give us the things we need and one of those things we need is our families. Think of the people in your family. What special things do the people in your family do? I want each of you to describe a certain person in your family but don't tell us who you are describing. We will talk into the recorder. Then during the devotion we will play the tape and the other children will guess who the person is you are describing.

An example follows: I cook breakfast. I make the beds. I pack the lunch boxes. Who am I? (Mother.) Allow each child to record.

During *Sharing in Worship*, play the tape and ask the large group to guess each family member.

6. Personal Praise. This group will create collages to be presented during the worship time. You will need old magazines, scissors, poster board, markers, and glue.

God has promised to give us everything we need? What are some of the things God has promised to give us? (Children respond—families, homes, food, clothing.) **I want you to choose one of these items and make a collage to show your praise to God for always keeping His promises.**

Have the children print on the poster board, "I worship you God because You give me (item they chose)." Then ask the children to cut out pictures to correspond with their worship statements about giving.

During *Sharing in Worship*, the children will display their poster and read the sentence on their poster board.

Sharing in Worship
(20-25 minutes)

Omit any of the following sections if you did not offer the corresponding activity. The devotional may be given without the presentation of Group 5.

Call to Worship (Group 1)**: The call to worship is the time for us to stop thinking about other things and start thinking about worshiping God. The children in Group 1 are going to help us worship God for keeping His promises.** Group 1 presents their choral reading.

Song: Sing "God's Promise Is a Promise" from page 180.

Lord's Supper: God promises to give us the things we need. The most important thing we need is to saved from our sins. Jesus died on the cross to save us from our sins. We remember Jesus when we take the Lord's Supper. Play quiet, worshipful music in the background as the Lord's Supper is served.

Offering: God has given us so many things. Let us give something back to Him. We worship God when we give our offerings to Him. Choose two children to pass the offering basket to those who did not give their offering during the Sunday school hour.

Special Music (Group 2)**: Group 2 will sing to us a song you are probably familiar with. But they have added some new verses. Let's listen to them sing.** Let these children come to the sharing space and sing "God Is So Good" to the class. Have the class join in singing the new stanzas of the song together.

Prayer (Group 3)**: Group 3 has created some pictures to remind us of how God gives us what we need. Let's pray with them now.** Group 3 presents.

Scripture (Group 4): Group 4 presents their Scriptures and story.

Devotional (Group 5): You will need the tape-recorded question and answer game made by Group 5.

God has promised to give us the things we need. One of the most important things He has given us is our families. Listen to the tape that Group 5 made and try to guess which family member the child is describing. Play one recorded message at a time. Stop the tape after each message and have the group guess the family member that is being described. If you did not offer this activity, provide your own clues for the following family members: Mom, Dad, Grandpa, Grandma, sister, brother.

There are many different people in a family. And we need each and every one of them. God promised to give us families. And God has kept His promise.

Personal Praise (Group 6)**: God has promised to give us many things. Group 6 has prepared Praise Posters to show some of the things God has promised to give us. We worship God because He keeps His promises to give us everything we need.** Group 6 presents their posters to the large group.

Closing Prayer: Have one child from each group offer up a worship sentence prayer to God. Then close out the prayer time. **Thank You, God, for keeping Your promise to Abraham and Sarah. Thank You from keeping Your promise to us by giving us the things we need. Thank You for our families, homes, food, and clothing. In Jesus' name, amen.**

Closing Moments
(10-15 minutes)

Family Portraits. Give each child a large sheet of construction paper with the words "Thank You, God, for my family" printed at the top. Then have the children draw the people in their family. Provide crayons or markers. Have the children write the names of the family members on their pictures as well. Arrange these family portraits on a wall or bulletin board with the caption "We worship God for our families." **Drawing pictures about things we are thankful for is another way to worship God. We worship God for giving us our families.**

For Next Week

Collect enough small rocks or stones for each member of your class to have one. Paint the stones in six different colors to correspond to the six activity groups for *Building the Theme*.

God Keeps His Promise to Provide Our Needs

Worship Focus
Worship God because He keeps His promise to provide our needs.

Transition Time
(10-15 minutes)

As children assemble for second-hour worship, allow them to go to the rest room and to get a drink of water. Prepare your room for Jacob's Walk.

Jacob's Walk. Before class hide small stones or rocks around your room—enough for each child to find one rock. Paint or color these rocks in six different colors. The rocks will be used to divide the class into their small groups for *Building the Theme*. Hide the rocks so just a small part of each rock is showing. Choose a child to be Jacob. He or she will lead the other children in a "Follow the Leader" fashion. As the children follow Jacob around the room have them look for a rock. Instruct the children to only pick up one rock so that all the children will get one. Continue Jacob's Walk until all the rocks have been found. The children should keep their rocks with them.

Launching the Theme
(10 minutes)

Jacob's Rock. The children should have the rocks they found earlier with them.

Are you all ready to take another trip? This time we are going along with Jacob. Is Jacob taking anybody on his trip? (No.) **Does this make Jacob feel scared.** (No.) **Why isn't he scared?** (Because God promised to take care of Jacob and always be with him.) **When did God made a promise to Jacob?** (When he slept with a stone for a pillow and saw angels on a stairway reaching to Heaven.) **What did God promise Jacob?** (I am with you; I will not leave you.) **Did God keep His promise to Jacob? What did Jacob use to remember this promise?** (A rock.) **God promised to take care of Jacob's needs. And God promises to provide for our needs too.**

Describe the small-group activities to the children. Then ask them to go to the activity that matches the color of their rock.

Building the Theme
(30 minutes)

1. Call to Worship. This group will prepare a poster that shows the difference between our wants and our needs. You will need a large piece of poster board, markers, old magazines and catalogs, scissors, and glue. Print *Wants* on one side of the poster board and *Needs* on the other side of the poster board.

God has promised to provide for our needs. But that doesn't mean He'll give us everything we want. We need to understand and decide whether something we want is something we really need.

The children will look through the magazines and catalogs for pictures that represent *Wants* or *Needs*. For example a picture of expensive tennis shoes would be glued to the *Wants* side and a pair of plain tennis shoes would be glued to the *Needs* side. Other examples would be houses, food, toys, transportation. The children will then glue the pictures to the appropriate sides of the poster board.

During *Sharing in Worship*, ask each child to tell about the items he or she chose. For example, "I want expensive tennis shoes that cost a lot of money. I need a new pair of shoes. God will provide my shoes."

2. Special Music. The children in this group will sing this song as special music during the worship time. You will need "Praise Him, Praise Him, All You Little Children" from page 182, a poster board, and markers. Before class print the words to the song on poster board using bright colored markers. Leave room on the poster board for new stanzas to be added.

"Praise Him, Praise Him, all ye little children.
God is love. God is love.
Praise Him, Praise Him, all ye little children.
God is love. God is love."

"Thank Him, Thank Him, He provides our food.

Thank You, God. Thank You, God.
Thank Him, Thank Him, He provides our food.
Thank You, God. Thank You, God."

"Thank Him, Thank Him, He provides our water.
Thank You, God. Thank You, God.
Thank Him, Thank Him, He provides our water.
Thank You, God. Thank You, God."

Sing the song for the children. Then ask them to sing with you. **What other things does God provide for us?** Encourage the children to be specific in their answers—Moms, Dads, friends, and so on. Write new stanzas for the song, substituting the items the children named for *food* and *water* in the second and third stanzas. Practice singing the new stanzas. An example follows:

"Thank Him, Thank Him, He provides peanut butter.
Thank You, God. Thank You, God.
Thank Him, Thank Him, He provides carrots.
Thank You, God. Thank You, God."

"Thank Him, Thank Him, He provides milk.
Thank You, God. Thank You, God.
Thank Him, Thank Him, He provides apple juice.
Thank You, God. Thank You, God."

During *Sharing in Worship*, the children will sing the song with the new words that they have written.

3. Prayer. The children in this group will create a wall montage to lead the prayer thoughts during the worship time. You will need crayons, markers, construction paper, scissors, glue, adhesive tape, and Plasti-Tak.

Why are we worshiping God today? (He keeps His promise to provide our needs.) **To whom did God keep a promise to be with him and not leave him?** (Jacob.) **How did God keep His promise?** (By taking care of Jacob on his trip and by giving him a family and bringing him home safely.) **What other Bible people have we talked about to whom God made promises?** (Noah, Abraham and Sarah.) **What promises did God make to them?** (Noah—to save him from the flood, never to destroy the earth again; Abraham—to be with him, to give him a new home; Abraham and Sarah—that they would have a baby boy.)

Ask the children to think of something to draw about each promise. Suggestions follow: Noah—an ark, a rainbow; Abraham—a tent, a baby; Jacob—a rock. Assign a picture to each child to draw. Attach the pictures around the **God Keeps His Promises** title used the last four weeks.

What can you say to thank God for keeping the promise you drew about? Ask each child to think of a short prayer to say to God.

During *Sharing in Worship*, each child will point to his or her picture and say a sentence prayer, thanking God for keeping that promise.

4. Scripture. This group will prepare a story and Scripture for the worship time. You will need copies of activity page 8A, scissors, glue, construction paper, and crayons or markers.

Why are we worshiping God today? (He keeps His promise to provide our needs.) **What promise did God keep to Jacob?** (I will be with you. I will never leave you.) **Let's read about that promise and how God kept His promise.** Read Genesis 28:10-15; 31:17 with the children. Distribute activity page 8A. Ask the children to color and cut out the pictures and glue them in order to a piece of construction paper. Assign each pupil a verse or verses from the passage above to read aloud during the worship time. Allow the children to practice reading the verses.

During *Sharing in Worship*, the children will display the pictures and read the Scripture verses in order.

5. Devotion. This group will make up endings to modern-day stories to be used as the devotion during the worship time. You will need copies of activity page 8B and crayons or markers.

Distribute activity page 8B. **Why are we worshiping God today?** (He keeps His promise to provide our needs.) **The children on this page have some needs.** Read about Carrie and David with the children. **How might God provide for Carrie and David's needs?** (Pupils respond. Suggestions follow: someone might give Carrie a coat she has outgrown; Carrie's parents might get some extra money; David might find new friends; David's new house might have a park nearby.) Record the children's suggestions on chalkboard or poster board. **Think of a time you needed something. Draw a picture of it on your activity page. How did God provide your need?** Share with the children a time when God provided something you needed. Ask two children to read about Carrie and David.

During *Sharing in Worship*, two children will read about Carrie and David. The large group will tell how God might provide for them. You will share the pupils' suggestions recorded on poster board. Then the pupils will tell about the time God provided a need that they drew about on their activity page.

6. Personal Praise. This group will prepare a praise scroll to present during the worship time. You will need shelf paper, markers or crayons, construction paper, and Plasti-Tak or cellophane tape.

Before the session, cut a length of shelf paper. Roll both ends and tape them so that they look like the ends of a scroll. Print **Our Praise Scroll** at the top of the paper. Underneath the title **Our Praise Scroll** print "God has used his riches in Christ Jesus to give me . . . "

Read Philippians 4:19 *(ICB)* to the children. "God will use his riches in Christ Jesus to give you everything you need." **What are some things we need?** (Food, clothes, home, families, friends.) **What is one person or thing God has given you?** (Allow the children to respond.) Ask each child to draw a picture of the thing God has given him or her. Use tape or Plasti-Tak to attach the pupils' drawings to the scroll you prepared.

During *Sharing in Worship,* each child will point to his or her picture on the scroll and say, "God has used his riches in Christ Jesus to give me (person or thing he or she drew)."

Sharing in Worship
(20-25 minutes)

Omit any of the following sections if you did not offer the corresponding activity. The devotional may be given without the presentation of Group 5.

Call to Worship (Group 1): **Group 1 will lead us in the call to worship.** Group 1 presents their poster.

Lord's Supper: Jacob set up a rock to remember the place where he had a dream from God. We remember Jesus when we see the bread and the cup. Jesus died to save us from our sins. Let's remember Him as we take the Lord's Supper. Play some quiet, worshipful music in the background as the Lord's Supper is served.

Offering: God gives us so many things. Let's give something back to Him. We worship God when we give our offerings to Him. Choose two children to pass the offering basket to those who did not give their offering during the Sunday school hour.

Special Music (Group 2): **Group 2 will sing to us a song they been practicing. You will probably know this song but they have added several new verses. Let's listen to them sing.** Have the children in this group come to the sharing space and sing "Praise Him, Praise Him." Have them sing it several times so the whole class can learn the words to the new verses. Then have everybody stand and sing it together.

Prayer (Group 3): **We have learned about several Bible people to whom God kept His promises. Group 3 will help us thank God for them now.** Group 3 presents their Promise Wall and prayers.

Scripture (Group 4): **How did God make His promise to Jacob? How did God keep His promise? Group 4 will read to us from the Bible.** Group 4 displays the Bible-story pictures and reads Scripture verses.

Devotional (Group 5): **God provided Jacob's needs. And God will provide our needs. We're going to think about ways God provides our needs now.** Ask children from Group 5 to present the open-ended stories and their personal experiences. If you did not offer this activity, read about Carrie and David from activity page 8B and ask, "How might God provide Carrie and David's needs? Then ask children to tell about times God provided for their needs.

Personal Praise (Group 6): **The children in Group 6 made a praise scroll to thank God for some things He has given them.** Ask children from Group 6 to present.

Closing Prayer: Choose three or four children to say a short sentence prayer to God. Then close out the prayer time. **Thank You, for keeping Your promises to Jacob. And thank you for keeping Your promise to us to provide our needs. Help us to know the difference between our wants and our needs. In Jesus' name amen.**

Closing Moments
(10-15 minutes)

Treasure Hunt. Before class write 10 "true treasures—needs" and 10 "false treasures—wants" on small pieces of construction paper. Hide these "treasures" around your room. Here is a sample of "true treasures—needs": warm coat, tennis shoes, storybooks, station wagon, mothers and fathers, orange juice, carrots, warm house, sweatshirt, Bibles. Here is a sample of "false treasures—wants": fur coat, expensive tennis shoes, Nintendo, Rolls Royce, TV stars, Coca Cola, potato chips, 10 room mansion, designer sweater, videos.

Divide the class into two teams. Give them five minutes to hunt for the hidden treasures. When the time is up have each team decide if the treasures they found are "true treasures-needs" or "false treasures—wants." Then have each team turn in the "true treasures. Each "true treasure is worth 2 points and each "false treasure" chosen as a "true treasure" takes away 1 point.

God will keep His promise to provide for all of our needs. We worship God for keeping His promises to us.

God Gives Us Families

Worship Focus

Worship God because He cares for us by giving us families.

Transition Time
(10-15 minutes)

Allow time for the children to use the rest room and drinking fountain.

Attendance chart. Put the children's names on a large poster board. Place miniature seals next to each child's name for attendance, bringing a Bible, and memory work.

Moses-Miriam relay. Divide the children into two teams and ask each team to line up in a straight line behind a starting point. The first child in each team will be Moses, the second child Miriam, the third child Moses, and so on to the end of the line. Explain that all the Moseses will take tiny baby steps, one foot in front of the other, and all the Miriams will run. At the starting signal, the first child in each team must walk with tiny steps to the goal (a wall or chalkboard), walk back to the team, and tag the next person in line. That person (a Miriam) will run to the goal, run back, and tag the next person, and so on. The first team to have all their players back in place wins. If you have time, play again and switch the Moseses and Miriams.

Mother or Father Says. For a smaller group of children, choose one child to be the leader. The leader could be "Mother" if a girl and "Father" if a boy. The leader gives commands to the others such as "touch your feet," "rub your tummy," "jump up and down." The others are to obey the commands only if the command is preceded by "Mother says" or "Father says." If the leader gives a command without saying, "Mother says" or "Father says" first, and if anyone obeys the command, they are "caught." Continue, letting all pupils participate even if they have been "caught." Let the children take turns being the leader.

Launching the Theme
(10 minutes)

You will need a paper plate and scissors. Fold the paper plate in half and cut it according to the pattern on page 84. You may wish to color the scene of Moses with Pharaoh's daughter and Miriam. Fold back the figures of the basket, Pharaoh's daughter, and Miriam. Pop up the figures when indicated as you say the following poem.

"I can't let my baby die," Moses' mother said.

She got a basket, covered it with tar, and made a bed. (Pop up figure of basket.)

The baby in the basket was set in the Nile to float.

His sister stood beside the Nile to watch the tiny boat.

The princess came to bathe and saw the baby in the reeds. (Pop up figure of princess.)

Miriam quickly ran to say, "A nurse is what he needs." (Pop up figure of Miriam.)

Moses' mother cared for him and nursed him till he'd grown.

Then Moses went to Pharaoh's house to be the Princess' own.

In the river, home, or palace, with his mother or the king,

God cared for baby Moses as He cares for everything.

God took care of baby Moses. Moses had a home with his mother and a home with Pharaoh's daughter. God provided a family for Moses wherever he was. God cares for us too by giving us families. Let's worship God today because He cares for us. He gives us families.

Briefly explain the choices of preparation for worship. Allow the children to choose which group in which they would like to participate. Or cut baskets from six colors of construction paper before the session. Children will draw a basket and go to the small group whose color corresponds with their baskets.

Building the Theme
(30 minutes)

1. Call to Worship. This group will prepare a choral reading to introduce the worship time. You will need poster board and a marker. Before the session, print the following verses from Psalm 100 (*ICB*) on the poster board.

Group 1: Shout to the Lord, all the earth.

Group 2: Serve the Lord with joy.

Group 1: Come before him with singing.

Group 2: Know that the Lord is God.

Group 1: He made us, and we belong to him.

Group 2: We are his people, the sheep that he tends.

Groups 1 and 2: Shout to the Lord all the earth.

Group 1: Go into his gates with thanksgiving.

Group 2: Go into his courts with praise.

Group 1: Give thanks to him.

Group 2: Praise his name.

Group 1: For the Lord is good.

Group 2: His love will be forever.

Groups 1 and 2: He is faithful forever.

Ask the children to find Psalm 100 in their Bibles. Read the Psalm with the children. **We belong to our parents, and they take good care of us. But who else do these verses say we belong to? Look in verse three if you need help remembering.** (Allow children to respond.) **These verses say we were made by God and we belong to Him. God made us and He takes care of us. He gives us our parents and other people like teachers, doctors, and baby-sitters to take care of us. Let's worship God because we belong to Him.**

Display the poster board. Read the choral reading once for the children. **We are going to say these verses antiphonally. That is a special way to say the verses in two groups. That means that Group 1 will say the first sentence and all the other sentences that say "Group 1." Group 2 will say the second sentence and all the sentences that say "Group 2." We will take turns going back and forth from Group 1 to Group 2, back to Group 1, and so on. When we say God's Word to each other, we are helping each other to worship God.**

Group 1 should begin very softly. Each sentence should be said louder and louder with "Shout to the Lord all the earth" being shouted by both groups. In the second set of verses, Group 1 should again begin very softly with each sentence increasing in volume. Again, end with "He is faithful forever" being shouted by both groups. Practice the reading many times.

During *Sharing in Worship*, the group will present the choral reading as the Call to Worship.

2. Special music. This group will sing and illustrate a song for the worship time. You will need "God Cared for Moses" from page 183, poster board, and markers.

Before the session, write the words to "God Cared for Moses" on poster board.

One way we can worship God is through singing. We are going to learn a song today that tells about how God took care of Moses. Then during our worship time together we can sing this song for the others and teach it to them.

Play the song through several times for the children, pointing to the words as they are sung. The tune is "Turkey in the Straw." When the children are familiar with the words, ask them to sing along with the tape. Practice the song many times until the children are comfortable singing it.

Ask the children to think of pictures that illustrate the song. Suggestions follow: a baby in a basket, Pharaoh, Red Sea, manna, quail, rock, Ten Commandments. Ask the children to draw the pictures on the poster board.

During *Sharing in Worship*, the children will display the poster board and sing "God Cared for Moses."

3. Devotional. This group will prepare puppets to present the story of Moses during the worship time. (Limit six children to this group.) You will need copies of activity pages 9A and 9B, crayons or markers, scissors, glue, and six craft sticks for each child. Use a table turned on its side for a puppet stage.

Do you remember what happened to baby Moses in the poem we just heard? (Allow children to respond.) **Why do you think Moses' mother put him in a basket and set him in the Nile River?** (She loved and cared for him and didn't want him to die.) **Who watched baby Moses while he was in the river?** (His sister, Miriam.) **Why do you think she watched him?** (She loved and cared for him too and wanted to make sure he was safe.) **Who found Moses?** (Pharaoh's daughter, the princess.) **How did she care for Moses?** (She listened to Miriam's suggestion and hired his mother to take care of him for her.) **God cared for Moses and always made sure there was someone to take care of him. When he was a little baby his mother took care of him and when he grew older, he was taken care of by the princess.**

Distribute activity pages 9A and 9B. Ask the children to color the figures. Then ask them to cut out each figure and glue it on a craft stick. The children can practice telling the story using their stick puppets.

Assign each child one puppet part. Ask them to tell how the person cared for Moses, or if the puppet is Moses, ask them to tell how God cared for Moses.

During *Sharing in Worship*, each child will use his or her puppet to tell about God's care for Moses.

4. Personal Praise. This group will prepare a praise mural for the worship time. You will need butcher paper and markers or crayons.

How did God take care of baby Moses? (He provided Moses' mother and sister to care for him when he was a little baby and then Pharaoh's daughter took care of him when he was older.) **God also gives us families to take care of us. What are some ways that your family cares for**

you? (Allow children to respond. Some suggestions follow: gives me food; gives me clothes; teaches me about God; gives me a home; loves me; and listens to me.)

Ask the children to choose one way their families care for them. Spread the butcher paper on the floor or table and ask the children to draw a picture of the way their family cares for them. Children who finish early may letter the title on the mural: **Thank You, God, for Families!** Choose two children to display the mural during the worship time.

During *Sharing in Worship*, the children will display the mural. Each child will point to his or her picture and tell the way the family cares.

5. Offering. This group will prepare banks for the large group to introduce the offering time. You will need an empty plastic container with a lid (such as a margarine container) for each child, construction paper, crayons or markers, scissors, Tacky glue, tape, and stickers (optional).

Before class, cut a slit in the lid of each container. Make a large "Harvest Bank" out of a coffee can to keep in the worship area.

How did God care for Moses? (His mother took care of him; He sent Pharaoh's daughter to care for him.) **Our church helps take care of many missionaries who work for Jesus and many poor people who have no money. One way God cares for them is through our money we give to him in the offering. Sometimes we need to help other people because they don't have a family to help them. Or maybe they need more help than their family can give them. Today we are going to make banks for everyone in our class. This month we are going to collect money every week to help care for the people our church helps.**

Distribute the containers. Ask the children to use the construction paper, crayons, markers, and stickers to decorate the banks in any way they wish. Make sure there are enough banks for everyone in the class.

During *Sharing in Worship*, the children will give each child in the large group a bank.

6. Prayer. This group will write letters to missionaries to introduce the prayer time. You will need lined paper, pencils, and crayons or markers. Before the session, gather some information about a missionary family your church supports. Find out an address where they can receive mail and some background information, such as names and ages of children. Be prepared to show the children on a map where the missionary family is living. Display photographs of the family.

Do you ever get letters or cards in the mail from someone in your family, like your grandparents or maybe a cousin? It is fun to get mail, and it is also fun to write a letter to someone.Our church helps the Smith family that lives in Africa. (Insert appropriate name and place.) **This family doesn't get to see their grandparents, aunts, uncles, and cousins very often since they live so far away. They love and miss their family. They are very happy to get letters from their family back here to find out how they are doing. Since Christians are all part of God's family, we can pray for our family, the Smiths, in Africa. We can also show the Smith family how we care for them by writing letters to them. We can tell them we are praying for them. We can draw them pictures showing them things we are doing and learning.**

Distribute the papers and pencils and crayons. It might be helpful to have a few words the children may want to use written ahead of time on a poster board or chalkboard to aid them in spelling. When the letters are completed, ask one or two children to read their letters during the worship time. Ask other children to tell about the family, show where they live on a map, and display their photographs. Practice the presentation.

During *Sharing in Worship*, the children will read the letters and tell the large group about the missionary family.

Sharing in Worship
(20-25 minutes)

Omit any of the following sections if you did not offer the corresponding activity. The devotional and offering may be completed without the presentations of Groups 3 and 5.

Call to Worship (Group 1): **One way we can worship God is to say His Word aloud to each other. Group 1 is going to say a section of God 's Word to us today. It is from Psalm 100:1-6.** Group 1 presents their choral reading.

Who made us? (God.) **Does God take care of us?** (Yes.) **Who does God give to take care of us?** (Our parents and family.)

Special Music (Group 2): **God gave Moses people to take care of him too. Listen to this song about Moses. See how many ways God cared for Moses you can find.** Group 2 sings "God Cared for Moses." After the song, ask the group to name ways God cared for Moses.

Devotional **(Group 3): Group 3 will help us remember all the ways God cared for Moses. Let's listen to them now.** Ask Group 3 to tell about Moses, using their puppets.

How many of you have younger brothers or sisters? Do you remember how tiny they were when they were just born? Remember how that little tiny baby couldn't do anything

without your mom or dad or maybe even you helping him? Little baby Moses was just like your baby brother or sister. He couldn't take care of himself because he was brand new and didn't know how. Somebody had to take care of baby Moses. God loved him very much and made sure there was always someone to take care of him. Who took care of baby Moses? His mother. His mother loved him and took very good care of him. She made sure he had enough to eat and was warm and happy. She had to hide Moses though because there were some people who didn't want him to live. When Moses got older, she couldn't hide him any more, so she put him in a basket and set him in the Nile River. God provided someone else to watch Moses in the river. Who was it? His sister, Miriam.

One day the Pharaoh's daughter was down by the river and heard Moses crying. She saw poor Moses and felt sorry for him. What did the Pharaoh's daughter decide to do with Moses? Let the children tell the rest of the story—the Pharaoh's daughter kept Moses and at Miriam's suggestion hired his own mother to take care of him. **God loved Moses and took care of him by making sure there was always someone to take care of him. God made each one of you and loves you and cares for you. God takes care of you by giving you a family to care for you. He provides parents to make sure you eat right and have clothes to wear and a place to sleep. He gives you brothers and sisters, aunts, uncles, cousins, and grandparents to help care for you. Our family is a wonderful gift God has given to each of us. We can worship God for caring for us by giving us our family.**

Personal Praise (Group 5): **Let's praise God for our families now. The children in Group 5 thought of some ways their families care for them.** Group 5 presents the mural. **Can you think of ways your family cares for you?** Allow the large group to respond.

Lord's Supper: The best way that God cared for us was by sending His only Son, Jesus, to die for us. God loves us so much that He gave us the best gift He had, Jesus. Let's think about Jesus now as the bread and juice are passed.

Offering (Group 5): **When we put money into the offering each week, we are giving our money to God. Our church uses that money to help missionary families and poor people. We are going to help our church care for others by collecting money each week.**

Children from Group 5 distribute the banks. **Save your money in your bank during the week. Then bring it to the worship time each Sunday. We will have a large Harvest bank where we will collect all of the money throughout the month.** Show the children the class Harvest bank.

Prayer (Group 6): **There is another way we can help our church care for others. We can pray for them. Group 6 found out about some missionaries our church cares for. They wrote letters to let them know we are praying for them.** Group 6 shares their letters and information now. **Let's pray for the missionaries now.** Ask several children to pray. Close with prayer, thanking God for caring for us.

Closing Moments
(10-15 minutes)

"God Cares for Me" folder. The children will make folders to keep take-home projects for this month. You will need a colored folder with pockets for each child, construction paper, the cornucopia pattern on page 88, scissors, glue, felt-tip markers, and an instant-picture camera with film (optional).

Before class, trace the cornucopia pattern onto pieces of construction paper. Ask the children to cut out the cornucopias and glue them to the front of the folders. Print "God Cares for" on the chalkboard. Ask the children to copy the words on the front of their folders, filling in their names. Take a picture of each child if you have a camera, and ask the children to glue the picture to the opening of the cornucopia. If you do not have a camera, the children may draw their pictures on the front of the cornucopias.

God Cares for Us Night and Day

Worship Focus

Worship God because He cares for us night and day.

Transition Time

(10-15 minutes)

Send the children in small groups to the rest room and water fountain. Welcome newcomers and involve them in the following game.

Follow the Leader. You will need to make a pillar of cloud and a pillar of fire before this session. Draw a cloud and flames of fire on poster board. Cut them out and use masking tape to attach each one to a dowel rod or yardstick.

To play the game, choose one child to be Moses. Moses will march around the room with the rest of the children behind him or her in single file. The children will imitate whatever actions Moses does. Moses could clap his hands above his head, put his hands on his hips, and so on. While the children are marching around the room, another child will be in charge of night or day. If the child holds up the pillar of cloud, indicating daytime, the children should continue to follow and imitate Moses. When the child holds up the pillar of fire, indicating nighttime, everyone should sit on the floor and pretend to be asleep. When the pillar of cloud is held up again, the marching will continue. Give several children the chance to be Moses and a chance to be in charge of night and day.

Launching the Theme

(10 minutes)

You will need a map, a large piece of cotton, a candle, and matches.

If I told you to start walking to Disneyland, how many of you would know which way to go? What could we use today to show us how to get to places if we don't know how to get there? (Allow children to respond. Then display the map.) **Today we have many maps of lots of different places in the world. We can look at them and they can guide us to wherever we need to go. Maps haven't always been available for people to use. When God's people, the Israelites, were leaving Egypt going toward the Red Sea, they had no map. But God cared for His people by guiding them in a special way. During the daytime He made a big pillar of cloud for the people to follow. Hold up cotton. The people could always see the pillar of cloud and know which way to go. Do you think the people could see the pillar of cloud at night?** (Allow children to respond.) **It would be hard to see a cloud when it is dark outside. But God cared for His people during the night too. He made a pillar of fire for them to follow at night.** (Light and hold up the candle.) **The people could see the pillar of fire all night long. God cared for His people all day and all night. He made sure they wouldn't get lost. God cares for us night and day too. We have some helpers who are going to pantomime or act out some different activities. The rest of us are going to try and guess what they are doing.**

Before the session, print the following activities on index cards:

- waking up in the morning
- brushing your teeth
- sleeping
- eating breakfast
- playing jump rope
- saying the pledge to the flag

Ask for volunteers to pantomime one of the activities you have printed on the cards. You may need to help beginning readers read the activity. After each child has pantomimed, ask the rest of the children to guess what he or she was doing.

Lead a discussion with questions like these: **What kinds of things did the children act out? Do you think God knows about all the things we do every day? Is there anything we do that God doesn't know about? Isn't it great that God knows what we do and cares for us day and night? He even cares for us when we are sleeping. We will worship God today because He cares for us night and day.**

Briefly explain the choices of preparation for worship. You can allow the children to choose which group in which they would like to participate.

Building the Theme

(30 minutes)

1. **Call to Worship.** This group will prepare a poem to read for the call to worship. You will need a poster board and marker. Before the session, print the two

repeating lines in bold type from the poem on page 80 by Vicki Ziese on the poster board.

God had a special group of people called the Israelites. The Israelites were slaves in a country called Egypt. The leader, Pharaoh, would not let the Israelites go to worship God. So God sent some terrible events, or plagues, to happen to the Pharaoh and Egyptians. It took ten different plagues before the Pharaoh finally let the people go. God cared for the Israelites all during the plagues and then when the people were let go, God still cared for them by guiding them all day and all night.

I'm going to read a poem about the plagues aloud to you. See if you can hear all ten plagues in the poem. When you have finished reading the poem, display the poster board with the lines printed on it. **You will say these lines of the poem when I signal you.** Practice reading the poem with the children. Look at them or nod to them to let them know when to say their lines. When pupils are comfortable with their lines, practice the presentation with Group 2.

During *Sharing in Worship*, you will read present the poem with the children as Group 2 displays their paper chains.

2. Call to Worship. This group will prepare paper chains, illustrating the ten plagues to present during the call to worship. You will need copies of activity page 10B, crayons or markers, scissors, and glue or paste.

God had a special group of people called the Israelites. The Israelites were slaves in a country called Egypt. The leader, Pharaoh, would not let the Israelites go to worship God. So God sent some terrible events, or plagues, to happen to the Pharaoh and Egyptians. It took ten different plagues before the Pharaoh finally let the people go. God cared for the Israelites all during the plagues and then when the people were let go, God still cared for them by guiding them all day and all night.

We are going to make a paper chain showing the ten different plagues God sent to Pharaoh and the Egyptians. We will color the strips and then cut them out and glue them where shown to make the chain. If you look at each strip you will see a pillar of cloud on one end and a pillar of fire on the other to remind us how God cared for His people following the plagues. When Group 1 reads their poem, we will show our paper chains. When children complete their paper chains, practice the presentation with Group 1.

During *Sharing in Worship*, children will hold up the appropriate link of their chains as Group 1 reads the poem.

3. Scripture. This group will illustrate Psalm 23 with pictures about God's care. You will need activity page 10A, drawing paper, crayons, markers, tape recorder, and a blank tape.

Distribute activity page 10A. Read Psalm 23 together. Explain that these verses tell how God watches over us and cares for us. **God gives us everything we need. He gives us rest and food. God helps us when we're afraid. We will live with God forever.**

Ask each child to choose a word in bold type from the psalm to illustrate. Be sure each word has been chosen by at least one child.

When the children have completed their pictures, record Psalm 23 on the blank tape. Allow each child to read a verse or part of a verse on the tape.

During *Sharing in worship*, children will display their pictures at the appropriate times as the tape is played. Practice the presentation during the small-group time.

4. Devotional. This group will present role plays about times God cared for His people. You will need poster board and a marker. Print the title "God Cares for Us" on the poster board.

God cares for us in many different ways. He provides people to take care of us. He provides things we need to help us too. We are going to act out four different situations. I will read you the situation and then we will act it out. Then we will try to think how God cared for that person.

Involve the children in this activity by helping them role play the following situations. You may need to help them by suggesting words for them to say while role playing.

1. A child is frightened by a storm at night and goes to a parent for comfort. The parent calms the child and helps her get back to sleep.
2. Two children are on the playground. One falls and badly skins her knee. The other child helps his friend to the teacher. The teacher helps the child go to see the school nurse. The nurse cleans the knee and puts a bandage on it.
3. A new child comes to Sunday school and doesn't know anyone. He sits alone and doesn't have a Bible. One of the other children goes to him and asks him to sit by him and share his Bible.
4. A child is sick with a bad stomachache. His mother or father drives him to the doctor. The doctor looks at him and gives him some medicine to help the child get better.

After each situation has been practiced in the small group, ask the children, **"How did God care for the person in this situation?"**

During *Sharing in Worship*, children will present the role plays. After each role play, ask the large group how God cared for that person. Write the children's' responses on the poster board. Include the following answers: Situation 1—home, parents; Situation 2—friend, teacher, nurse, clean water, bandage; Situation 3—friends; Situation 4—parents, car, doctor, medicine.

5. Personal Praise. This group will draw pictures of times God cares for them. You will need large sheets of paper, crayons, thinned black tempera paint, paint brushes, newspapers to cover the table, and old shirts for children to wear as smocks to protect their clothing.

Ask the children to draw pictures of people and things God has given them to show He cares for them every day. The pictures could include homes, food, parents, family, or items from God's creation. Tell the children they need to press very hard with the crayons while drawing their pictures.

Focus a discussion on God's care for us as the children work. **How does God care for us?** (By providing things we need.) **What has He given us that shows He cares?** (Food, clothes, family, and so on.) **How do our families care for us?** (They provide things we need like meals and clothes, take us to the doctor when we are sick, and so on.) **Did God care for His people in the daytime? How?** (By providing a pillar of cloud to follow.) **Did God care for His people in the night? How?** (By providing a pillar of fire to follow.) **Does God care for you in the day and the night?** (Yes.)

When the children have finished their pictures, help them paint over their pictures with the thinned paint. As the pictures dry, remind them that all that God has given us each day is also there at night. **He cares for us day and night.** Read Psalm 13:6—"I sing to the Lord because he has taken care of me" (*ICB*). Practice saying the verse a few times together with the children.

During *Sharing in Worship*, children will display their pictures. After each child tells about his or her picture, the children will say Psalm 13:6 together.

6. Prayer. This group will write a prayer, thanking God for His care day and night. You will need Bibles for each child, a globe or an atlas, marker, and poster board.

Read Psalm 86:9 (*ICB*) to the children. "All the nations you have made will come and worship before you, O Lord; they will bring glory to your name."

Explain that God has made all the nations. Examine the globe or atlas with the children. **What is a nation?** (Allow children to respond.) **A nation is the same thing as a country. What country do we live in? Our country, or nation, is the United States of America. Can anyone show me the United States on the globe?** (Allow children to respond.) **There are many nations or countries in the world. Let's look at this globe. What are some other nations?** Allow children to tell names of countries they know. Point out some countries on the globe and tell a little about them. **Here is the country of Brazil. There is a big tropical rain forest in Brazil. Over in Africa is a country you may have heard of called Ethiopia. You may have seen pictures of Ethiopia on television. It hasn't rained in Ethiopia for a long time, and they can't grow much food to feed the people. Over in the country of India there are many elephants and snakes. And way up in the country of Greenland it is very, very cold.**

Who made all these nations? (God made them.) **Do you think God cares about the people in all these nations?** (Yes, He does.)

When it is daytime in our country, the United States, it is nighttime in a country on the opposite side of the globe. God watches over all the nations all the time. The Bible says God never sleeps. Read Psalm 121:4 (*ICB*). **God cares for us day and night. He never rests or sleeps. He cares for people in other countries too and in the countries where our missionaries live. God loves us very much and cares for us day and night.**

Help the children to write a prayer thanking and praising God for His care. Write their sentences on a poster board to be shared with the large group. Some possible suggestions are: Thank You, God, for never sleeping. We praise You, God, that You care for us. Thank You, God, for giving us homes. Thank You, God, for giving us families. If children have time, they may use crayons or markers to illustrate the prayer.

During *Sharing in Worship*, each child will read his or her sentence of the prayer.

Sharing in Worship
(20-25 minutes)

Omit any of the following sections if you did not offer the corresponding activity. The devotional may be completed without the presentation of Group 4.

Call to worship (Groups 1 and 2): **God cared for His people when they were in Egypt, and God cared for them when they left Egypt. Groups 1 and 2 will present a poem about God's care for His people.** Groups 1 and 2 present their poem and paper chains.

Song: Sing "Praise Him, Praise Him, All Ye Little Children" from page 182.

Lord's Supper: We are so thankful that God cares for us. He shows us His care in many ways. One way God showed His care for us was when He sent Jesus to earth to die for us. Christians take the Lord's Supper each week to remember what

Jesus did for them.

Offering: Last week we discussed our "Harvest Banks" and how our church uses our offerings to help missionary families and poor people. God cares for these people and us happy when we give our money to help these people know that God cares for them. Children should put their offering into the "Harvest Bank" made in Worship session 9.

Scripture (Group 3)**: This group read a Psalm telling how God watches over us and cares for us. As you listen to this 23 Psalm watch the children show how they have illustrated these verses.** Group 3 will share their drawings as the tape recording of Psalm 23 is played.

Devotional **(Group 4)**: **Has anyone ever stayed up all night long? If you ever have or if you have stayed up very late you know how tired you felt the next day. We all need our sleep. God made us to need to sleep. Does God ever sleep? No, God is always awake. That is how He can take care of us all day and all night, every day and every night.**

We heard a poem from Groups 1 and 2 about how God took care of His people. When God sent the plagues to Pharaoh and the Egyptians, He took care of His people. And when they were finally allowed to go, God took care of them by providing the pillar of cloud in the day to guide them and a pillar of fire in the night to guide them. God never got tired of taking care of His people.

God is always taking care of us. He never gets tired or forgets about us. Today we are worshiping God because He cares for us every day and night.There are many ways God cares for us. He provides people and things that we need. We are going to watch Group 4 share four skits. Then we will talk about how God cared for these people.

Allow Group 4 to present their role plays. If you did not offer this activity, read the situations found in Group 4 to the children and ask them to tell you how God cared for each person.

Personal Praise (Group 5)**: God has given us many people and things to show He cares for us. Group 5 drew some of those things.** Group 5 shares their drawings.

Prayer (Group 6)**: We talked about how God takes care of His people everywhere, in all nations. When it is day in one country it is night in another. But God is always taking care of His people everywhere. We will end our sharing time with the prayers we wrote.** Group 6 will share their prayers.

Closing Moments
(10-15 minutes)

"God Cares for Me"folder. Today's addition to the folders will be a silhouette picture of each child. You will need a large roll of white paper, 8" x 10" sheets of both black and white paper, pencil, masking tape, scissors, glue, chalk, chalkboard, and a high-intensity light (either a projector light or high-beam flashlight).

Tape the roll paper to a blank, smooth wall. Set the child in front of the wall and shine the light at him or her. Carefully trace around the shadowed profile.

Cut out the silhouette and have the child trace his or her image onto the black paper. Then glue it to the white paper. At the bottom of the picture, help the child carefully copy from the chalkboard, "God cares for ________ day and night." Fill in the blank with the child's name.

Special Note: This activity needs a great deal of adult supervision. You may want to start this today and extend it through the rest of the sessions. The finished product will be something parents will enjoy, but you will need at least one person to hold the light (depending on which type you use), one to make sure the child sits still, and one to trace.

Unit Three
Worship God for His Care

Session 11

God Cares for Us Wherever We Go

Worship Focus

Worship God because He cares for us wherever we go.

Transition Time

(10-15 minutes)

Allow time for the children to use the rest room and drinking fountain.

With the children's help, arrange the chairs in two semicircles with an aisle in the middle. Involve children in the following activity.

Miriam's tambourines. You will need dessert-size paper plates, paper clips, crayons, yarn, and a paper punch. Have each child color the bottoms of two paper plates and put his name on one. Punch holes around the two plates at one time. Sew the plates together with the yarn, tops facing. Just before finishing the sewing, put several metal paper clips inside. Sew the plates completely closed. Save the tambourines for later.

Launching the Theme

(10 minutes)

Action play. Divide the children into five groups and assign each group a part in the play. Each group will add a sound effect to the story. The leader should read the story in an exaggerated and excited "Radio Announcer" voice. When the children hear their "character" mentioned, they should make the appropriate sound. Have each group practice making their sound once before beginning the story.

The Crossing of the Red Sea

Cast:
Announcer (Leader)
Moses – "Yea!"
Grumbling Hebrews–"Grumble, grumble, grumble!"
Chariots and Horses – "Whir, whir, clop, clop, neigh!"
Wicked Pharaoh – "Boo!"
Red Sea – "Whoosh!"

Now **Moses** obeyed God and led those **grumbling Hebrews** out of Egypt toward the **Red Sea.**

But the wicked Pharaoh got to thinking, "Who is going to do all the work around here?" So the **wicked Pharaoh** called his army with their **chariot and horses** and told them to bring those **grumbling Hebrews** back.

When the **grumbling Hebrews** saw the **wicked Pharaoh's** army with their **chariots and horses** was following close behind them, they became afraid. They asked **Moses,** "Why did God bring us out here to die? The **Red Sea** is in front of us and **wicked Pharaoh's** army is behind us with chariots and horses."

But **Moses** replied, "God says to be quiet, you **grumbling Hebrews,** and move on toward the **Red Sea.**"

So Moses lifted up his staff, God parted the Red Sea, and the **grumbling Hebrews** crossed over to the other side on dry ground.

Meanwhile, the **wicked Pharaoh** ordered his army with **chariots and horses** to follow those **grumbling Hebrew.** But, Moses lowered his staff and wicked Pharaoh's army was buried in the Red Sea.

God took care of His people and helped them to be able to leave Egypt. What did the Hebrews do? (They grumbled, or complained.) **God still cared for them and helped them escape from Pharaoh and his men when they were chasing the Hebrews. How did God help His people then?** (God parted the Red Sea and allowed the Hebrews to cross, but caused the Red Sea to close up and drown Pharaoh's army.) **When the Hebrews saw this miracle, they were reminded of God's power and His love and care for them.**

Sometimes we sound like those "grumbling Hebrews." We complain about things and we need to be reminded of God's love and care for us. Today we will talk about God's care for us wherever we go. We will worship God because He cares for us wherever we go.

Briefly explain the choices of preparation for worship. You can allow the children to choose in which group to participate. Group 6 will need five pupils to participate in the skit.

Building the Theme

(30 minutes)

1. **Call to Worship.** This group will present a choral reading

during the worship time. You will need poster board and markers. Before the session, print the following choral reading on the poster board.

Leader: I will sing to the Lord, for He is great!

Group: The horse and its rider He has cast into the sea.

Leader: The Lord makes me strong and gives me a song to sing.

Group: The horse and its rider He has cast into the sea.

Leader: I will praise the Lord, for He is God.

Group: The horse and its rider He has cast into the sea.

Leader: Pharaoh's chariots and his army He has cast into the sea; they sank like stones.

Group: The horse and its rider He has cast into the sea.

Leader: All people everywhere, in every nation, will know the Lord is God.

One way we can worship God is by reciting a choral reading. This means I will say a sentence and then you all will say a sentence. You will always respond with the same sentence. Display the poster board. **We will practice saying our lines while we look at the words on the poster board. Who are we talking about when we say, "the horse and its rider"?** (Pharaoh's army and their horses and chariots.) **Who cast them into the sea?** (God.) Read again, asking the children to read their lines. When the children are comfortable with their lines, ask them to practice playing their tambourines as they say their lines.

During *Sharing in Worship*, children will say the choral reading as they play their tambourines.

2. Scripture. This group will make a sandpaper painting of a Scripture verse. You will need a poster board to which you have glued several sheets of sandpaper (sand side up), a soft pencil, salt, glitter, paprika, a can of clear spray varnish, and Bibles.

Look up Psalm 86:10 (ICB) in your Bible. Have the children look up the verse in their Bibles. Read the verse aloud, **"Only you are God."**

What does this verse mean? Allow pupils to respond. Help them to understand that there is only one God, and only He is more powerful than anyone or anything.

In large block letters, print the words, "Only You are God" on the sandpaper with a soft pencil. Then show the children the salt, glitter, and paprika. Ask the children to choose which colors they will sprinkle on the background and on each letter. Make small paper cones by rolling a piece of paper to sprinkle the salt, glitter, and paprika.

When the children have finished, hold the spray can about ten inches from the painting. Spray and let dry, and spray again.

During *Sharing in Worship*, the children will display the painting and say Psalm 86:10 together.

3. Lord's Supper. This group will prepare a coded message to introduce the Lord's Supper. You will need the code below, poster board, and a marker. Before the session, copy the code across the top of the poster board.

A=!	C=#	D=$
E=%	F=^	G=&
H=*	O=)	R=?
S=/	U=+	V=(
W=>		

Does God see us in church? Home? School? Outside playing? When we are alone? When we are with friends? When we obey? When we disobey? Allow children to respond after each suggestion. God sees us all the time, wherever we go. We can never go any place where God cannot see us. Does God always care for us? (Yes.) **God made us and loves us and He cares for us always, wherever we go. Today we are worshiping God because He cares for us wherever we go.**

We will make a coded message to remind the large group that God cares for us. Ask the pupils to print the message "God cares for us wherever we go" in code on the poster board. Leave room above the coded message to write in the letters of the message. Use tape or Plasti-Tak to attach the poster to the wall.

During *Sharing in Worship,* display the poster board and ask the large group to decode the message.

4. Prayer. This group will prepare a mural to introduce the prayer time. You will need a large sheet of blank newsprint, crayons, old magazines and catalogs, scissors, Plasti-Tak or tape, and glue.

Where are some different places you go in your neighborhood? (Allow children to respond.) **Does God see you when you are at these different places? Does God ever not see you? God made us and loves us. He always sees us wherever we go. He cares for us no matter where we are. It makes us feel safe to know God is always watching over us. We are worshiping God today because He cares for us wherever we go.**

Have the children draw pictures of places they go. Many environments can mesh, rural and city, to create a special neighborhood where they are reminded that God is there watching over them. Pictures should include such things as homes, schools, church buildings, parks, and barns. Encourage the children to add details to their drawings such as trees, park benches, play equipment, animals and so forth.

Ask the children to cut

magazine or catalog pictures to represent people in their lives such as parents, teachers, preachers, friends, and so on. Then ask them to glue these pictures on the mural. Attach the completed mural to the wall using tape or Plasti-Tak.

During *Sharing in Worship*, each child will point to a place he or she drew on the mural and say a sentence prayer, thanking God for caring for him or her at that place. Practice the presentation during the small-group time.

5. Devotional. This group will present a skit about God's care during the devotional time. You will need copies of activity page 11A and a few sticks.

Distribute activity page 11A to the children and assign parts. Be sure to have a good reader for the narrator.

Where does God care for you? (Home, school, play, and so on.) **Is there a time when God does not care for you?** (No.)

We are going to practice a skit to present during our worship time together. It is about a boy and girl who become lost and how God watches over them even when no one else sees them or knows where they are. Practice the skit several times with the children.

During *Sharing in worship*, children will present the skit.

6. Personal Praise. This group will prepare puzzles, praising God for His care. You will need copies of activity page 11B, crayons or markers, scissors, and glue.

Distribute the materials to the children. **Where does God care for you?** (Allow children to name places.) **God cares for us wherever we go.** Ask the children to cut out the puzzle pieces and glue them together onto a piece of construction paper. Then ask them to write a place where God cares for them on the blank line. They may use crayons or markers to color their puzzle.

During *Sharing in Worship*, each child will display his or her puzzle and thank God for caring for him or her at that place.

Sharing in Worship
(20-25 minutes)

Omit any of the following sections if you did not offer the corresponding activity. The Lord's Supper and devotional may be completed without the presentation of Groups 3 and 5.

Call to Worship (Group 1): **One way we can worship God is by saying and listening to a choral reading. Group 1 has prepared a choral reading that they would like to share at this time. You might all want to get out your tambourines to join us in praising God.** Group 1 will share their choral reading at this time.

Song: Sing "God Cared for Moses " from page 183 and "God Is So Good" from page 181.

Scripture (Group 2): Group 2 displays their poster and says the Scripture verse. **God is the only God. What are some things that only God can do?** (Allow the children to name things.)

Lord's Supper (Group 3): **Group 3 has a message about God's care for us, but their message in in a code. Let's decode the message to find out about God's care.** Display the coded message made by Group 3 and ask the children to decode the message: "God cares for us wherever we go." If you did not offer this activity, continue with the following discussion.

God sees us all the time. He watches over us and cares for us. Since God sees us always, He also sees the things we do that do not please Him. We need to ask God's forgiveness for those things. Jesus died on the cross so we could be forgiven for those things we have done that do not please God. Let us think about Jesus' dying on the cross for us and let us also think of anything for which we need to ask forgiveness. As the bread and juice are passed, think about these things and talk to God.

Offering: We are collecting money to help poor people and missionaries. God knows where these people are. He cares for them wherever they are. Let's praise God for caring for these people. Let's pray that our offerings can be used to help these people. Children should put offering into "Harvest Bank."

Prayer (Group 4): **Can you think of some places where God cares for you? Group 4 made a mural of places where God cares for them. Let's pray with them now and thank God for caring for us wherever we go.** Group 4 displays their mural and prays.

Devotional (Group 5): Ask Group 5 to present their skit. If you did not offer this activity, make five copies of activity page 11B and ask five good readers to read the skit to the large group. **Have you ever been lost?** (Allow a few children to share about a time they have been lost.) **We saw in the skit how Mike and Amy became lost on their camping trip. It is easy to get lost in a new school or any new place. Sometimes we might get lost in a crowded place, like a grocery store or a shopping mall. We might feel afraid when we are not sure where we are.**

Think how the Hebrews must have felt when they were walking towards the Red Sea. How do you think they felt when they knew Pharaoh's army was coming behind them and the big Red Sea was in front of them? I think they were afraid. Did the Hebrews need be be afraid. (No.) **Who was watching over them?** (God.) **Did God take care of them no matter where they were?** (Yes.)

God always knows where we are, even if we don't know. God

is always watching over us. God cares about what happens to us. God cared about His people when Pharaoh's army was after them. God cares about you wherever you are. We are worshiping God today for caring for us wherever we are.

Personal Praise (Group 6): Ask Group 6 to display their puzzles and tell the places they are thankful God cares for them.

Prayer: Ask a child to pray, asking God to keep the class safe as they travel to their homes.

Closing Moments
(10-15 minutes)

"God Cares for Me" folder. To make a "trip mobile," you will need small rings, string (cut in 18" to 25" pieces), paper plates, paper, crayons, and scissors.

Encourage each child to think about a trip (far or near) he has taken. Ask each child to draw reminders of the trip on the paper. Examples might be, the vehicle in which he or she rode (car, plane, bus), special sights he or she viewed (a ship, mountains), people he or she visited (Grandma, a new baby).

When the children have several "reminders" colored, ask them to cut them out and set them aside. Distribute the paper plates and ask the children to write, "God Cares for Me Wherever I Go" around the bottom. Make as many small cuts around each plate as each child has "reminders." Ask the children to tie pictures to pieces of string and thread through the individual slots in the paper plate. Bring all the strings together at the top of the plate and tie to the ring for hanging. Children can put their mobiles into their folders to take home at the end of the month.

For Next Week

You will need different kinds of dry cereal, juice, or pop, and small paper cups. See *Transition Time* in Session 12.

God Gives Us Food and Water

Worship Focus

Worship God because He provides food and water.

Transition Time

(10-15 minutes)

Allow time for the children to use the rest room and drinking fountain. Prepare the room for the following game.

Taste Test. Before the session, gather different kinds of dry cereal, juice, and pop that your children will be familiar with. Place small amounts of the cereal or liquids in unmarked containers. Set up a cereal station, a juice station, and a pop station with a leader at each station. Divide the children into three groups. Send each group to a different station. The children in the group will take turns being blindfolded, tasting one food or drink, and guessing what it is. When groups are finished at one station, ask the groups to switch stations, so that each group has a turn at each station. If you wish to keep score, leaders may record points for each food item guessed correctly. The group with the most points, wins.

Launching the Theme

(10 minutes)

Cut-and-Tell story. You will need a dessert-sized paper plate, scissors, and felt markers. As you tell the story, cut the folded plate according to the pattern on page 24. See the illustration on this page. Fold and add eyes to the quail. Practice cutting the quail as you say the following poem.

"Something to eat, something to eat!"
The Hebrews complained,
"We're quite dead on our feet.
We've got to have something, something to eat!"

"Manna to eat, manna to eat!
We're so very sick of this heavenly treat,
We'd rather be in Egypt than have more manna to eat!"

"Give us some meat, give us some meat!"
"Surely God," they whined,
"You could manage this feat.
We're tired of manna, so give us some meat!"

So God sighed and said, "Quail to eat, quail to eat.
Can't you ever be grateful?
Must you always repeat,
'We're so bored with just manna!' So here's quail to eat."
(Show finished quail.)

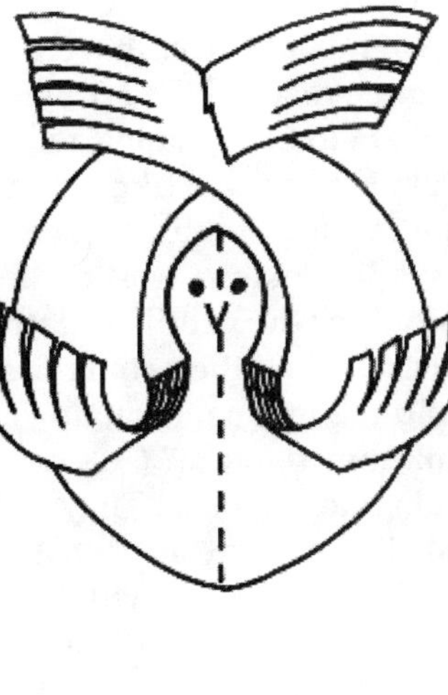

God must have gotten tired of hearing His people complain when He was taking care of them. He helped them cross over the Red Sea. He guided them with a cloud and fire. He gave them manna every morning to eat. But they still whined.

Sometimes we are like God's people. Have you ever complained about the food you had to eat? What if your mom fed you spinach or lima beans or liver? (Allow children to respond.) **We need to thank God for all our food. Think about the foods you tasted this morning. God gave us many different kinds of food, and He made us able to taste each food! Our God is wonderful! Today we are going to worship God for giving us food and water.**

Briefly explain the choices of preparation for worship. You can allow the children to choose in which group they would like to participate. To divide the children more evenly, ask them to draw out slips of torn white paper (manna) that have numbers written on them. The children would go to the group that corresponds with the number on the paper.

Building the Theme

(30 minutes)

1. **Call to Worship.** This group will make a mural showing where our foods come from. You will need a large sheet of newsprint, crayons, cotton balls, and baby oil.

Think of all the different kinds of food God gives us. God

gives us many kinds of food. Some foods we like to taste, and other foods we don't like so well. What are some of your favorite kinds of foods? (Allow the children to respond.) **Your mom or dad probably gets most of your food from the grocery store. But where do these foods come from before they get to the grocery?** Allow time for the children to discuss the origins of foods. Help them to understand how some fruits come from trees; cheese, yogurt, and ice cream come from milk; flour comes from wheat; beef comes from cattle; and so on. Help them to understand that God is the originator of our foods.

Ask the children to choose a section of the newsprint. They will draw a picture of their favorite food. Ask them to push hard on the crayons and fill in their entire space, leaving no part of the paper uncolored.

When the pictures are completed, turn the paper over and lightly rub oil on the back with a cotton ball. The finished mural will have a stained-glass appearance, especially if you mount it on a window.

During *Sharing in Worship,* each child will point to his or her picture on the mural and say, "I thank God for (favorite food they drew)." Then he or she will say a sentence about the origin of the food. For example, "I thank God for ice cream. God made the cows that give us milk to make ice cream."

2. Personal Praise. This group will make bookmarks to remind the group that God cares for us. You will need brightly-colored construction paper cut into 3" x 7" strips, glue, glitter, toothpicks, and a chalkboard with chalk. Before the session, cut enough 3" x 7" strips of construction paper for every child in the session.

Let's open our Bibles to 1 Peter 5:7. Help those children who need help to locate the verse. Read the verse aloud with the children. **"Cast all your anxiety on him because he cares for you. Who cares for us?"** (God does.) **What are some ways God cares for us?** (He gives us food, homes, families, friends, and so on.) **How did God show that He cared for His people in our Bible story today?** (He took care of them by providing food and water for them.) **Today we are going to make a bookmark to remind everyone in our session that God cares for us.**

Print "God cares for you" on the chalkboard. Pass out the strips of construction paper. Ask the children to write "God cares for you" on each bookmark and trace the letters using a toothpick dipped in glue. Then ask them to sprinkle the letters with glitter and allow it to dry.

During *Sharing in Worship,* ask the large group to form a prayer circle and ask the children from the small group to give each child a bookmark. Go around the circle and ask each child to thank God for a way He cares for him or her.

3. Devotion. This group will prepare a skit, showing how God's people might have acted when they first found manna. You will need a large, clean sheet; an air-pop popcorn popper (a regular popper will leave oil on the carpet); and popcorn. If you use a regular popcorn popper, use a large plastic sheet under the cloth sheet.

When God's people were hungry, what did God provide for them to eat? (Manna and quail.) **Manna was like a thin wafer. When the early morning dew dried, manna was left on the ground for the people to gather and eat. When the people first found the manna, what do you think they thought?** (Allow children to respond.) **They probably weren't sure what it was. In fact, they named it "manna" because "manna" means, "What is it?" We are going to write a skit showing how the people might have acted when they first found the manna.** Help the children to create the skit. The skit can be very simple. An example follows: Some Israelites wake up in the morning. They are rubbing their eyes and yawning. Then they notice some white stuff at their feet. They say, "What is it?" Someone tastes some and tells everyone, "It's good to eat!" Everyone tastes the manna and runs and grabs containers to gather it in. Someone says, "What shall we call this food?" One person says, "White wafers." Everyone says, "No." Another person says, "Food from God." Everyone says, "No." A third person says, "Let's call it *manna* because we asked what it was." Everyone says, "Yes."

During *Sharing in Worship*, spread out the sheet and set the popcorn popper on it. Allow the popcorn to pop freely into the air and out onto the sheet as the children watch from a safe distance. The group can then perform the skit and pretend the popcorn is manna.

4. Scripture. This group will present a responsive reading from Psalm 104. You will need poster board and markers. Before the session, print the following reading on the poster board.

Child 1: My whole being, praise the Lord.

Group: Lord my God, You are very great.

Child 2: The earth is full of things you made.

Group: Lord my God, You are very great.

Child 3: You make the grass for cattle and vegetables for the use of man.

Group: Lord my God, You are very great.

Child 4: You make food grow from the earth.

Group: Lord my God, You are very great.

Child 5: You give us bread that gives us strength.

Group: Lord my God, You are very great.

Read Psalm 104:1a, 13b, 14, 15b (ICB) with the children. "My whole being, praise the Lord. . . . The earth is full of the things you made. You make the grass for cattle and vegetables for the use of man. You make food grow from the earth. . . . You give us bread that gives us strength."

Who is being praised in these verses? (The Lord.) **What are some of the things mentioned in these verses that God has made?** (Grass for the cattle, plants for man, food, bread.) **Why should we praise God for making these things?** (Without food for the animals or food for us, we would all die because we need food to live.)

We are going to do a responsive reading. Someone will say a sentence and then everyone will respond by saying, "Lord my God, you are very great." This is one way we can worship God.

Display the poster board. Read the responsive reading for the children. Then ask them to read it with you. Assign each child a sentence to say. After each child says his or her sentence, the whole group will say, "Lord my God, you are very great." If they have time, children may use markers to illustrate the responsive reading.

During *Sharing in Worship*, children will display the poster board and read the responsive reading.

5. Offering. This group will prepare a story wheel showing how God cared for God's people and how He cares for us. You will need copies of activity page 12A, crayons or markers, scissors, and paper fasteners.

How did God care for His people by giving them food and water? (He sent manna in the morning and quail in the evening. He made water come from a rock.) **Does God care for us by giving us food and water too?** (Yes) **How does God care for us?** (Allow children to share their ideas.)

Distribute activity page 12A. Ask the children to color the two wheels, cut them out, and fasten them together using a paper fastener. Then ask them to match the Bible-times pictures to the modern-day pictures. **Which picture shows how God gives the Israelites bread?** (Gathering manna.) **Which picture shows one way God gives us bread?** (Mom bakes rolls.) Continue with the other pictures: The Israelites asked Moses for food, we pray to God for food; God sent the Israelites quail for meat, we go buy meat at the grocery; God gave the Israelites water from a rock, we drink water from faucets and drinking fountains. Assign each child one picture or pair of pictures to explain during the worship time.

During *Sharing in Worship*, children will tell each way God cared for the Israelites followed by the corresponding way He cares for us.

6. Prayer. This group will thank God for foods from each of the four food groups. You will need copies of activity page 12B and crayons or markers.

We are worshiping God today for giving us food and water. What would happen if we didn't have food to eat or water to drink? (We would die.) **Our bodies need certain kinds of foods to stay healthy. If we ate only candy every day, what would happen?** (We would be unhealthy and get sick.)

There are four different food groups. What are the four food groups? (Fruits and vegetables, meats and legumes, bread and cereal, dairy products.) Distribute activity page 12B. Ask the children to follow the instructions on the page to find the hidden foods from the four food groups. They will find an apple, cheese, a fish, and a piece of bread. **What fruit or vegetable are you thankful for? What meat? What bread or cereal? What dairy product?** Ask the children to write a food from each of the four food groups in the pictures on their activity pages.

During *Sharing in Worship*, children will lead a prayer time thanking God for the foods they wrote.

Sharing in Worship

(20-25 minutes)

Omit any of the following sections if you did not offer the corresponding activity. The devotional and offering may be completed without the presentations of Groups 3 and 5.

Call to worship (Group 1): **Group 1 has made a mural showing us where some foods come from.** Group 1 presents their mural.

Song: Sing "All the World Was Made by God" from page 182.

Personal Praise **(Group 2)**: Let's all make a prayer circle. Group 2 is going to give everyone a bookmark that says, "God cares for you." This will remind us how God provides for us. Let's go around our prayer circle and each take a turn thanking God for a way He cares for us. **Group 2 distributes bookmarks.**

Devotional (Group 3): **We heard earlier about how God provided food and water for His people. Do you wonder what the people must have thought when they first saw the manna? Group 3 has written a skit and will present it to us at this time.** Pop the popcorn and ask Group 3 to present the skit. If you did not offer this activity, discuss how the people might have felt when they first saw manna and continue with the following discussion.

Have you ever skipped a meal? Maybe you were busy or just forgot to eat. How did you feel? (Allow children to respond.) **We saw today how the Hebrews, God's people, complained about being hungry and thirsty. Did God love His people?** (Yes, He did.) **Does God take are of people He loves?** Yes. **How did God take care of the Hebrews?** (Allow children to respond.) **He provided manna and quail and water. Does God love us?** Yes. **Does He take care of us?** (Yes.) **How does God provide food for us?** (Allow children to respond.) **He allows our parents to have jobs for money to buy food. He sends sunshine and rain for farmers to grow food. God takes care of us by providing the many different kinds of foods our bodies need to stay alive and healthy. We are worshiping God today for providing us with food and water.**

Scripture (Group 4)**: One way we can worship God is by telling Him how great He is. Group 4 has read some verses that tell how God has provided food for us. They will take turns saying a sentence about these verses. Then we will all say, "Lord my God, you are very great."** Group 4 shares their responsive reading.

Offering (Group 5)**: Many times poor people don't have money to buy food they need. Let's thank God for providing food for the Israelites and for us and pray that our offering might be used to help provide food to someone who needs it.** Group 5 presents their wheels. When they are finished, choose two children to collect the offering and put it in the "Harvest Bank."

Lord's Supper: God cares for us by giving us food and water. But God loves us so much that He gave us something much better than food or water. God sent His Son, Jesus, to die for the wrong things we do. Let's thank God for Jesus now.

Prayer (Group 6)**: We need different kinds of foods to stay healthy. Does anyone know from what four food groups we need food?** (Allow response.) **Group 6 will lead us in prayer, thanking God for foods from the four food groups.** After Group 6 completes their prayer, close with prayer, thanking God for providing our food and water.

Closing Moments
(10-15 minutes)

"God Cares for Me" folder. Help the children make their own quails (like the one you made in the cut-and-tell story) to tuck into their folders. Or punch holes in the top of the quail and hang them from the ceiling.

Bottled manna. You will need an empty baby food jar for each child, silicone glue, fine sand, white glitter, and small containers of water. Begin to collect baby food jars early in the week.

At least one day before the session, put a thick layer of glue on the inside of each lid to resemble "sand dunes." Sprinkle a light layer of sand on the glue for color. Dry overnight.

Allow children to fill the baby food jars with water. Add one or two teaspoons of white glitter to the water. Help them spread a thick layer of glue along the inside rim of the lid, and spread some more around the outside rim of the jar. Tightly screw the lid on the jar and allow the glue to dry, making the jar watertight.

Once the glue has dried, turn the jar upside down. Shake the jar to watch the "manna" fall from "heaven" to the "desert sand."

God Cares for Us by Giving Us Rules

Worship Focus

Worship God because He gives us rules.

Transition Time

(10-15 minutes)

Send the children in small groups to the rest room and water fountain. Welcome any newcomers and involve them in the following game.

Red Light, Green Light. Choose one child or adult to be the leader. The leader will stand at one end of the room. The rest of the children will stand in a line across the other end of the room. You may need to move chairs and furniture out of the way. The leader will turn his or her back to the large group and say, "green light." As long as the leader's back is turned, the large group may quietly walk toward him or her. As soon as the leader turns around and says, "red light," everyone freezes wherever he or she is. If the leader sees anyone move after he or she says, "red light," the leader may send that person back to the starting place. The game ends when one person reaches the leader and taps him or her on the shoulder. That person becomes the new leader for the next game.

Launching the Theme

(10 minutes)

I am going to list some rules. After I say each rule, you tell me where you usually are when you obey these rules. Following is a list of rules. You may wish to add some that you know your children are familiar with.

1. Don't run in the hall. (School)
2. You must go to bed at 8:30. (Home)
3. Walk with the green light. (Traffic)
4. Sharpen your pencils before the first bell rings.(School)
5. No fighting on the playground. (School)
6. Eat everything on your plate. (Home)
7. Use hand signals when riding your bike. (Traffic)
8. Put your clothes away. (Home)
9. Walk quietly and in single file. (School)
10. No jumping on the beds. (Home)
11. Don't play in the street. (Home)
12. Wash your hands before you eat. (Home)
13. Don't push in line. (School)
14. Don't talk when the teacher is talking. (School, church)

We have rules at home, rules at school, and traffic rules. Do we have any other kinds of rules? (Allow the children to respond with any other kinds of rules they can think of.) **Why do we have rules at all?** (Allow children to respond.) **We have rules for many reasons. One reason we have traffic rules is for our own safety. If nobody obeyed traffic rules we would have many accidents and many people would get hurt. We have rules at home because our parents know what is best for us. They want us to get our proper rest and meals, and don't want us to get hurt. Our school rules are so we don't get hurt and so we can all be able to learn. Think what it would be like to go to school and have no rules. It would be so noisy and crazy and wild that no one would be able to learn.**

God knew a long time ago that people would need rules. Moses went up the the top of Mount Sinai where God gave Moses ten rules, or commandments, to give to His people. God loved His people and knew they would need some rules to help them know how to love God and how to love each other. Does anyone know what we usually call these rules God gave Moses? (The Ten Commandments.) **Can anyone name any of those commandments?** (Allow children to respond. Then list some of the following rules God has given us: Make me your only God; Don't make or worship any idol; Use my name the right way; and so on.)

How do traffic rules help us? (Keep us safe.) **How do rules at home help us?** (Keep us healthy and safe.) **How do rules at school help us?** (Keep us safe and help us to learn.) **How do God's rules help us?** (Help us to know how to love God and each other.) **God gives us rules because He loves and cares for us. We will worship God today because He gives us rules.**

Briefly explain the choices of preparation for worship. Allow the children to choose in which group they would like to participate.

Building the Theme
(30 minutes)

1. Call to Worship. This group will tell God's rules in their own words for the call to worship. You will need ten cards; poster board and marker or chalkboard and chalk; a tape recorder and blank tape (optional). Before the session, print each of the following simplified forms of the Ten Commandments on a card and number the cards 1 to 10.

1. Make me your only God.
2. Do not make or worship any idol.
3. Use my name in a proper way.
4. Have a special day for God.
5. Honor your father and mother.
6. Do not kill.
7. Do not break your marriage promises.
8. Do not steal.
9. Do not tell lies.
10. Do not want to take something that is not yours.

Discuss each of God 's rules with the children. Give examples when necessary to help them understand the rules. Allow children to respond during the following discussion.

What do the first two rules mean? (We are to put God first, always. Whatever God wants us to do should always be more important than anything else.) **God's third commandment tells us to use God's name in a proper way. When is it proper to use God's name?** (Whenever we are talking to God or about God it is proper to say God's name.) **We are supposed to have a special day for God so we take time to worship Him and to rest. How do we honor our father and mother?** (By obeying them.) **Rule 6 means God does not want us to kill, and rule 7 means when we get married we should promise to stay married to that person. We should not take things that aren't ours and we shouldn't say things that are not true. Finally, we should be happy with what we have and not wish we had someone else's things.**

Ask for volunteers to read one of the rules for the worship time or record their reading on tape. Then print on the chalkboard or poster board Psalm 119:167 (ICB)—"I keep your rules. I love them very much."

During *Sharing in Worship*, ask the child with rule #1 to read his or her rule (or play the tape). Then ask everyone to say Psalm 119:167. Repeat this until all the rules have been read.

2. Call to Worship. This group will construct a mobile of the Ten Commandments. You will need copies of activity pages 13A and 13B, crayons or markers, scissors, yarn or string, a hole punch, and a hanger for each child.

We have talked about how God's rules are important to us. Why do we need God's rules? (So we know how to love God and how to love each other.) **Do you think it is important to remember God's rules?** (Yes, it is.) **We are going to make a mobile to remind us of God's rules.**

Distribute activity pages 13A and 13B. Ask the children to color the mobile pieces on the pages and cut them out. Punch a hole in each mobile piece where indicated. Tie one end of a piece of yarn on each tablet. Tie the other end to the hanger. As the children are working, focus a discussion on what each commandment means in their own words.

During *Sharing in Worship*, children will display their mobiles as Group 1 reads their paraphrases of the commandments. You may wish to hang the mobiles in the front of the room now rather than asking children to come forward and hold them during the worship time.

3. Special music. This group will sing a song, thanking God for His rules. You will need "Oh, How We Love God's Rules" from page 183, poster board or a song chart, and a marker. Before the session, print the words to the song on the poster board.

Oh, how we love God's rules.
(Repeat twice.)
Because God cares for us.

Oh, we will obey God. (Repeat twice.)
Because God cares for us.

Oh, help us keep your rules.
(Repeat twice.)
Because You care for us.

When we know how much God cares for us, we want to sing and praise Him for His care. We want to worship God today because He gives us rules to help us. Display the poster board for the children and sing the song for them. Then sing the song again, asking them to sing with you. If you have time, ask the children to create additional stanzas to the song by saying a rule God gave us for the first three lines. For example, "Oh, you tell us not to steal. Oh, you tell us not to steal. Oh, you tell us not to steal because You care for us." **Write the stanzas the children suggest on the poster board. Practice singing the song several times.**

During *Sharing in Worship*, the children will display the poster board and sing the song for the large group.

4. Scripture. This group will put motions to Psalm 119:1-3 for the Scripture time. You will need a Bible (*ICB*), tape recorder, and a blank tape.

Read Psalm 119:1-3 to the children from the *International Children's Bible.* "Happy are the people who live pure lives. They follow the Lord's teachings. Happy are the people who keep his rules. They ask him for help with their whole heart. They don't do what is wrong. They follow his ways."

The Psalms are about many different things, but one thing the Psalms talk about are God's rules. They tell us many good things about God's rules. They tell us we will be happy if we follow God's rules.

Ask the children to suggest motions for the Scripture verses. Suggestions follow:
Happy—point to smiles on their faces; are the people—point to different people in the large group; who live—march in place facing forward; pure lives—hand on top of head; They follow—turn to the left and march in place; the Lord's—point up; teachings—hands open to make a book; Happy—point to smiles on their faces; are the people—point to people in the large group; who keep—hands together to make a cup; his rules—point up; They ask him for help—arms held out in front, palms up; with their whole heart—hands over heart; They don't do—shake heads "no"; what is wrong—shake finger; They follow his ways—turn right and march in place, pointing up.

Assign a child or children to record Psalm 119:1-3 on the blank tape. Play the tape as the children practice the motions to the verses.

During *Sharing in Worship*, the children will play the tape of the verses as they do the motions.

5. Devotional. This group will present situations about keeping God's rules. You will need a poster board, marker, paper, crayons, and pencils. Before the session, print the following situations on the poster board.

1. Jerome stayed up too late and is tired at school.
2. Alicia ate a whole bag of candy. She feels sick.
3. David didn't stop his bike at the corner and a car bumped him.
4. Jenny and Tessa didn't hear the instructions for the test because they were talking.
5. James punched Russell on the playground.
6. Kristi's baseball knocked over her mom's lamp and broke it.

God gave us rules because He loves us. He knows what is best for us. Sometimes we don't always obey rules and many times we end up getting hurt because we don't obey. Display the poster board. **What rule is being broken in each of these situations? How are the children hurt because they disobeyed the rule?** (Allow children to respond.) Write the children's responses beside each situation. For example, in situation #1, Jerome stayed up past his bedtime. Now he won't think well at school. When you have discussed each situation, distribute paper and pencils or crayons. Assign each child or children one situation to tell about during the worship time. Children may draw pictures to illustrate their situation or write a few sentences about their situation.

During *Sharing in Worship*, each child will tell about his or her situation.

6. Prayer. This group will lead a prayer, thanking God for His rules. You will need Bibles, paper, and pencils.

We know God gave the ten rules, or commandments to Moses so that His people would know how to love God and how to love each other. The first four rules were made so the people would know how to love God. The last six rules were made so that people would know how to love each other.

Ask the children to open their Bibles to Exodus 20. Read Exodus 20: 3, 4a, 7, 8, 12-17a. **God's rules help us to be happy. Let's think about how these rules help us. How does the rule, "Remember the Sabbath day" help us?** (We go to church and learn more about God and how to do right.) **How does the rule "Honor your father and mother" help us?** (When we obey our parents, we please God. We learn the right way to live.) **How does the rule "Do not steal" help us?** (The things we own are safe as well as the things that belong to everyone else.) Continue with the other commandments. Ask each child to choose a commandment for which he or she is thankful and write a short prayer to God thanking Him for the way that commandment helps us.

During *Sharing in Worship*, the children will read their prayers to God.

Sharing in Worship
(20-25 minutes)

Call to Worship (Groups 1 and 2): **God gave us rules to help us! He gave us rules because He loves us. Let's listen as Groups 1 and 2 help us praise God for His rules.** Group 1 reads their paraphrases as Group 2 displays their mobiles.

Special Music (Group 3): Group 3 sings "Oh, How We Love God's Rules."

Lord's Supper: God's name is great because He is great! He is our Creator and Father, and He sent His only Son to be our Savior. Let's think about how good God has been to us, how much He cares for us, and how much we love Him and His Son. Pray and serve the Lord's Supper.

Offering: We have filled our "Harvest Bank" and will be

giving it today to help feed some people who are hungry. By worshiping God in this way, we are showing others that He cares for them. Giving our offering each week is one way we worship. Choose two children to collect the offering.

Scripture (Group 4): **Group 4 discovered some good things written about God's rules in Psalm 119. They have put motions to the first three verses. They are going to share these verses and motions for us now.** Allow Group 3 to share.

Devotional **(Group 5):** How many of you like to play games? What are some of your favorite games to play? **(Allow children to respond.)** There are many different games to play. Some of you like to play soccer or baseball, and some of you like to play board games. Do all of these games have rules? **(Yes, they do.)** Why do you think these games have rules? **(Allow children to respond.)** What would happen if there were no rules? If there were no rules to these games, they would be no fun. People would get angry if there were no rules because people wouldn't be playing "'fair." It could be dangerous to play sports if there were not rules. **You might get hurt.**

We have rules at other times in our lives too. We know we have traffic rules to keep us safe. We know we have rules at school to be safe and to be able to learn. We know we have rules at home to stay healthy and safe. We have these rules because people care about us.

Does God care about us? Of course He does. He loves us and wants us to be happy. God gave us rules to help us. Group 5 will tell us about some children who found out how disobeying rules can hurt us. Group 5 presents their situations. If you did not offer this activity, read the situations from Group 5 and ask the children, "What rules did the children disobey? How were the children hurt because they disobeyed?" **We know the Bible says we will be happy if we follow God's rules. God gave us rules to know how to love Him and how to love each other. We are worshiping God today for giving us rules.**

Prayer (Group 6): **Group 6 is thankful for ways God's rules help us. They will lead us in prayer now.** Group 6 leads the prayer time.

Closing Moments
(10-15 minutes)

"God Cares for Me folder." You will need large sheets of finger paint paper, finger paints, sponges, clip clothespins, scissors, small paint brushes, newspapers to protect tables, and old shirts to protect clothes. The children will be making wrapping paper to be used at Christmas or other special occasions.

Help the children cut the sponges into appropriate shapes and clip the clothespins on them as handles. They can stamp the designs on the paper and write messages with the brushes. Messages might include:

"God cares," "The Lord is God," or "He cares for you." Encourage the children to express on the paper what they have learned in the past month.

Send the folders home with the children today.

Joyfully Worship God for Jesus

Worship Focus
We joyfully worship God for the birth of Jesus.

Transition Time
(10-15 minutes)
Send the children in small groups to the rest room and water fountain. Welcome newcomers and involve them in the following game.

Bean-bag Toss. With masking tape, construct two large squares on the floor, one containing the letter *H* and the other containing the letter *S*. Ask the children to stand single file behind a line approximately 10′ to 12′ away from the squares. The children will take turns tossing a bean bag to the squares. then the bag lands in the square, the child must name one thing that makes him or her happy. If the bag lands in the *S* square, the child must name one way he or she shows others he or she is happy. Continue the game until everyone has had at least one turn.

Launching the Theme
(10 minutes)
Before class, print the following Scriptures on slips of paper for the children to read. These Scriptures are taken from the *International Children's Bible.*

"Sing a new song to him. Play well and joyfully." Psalm 33:33.

"Clap your hands, all you people. Shout to God with joy." Psalm 47:1.

"Everything on earth, shout with joy to God!" Psalm 66:1.

"I will shout for joy when I sing praises to you." Psalm 71:23.

"Sing for joy to God, our strength." Psalm 81:1.

"I will sing for joy about what your hands have done." Psalm 92:4.

"Shout with joy to the Lord, all the earth. Burst into songs and praise." Psalm 98:4.

"Shout with joy to the Lord, all the earth. Burst into songs and praise." Psalm 98:4.

"Let the rivers clap their hands. Let the mountains sing together for joy." Psalm 98:8.

"Serve the Lord with joy. come before him with singing." Psalm 100:2.

"Be full of joy in the Lord always. I will say again, be full of joy." Philippians 4:4.

Distribute the Scripture papers to you readers during *Transition time* and help them practice reading the verses out loud to a friend.

In the game we just played, we talked about things that make us happy and how we show our happiness to others. Can anyone think of another word we could use instead of *happy*? I am thinking of a word that has just three letters. The first letter is *J*. Print a *J* on the chalkboard with two lines beside it. Ask the children to guess the word. The word is *joy*. **You're right! The word is *joy*! To be *joyful* means to be filled with joy or to be happy. Today, we want to worship God because He gives us joy. Listen to some Scripture verses which tell us how we can show our joy to God. See how many different ways to show joy you can hear from these verses.** Ask the children to read the verses at this time. When all verses have been read, ask the children to list different ways to show joy to God. Answers follow: sing, play, clap hands, shout, sing praises, serve, pray, and be filled with joy.

We are going to joyfully worship God today for the birth of His Son Jesus.

Explain the choices of *Building the Theme* and allow the children to choose in which group to participate.

Building the Theme
(30 minutes)
1. Call to Worship. This group will create a banner to present during the worship time. You will need pieces of poster board; a marker; a piece of felt (or burlap) a few inches longer than you want the banner to be; a dowel rod a couple of inches longer than the width of the felt; rug or craft yarn; fabric glue; and scraps of felt in various colors. Before the session, fold the banner along the top edge to form a casing for the dowel rod. Machine-stitch close to the edge of the cloth. Print each of the following Scriptures on a piece of poster board: Luke 1:31, "You will name him Jesus." Isaiah 9:6, "A child will be born to us . . . His name will be Wonderful Counselor, Powerful God, Father Who Lives Forever, Prince of Peace." Luke 1:32, "He will be great, and people will call him the Son of the Most High." Scriptures are taken from the *International*

Children's Bible.

Display the Scriptures you have prepared. Read them with the children. We can be joyful because of the names that have been given to Jesus. His names show us different things about Him. He is the Wonderful Counselor because we can go to Him for help with problems. He is the Powerful God, because He has all power. There is nothing that is too hard for Him. He lives forever. He has promised that we will live forever with Him. He is the Prince of Peace. He helps make peace between God and men.

Ask the children to design a simple banner, and decide who will make which parts. For example, the children could glue the name *Jesus* on the banner with craft yarn or trace the letters on fabric to glue on the banner.

When the banner is completed, insert the dowel into the casing, cut a piece of yarn for a hanger, and tie it to the ends of the dowel. Ask two children to hang the banner on a hook at the appropriate time. Help the children practice reading the Scripture verses from the poster board.

During *Sharing in Worship*, children will display the banner and read the Scriptures.

2. Special Music. This group will learn and illustrate a song. You will need "Jesus Came" from page 184, poster board, construction paper, and markers. Before the session, print the words to the song on poster board.

Display the poster board for the children. Sing the song once for them. Then ask them to sing it with you. When they are familiar with the words, help them decide how they will illustrate the song. The first illustration could be a night sky with the silhouette of some hills and a tree or a dark, lonely scene. The next illustration could show Mary and the manger. Then the stable and animals could be drawn, and so on. Make four scenes for each stanza. Decide who will work on each picture.

When the illustrations are completed, practice filing up front and standing together, or simply have the children sit together and stand where they are to sing. Assign two children to hold up the illustrations while the others sing.

During *Sharing in Worship*, children will sing the song once for the large group. Then they will ask the large group to join them in singing the song a second time.

3. Scripture. This group will learn a portion of Scripture from Mary's praise to God. You will need poster board and a marker. Before the session print the following words from Luke 1:46,47, 54, 55, *ICB* on the poster board. Do not print the italicized actions.

My soul praises the Lord;

(*Point to self, then raise arms; look up.*)

My heart is happy because God is my Savior.

(*Cross hands over heart; point up.*)

God has helped his people.

(*Point up; extend hands, palms up*).

God has done what he promised.

(*Point up; extend hands as if holding Bible.*)

Display the poster board for the children. Read the words to them. Then ask them to read with you. **Mary spoke these words as she praised God for promising her baby Jesus. She was joyful to be chosen by God for this important role–the mother of the Savior. She was willing to do whatever God wanted her to do.**

Divide the children into two groups. Group 1 will learn the first and third lines. Group 2 will learn the second and fourth lines. Allow the children to practice saying the lines until they can say them without looking at the poster board. Then demonstrate the actions for the children and ask them to practice saying the lines with the actions.

Option: Ask someone who knows sign language to teach the children how to sign some of the words of the Scripture.

During *Sharing in Worship*, the children will say the Scripture with the actions.

4. Devotional. This group will prepare an interview with two Bible characters, Mary and Gabriel. You will need simple Bible-times costumes: a robe and head covering (a towel) for Mary and a white sheet for Gabriel.

Ask the children to find Luke 1:26-38, 46-55 in their Bibles. Read the verses together.

Choose two children to be Mary and Gabriel. The rest of the children will brainstorm questions to ask Mary and Gabriel. Suggested questions follow: **Mary**—What did you think when the angel came to you? Were you scared? How did you feel after he told you what God planned? What did you do after you heard this news? **Gabriel**—Who sent you to see Mary? What did you tell her? How did you feel about giving her the news? How did Mary take the news?

Write the suggested questions on paper. Ask Mary and Gabriel to answer the questions. The rest of the group may help them. Write Mary and Gabriel's answers after each question. Assign each child a question or questions to ask Mary and Gabriel. Practice the interview several times.

During *Sharing in Worship*, children will present the interview.

5. Personal Praise. This group will lead the group in a joyful praise time. poster board and markers. Before the session, print the following verses in large letters on the poster board.

"Sing a new song to him. Play well and joyfully." Psalm 33:3

"Clap your hands, all you

people. Shout to God with joy." Psalm 47:1

"Everything on earth, shout with joy to God!" Psalm 66:1

Display the poster board for the children. Ask them to read the verses with you. **We are going to present these verses to the large group. The large group will help us praise God as we read the verses.** Ask the children to think of ways the large group could participate as they read the verses. For Psalm 33:3, the children could think of a joyful song to sing following the reading of the verse. They could ask the large group to join them in singing the song. Suggestions follow: "Joy the the World," "The Joy of the Lord Is My Strength," "Rejoice in the Lord Always," "I've Got the Joy, Joy, Joy Down in My Heart." For Psalm 47:1, the large group could clap along with the verse. For Psalm 66:1, the large group could shout the last part of the verse with the small group. Practice saying the verses and singing, clapping, and shouting.

During *Sharing in Worship*, children will display the poster board and say the verses. Before each verse is said, they will ask the large group to join them in the appropriate action.

6. Prayer. This group will present praise prayers. You will need copies of activity page 14A, Bibles, poster board, small paper bags, scissors, markers, and glue. This activity is for older or gifted children.

Ask the children to find Luke 1:46-53. Read the verses with the children. **Mary is joyfully worshiping God in these verses. She is joyfully praying to God. We will prepare a joyful prayer like Mary did today.** Ask the children to put the ideas from Mary's prayer into their own words. Suggestions follow: He has been mindful of the humble state of His servant—God has remembered me; His mercy extends to those who fear Him—God is kind to those who obey Him; He has performed mighty deeds with His arm—God can do things no one else can do; He has filled the hungry with good things—God gives food to the hungry. Write the children's suggestions on the poster board.

Distribute activity page 14A. Ask the children to cut out the two pieces of the puppet and glue them to a paper bag. Then ask them to practice saying the prayer, using the puppets.

During *Sharing in Worship*, children will present the prayer.

Sharing In Worship
(20-25 minutes)

Omit any of the following sections if you did not offer the corresponding activity. The devotional may be completed without the presentation of Group 4.

Call to Worship (Group 1): Ask Group 1 to present their banner and Scripture verses.

Lord's Supper: This is a joyful time of year. We are joyful because Jesus was born for us. He came to earth so that He could show us how to live. Then He died for the wrong things that we do. But we can still be joyful, because He came to life again. Let's joyfully remember Him now. Pray and serve the Lord's Supper.

Offering: Ask four children to collect the offering at this time. Thank God that we can joyfully give so others will learn about Jesus.

Special music (Group 2): Ask Group 2 to present their illustrations as they sing "Jesus Came." Then ask the large group to join them in singing the song a second time.

Scripture (Group 3): Ask Group 3 to present the verses they have memorized with the actions.

Devotional (Group 4): **We have some special guests with us today who have some important information about Jesus' birth. Let's welcome our guests now.** Ask Group 4 to present their interviews. If you did not offer this activity, discuss how Mary and Gabriel might have felt, using the questions listed in that activity.

I imagine Mary and Gabriel must have been very excited and a little scared when they heard that Jesus was coming. They knew His birth was very important. Why was Jesus' birth so important? (Allow response.) **God sent Jesus so that we could be friends with God.**

What does your best friend want for Christmas? What is your best friend's favorite food? (Allow response.) **How did you find out these things about your friend?** (Talked to them.) **Imagine how hard it would be to have friends if you couldn't see them or talk to them. God knew how hard it was. That's the reason He sent Jesus. Before Jesus came, we couldn't be God's friends. We couldn't see God, and we couldn't talk to God. But Jesus helped us be God's friends. He helped us by telling us about God and showing us how God would act. And Jesus helped us by dying for the wrong things we do. Now we can be God's friends. That is a great reason to joyfully worship God!**

Personal Praise (Group 5): Ask Group 5 to present their Scriptures, asking the large group to participate in praising God with them.

Prayer (Group 6): Ask Group 6 to say their paraphrase of Mary's prayer, using the puppets. Close with prayer, thanking God for sending Jesus.

Closing Moments
(10-15 minutes)

You will need copies of activity page 14B and pencils.

Distribute the activity pages to

the children and ask them to complete the crossword puzzle. Answers follow: Nazareth, Gabriel, Joseph, sixth, marry, Mary, Galilee.

Option: Play the following match game about the birth of Jesus. Before the session, prepare sets of cards. You will need one set of cards for every six (or fewer) children. Each set will contain six pairs of cards—six question cards and six corresponding answer cards.

Questions/Answers: 1. In what city was Jesus born? (Bethlehem) 2. Who was Jesus' mother? (Mary) 3. Who appeared to Mary to tell her about the birth of Jesus? (Gabriel) 4. Why did Mary sing? (She was joyful about the angel's news.) 5. Who followed a star to see baby Jesus? (Wise-men) 6. Who came to see Jesus in the manger? (Shepherds)

To play the game, mix the cards and put them face down on the floor or table in three rows of four. The first person turns over two cards so everyone can see them. If they match, he or she keeps the cards and another person takes a turn. If they do not match, the cards are turned over in their original positions and another person takes a turn.

Thank God for Jesus

Worship Focus

We are thankful for the baby Jesus.

Transition Time

(10-15 minutes)

Bible hopscotch. Play a game of Bible hopscotch to review the details of the Sunday-school lesson. To prepare for the game, draw a hopscotch game board on poster board. For markers, provide buttons or circles cut from various colors of construction paper. This game is best played with 4 or 6 players, so prepare as many game boards as are necessary to accommodate your class. There should be one adult per group. Write the following review questions and Scripture references on index cards. Make one set of cards for each game board. Do not write the answers on the cards. 1. Who was the Roman emperor who said the census (counting) should be done? Luke 2:1 (Caesar Augustus.) 2. Who was Quirinius? Luke 2:2 (Governor of Syria.) 3. How did people know where to go for the census? Luke 2:3 (They had to go to their own town.) 4. Where did Joseph go? Luke 2:4 (He went to Bethlehem.) 5. From whose family did Joseph come? Luke 2:4 (He came from David's family.) 6. Who went with Joseph? Luke 2:5 (Mary.) 7. What happened while they were in Bethlehem? Luke 2:6, 7 (Mary gave birth to Jesus.) 8. In what was Jesus wrapped? Luke 2:7 (Cloths.) 9. Where was Jesus laid? Luke 2:7 (Manger or feeding box.) 10. Why was Jesus laid in a manger? Luke 2:7 (There was no room in the inn.)

To play, a player draws a card from the stack of question cards. If he or she answers the question correctly, he or she moves his or her marker one space on the hopscotch board. If the question is not answered correctly, help the child check his or her answer in the Bible. (Children begin playing with their markers off the board and answer only one question per turn.) The child who gets through the hopscotch first is the winner.

Launching the Theme

(10 minutes)

You will need copies of activity page 15A and pencils.

Distribute the activity pages to the children. Ask them to use the code to discover a special message from them. When children have discovered the message, ask a volunteer to read it aloud for the group.

Maybe some of you know that verse from memory. It is a wonderful verse because it tells us something very important that God did. God had a special message that He wanted all people to hear. He didn't want to trust that message to just anyone. Many times before, God had given His messages to those who already lived on the earth, and told them to tell everyone they could. Other times, God sent one of His angels to tell His message to people. But this time, God's message was so important that the only One who could bring it was Jesus, God's own Son. And so Jesus was born on Christmas to tell all people God's special message.

What do you think the message is that Jesus came to tell us? (Let the children give their ideas.) **The special message is: "I love you and I want to forgive you for all the wrong things you have done." God showed us His love by doing something very special–sending His Son Jesus. We can thank Him for His very special gift. We can also show our love and thanks by the things we do. We are going to learn about some of those things today.**

Explain the choices for *Building the Theme* and allow the children to choose in which group to participate.

Building the Theme

(30 minutes)

1. Call to Worship. This group will make sun-catchers thanking God for Jesus' birth. You will need two circle patterns, one 5″ in diameter and the other 4 or 4 1/2″ in diameter; scissors; construction paper; colored transparency sheets; hole punch; glue; yarn; paintbrushes; and markers or fingernail polish. Before the session, trace the 5″ circle on pieces of construction paper. Trace the other circle inside the 5″ circle. Trace enough circles for each child to have two circles.

Your birthday is a very special day because it is the day you were born. Christmas is when we celebrate Jesus' birthday. Today we will make sun-catchers to remind us to joyfully thank God

for Jesus' birthday.

Distribute the circles you traced. Ask the children to cut out each circle and the middle portion. Then ask each child to trace the 5" circle on a piece of transparency and cut it out. Glue the construction paper rings each has made on the front and back of the transparency. Make sure both rings match in size and width before gluing.

After the glue has been allowed to dry for a few moments, give each child some fingernail polish and a paintbrush or provide markers. Tell him or her to paint Happy Birthday Jesus on the transparency. If there is room, he or she may add extra decorations to his or her sun-catcher. Allow to dry. Punch a hole at the top of the sun-catcher and tie a piece of yarn through the hole for a hook.

Ask the children to practice singing "Happy Birthday" to Jesus.

During *Sharing in Worship*, children will display their sun-catchers and ask the large group to join them in singing "Happy Birthday" to Jesus.

2. Special Music. This group will present a tableau of the manger scene and sing "Away in a Manger." You will need "Away in a Manger" from page 185, poster board, and a marker.

Before the session, write the words to the song on poster board. Gather costumes for the children to wear. Included in the scene will be Mary, Joseph, and animals, such as cows, sheep, and donkeys. Make animal "ears" out of construction paper. Also, find a doll and a blanket for baby Jesus.

Let's think about what it must have been like for Mary to have her baby in a place where animals lived. Because there was no room for them in the inn, she gave birth in a stable or a barn. (Read Luke 2:6, 7 for the children.) **Mary and Joseph had just made a long, tiring journey. The distance from Nazareth to Samaria was about seventy miles. That might take us a little over an hour to travel in a fast car. But Mary and Joseph had to walk or ride a donkey. It was a long, hard trip. There were no fast food restaurants along the way, so Mary and Joseph had to take and cook all of their own food. They probably had to sleep on a hard floor or even outside on the ground during the nights. It must have been especially hard for Mary, since she was almost ready to have a baby. When they arrived at Bethlehem, it was already so crowded that they couldn't even find a room in the inn. Even if there had been, they wouldn't have had any privacy. So they ended up in the stable with the animals.** Explain to the children that they are going to put on costumes and pretend that they are the people and animals in the story. They are not going to do any acting. They will simply get in one position and stay that way while they sing the song. They are to sing as if they were Mary, Joseph, and the animals.

Display the poster board with the words of the song written on it. Practice singing both stanzas of "Away in a Manger."

During *Sharing in Worship*, children will stand in their positions and sing the song.

3. Lord's Supper. This group will prepare a poster about Jesus' birth. You will need poster board, old Christmas cards, construction paper, markers, scissors, and glue.

Why do we celebrate Christmas? (It is Jesus' birthday.) **What is the most important thing about Christmas?** (Jesus was born.) Distribute the materials. Ask the children to cut out pictures or words, telling things that people think are important about Christmas. Or they may draw pictures on construction paper. The children will glue the things to the poster board to make a collage.

During *Sharing in Worship*, the children will display the collage. Each child will name one thing people think is important about Christmas. Then the group will say, "But the most important thing about Christmas is that Jesus was born." Practice the presentation during the small-group time.

4. Devotional. This group will prepare skits showing ways to thank God at Christmas. You will need paper and pencils. Before the session, write the situations below on three separate sheets of paper. Do not write the answers.

- Your Sunday-school class is going to a nursing home to sing Christmas carols. You don't like to sing and don't like nursing homes. You would rather stay home and eat Christmas cookies. What would you do? (Go and sing to tell others about Jesus' birth and thank Him we can celebrate.)
- Your mom asked you to help clean the house to help her prepare for a Christmas visit from your relatives. You want to go Christmas shopping with your friend, and you hate to clean house. What would you do? (Help Mom clean house.)
- You want to be a shepherd in the Christmas play. But you are asked to be the lamb. You have to put on a dumb costume with ears and say, "Baa-baa." What would you do? (Do it and thank God that we can celebrate Jesus' birth.)

Are you thankful that God sent Jesus to be born? (Allow response.) **What are some ways we can show God we are thankful?** (Allow response.) **Listen to the following situations and tell me what the children in these situations could do to show God they are thankful for sending Jesus.** Read the situations for the children. Record their suggestions on the papers. Divide the children into three groups. Ask each group to prepare a skit, showing what they would do to thank God for sending Jesus. When groups have completed their skits, ask them to present them for the small group. Assign one child from each group to read the situation for the large group.

During *Sharing in Worship*, a child will read each situation. Then his or her group will act out how a child in that situation could show thankfulness to God.

5. Personal Praise. This group will draw things they can do to show God they are thankful for Jesus. You will need construction paper or drawing paper, colored chalk, newspaper or plastic, old shirts or aprons, and hair spray or clear fixative spray.

God showed His love for us by sending His Son. We want to show our love by saying and doing kind and loving things. We also want to show our love when we celebrate Christmas. We need God's help to do these things, because often we want to do the very things we *should* not do, don't we? What are some kind, loving things we should do to show God our love?

Help the children list things, such as share toys, don't hit or punch, forgive, obey, be kind , and so on. Ask the children to list special things they do at Christmas which show how much they love and thank God for Jesus. Spread newspaper or plastic over the work area and distribute materials. Ask each child to choose one thing to illustrate using the chalk. When the children have completed their illustrations, spray them with hair spray so the chalk will not rub off.

During *Sharing in Worship*, children will display their illustrations and tell the way they thank God for Jesus at Christmas.

6. Prayer. This group will make Christmas ornaments to remind them to thank God for Jesus' birth. You will need copies of activity page 15B, markers, scissors, glue, chenille wire, paper clips or Christmas bulb hangers.

What can we say to pray and thank God for sending Jesus? Allow response. **Today we will make Christmas ornaments to remind us to pray and thank God for sending Jesus.** Distribute the materials. Ask the children to color and cut out the six circles. Then ask them to fold the edges forward as shown on the page. They will then glue the edges of the circles together to make the ornament. Ask them to glue a piece of chenille wire between two of the edges. Attach a hanger to the chenille wire.

During *Sharing in Worship*, children will display their ornaments. Each child will say one sentence prayer, thanking God for sending Jesus. **Option:** If you have a Christmas tree in your room, ask each child to hang his ornament on the tree as he or she says his or her sentence prayer.

Sharing In Worship
(20-25 minutes)

Omit any of the following sections if you did not offer the corresponding activity. The Lord's Supper and devotional may be completed without the presentations of Groups 3 and 4.

Call to Worship (Group 1): Ask Group 1 to present their suncatchers and sing "Happy Birthday" to Jesus. Ask the large group to join them in singing.

Song: Sing "Jesus Came" from page 184.

Special Music (Group 2): Ask Group 2 to present their tableau and their song.

Lord's Supper (Group 3): **What is the most important thing about Christmas?** (Allow response.) **People have many ideas about what is most important. Listen as Group 3 shares them with us.** Ask Group 3 to share their poster of things people think are important about Christmas.

The most important thing about Christmas is that God sent Jesus to be born. God gave us a very special gift when He gave us His Son, Jesus. He showed us how much He loves us. Let's think about God's love for us and thank Him for sending Jesus now. Pray and serve the Lord's Supper.

Offering: When we give our offerings to God, we are showing Him that we are thankful for what He has done for us. Let's show our thanks to Him today by giving back to Him. Ask four children to collect the offering.

Devotional (Group 4): **When God sent Jesus, His own Son, to earth, He could have sent Him to a king's palace where Jesus would have been treated wonderfully. But God chose to send Jesus to a couple that didn't have much money. Instead of being born in a palace, God chose for Jesus to be born in a place where animals live. Imagine what it must have been like for Mary and Joseph that night. They had traveled for a long time. Finally they were in Bethlehem. Yet there was no room for them in the inn—the only place where visitors to the city were able to stay. In addition to being tired and hungry, Mary could tell it was almost time for her baby to be born. What was going to happen? How was God going to work this out? Mary and Joseph didn't know, but they knew God would take care of them. The innkeeper told them they could stay in the stable with the animals.**

A stable wasn't a pretty place. It was probably inside a cave, dark and cool. It probably didn't smell very good. But Jesus was born in a stable. And Jesus' first bed was a box that was used for feeding the animals.

God loved us so much that He was willing to send Jesus to earth to be born in a stable. What can we do to show Him we are thankful. Group 4 will share

some ideas with us. Ask Group 4 to present their skits. If you did not offer this activity, read the situations found in Group 4 and ask the group to tell you what they would do.

Personal Praise (Group 5): **We have just seen some ways we can thank God for Jesus' birth. Now Group 5 is going to share some ways that they will thank God for Jesus' birth. As you listen to them, think of a way that you will thank God for Jesus' birth this week.** Ask Group 5 to share their drawings and ways they will show God they are thankful for Jesus' birth.

Prayer (Group 6): Ask Group 6 to display their ornaments and pray, thanking God for sending Jesus.

Closing Moments

(10-15 minutes)

Allow children to choose favorite Christmas carols to sing.

Unit Four
Worship God for Jesus

Session 16

Tell Others About Jesus' Birth

Worship Focus

We can tell others why we celebrate Christmas.

Transition Time

(10-15 minutes)

Christmas poster. On a length of butcher or shelf paper, letter the partial statement, "Christmas is . . . ."Place the paper on a wall, a table, or the floor, being sure to put newspapers between the paper and work surface. Provide washable felt pens or crayons.

As the children arrive, let them respond to the statement either by writing something, drawing a picture, or selecting pictures from magazines or old Christmas cards to place on the paper. They may write captions or explanations for their pictures if they wish.

Launching the Theme

(10 minutes)

Discuss the poster the children made during *Transition Time.* **You gave some very good answers about what Christmas is. Christmas is a very special time because . . .** (give some of the children's answers). **At Christmas we remember that God sent His Son Jesus because He loved us so much. What happy news it is that "Jesus is born." Who were the very first people to hear this good news. That's right, the shepherds. Shepherds were common, simple people who took care of sheep. God chose these men to be the first people to hear about Jesus' birth? What a joyful, special night it was! The shepherds went to see this special baby and found Him lying in a manger, just as the angel had told them. They were so happy and excited when they left! They had seen God's own Son, and joyfully told others about this good news.**

Explain the choices of activities for *Building the Theme* and allow the children to choose in which group to participate.

Building the Theme

(30 minutes)

1. Call to Worship: Group 1 will learn a verse to present during the worship time. You will need index cards, craft sticks, a marker, glue or tape, and a rectangular pan filled with sand or cornmeal. Before the session, write one word of the following verse on each index card. "I will praise you, Lord, with all my heart. I will tell all the miracles you have done" (Psalm 9:1, *ICB*). Glue or tape each card to a craft stick.

Ask the children to find Psalm 9:1 in their Bibles. Read the Psalm with the children. Then ask them to use the cards to place the first sentence of the verse in the proper order in the pan. When they have done this several times, ask them to place the second sentence of the verse in order in the pan. Practice saying the verse together several times.

What miracle or other thing about Jesus can you tell other people at Christmastime? Who will you tell? Ask children to respond.

During *Sharing in Worship*, children will recite the verse. Then they will each tell something they can tell about Jesus at Christmas.

2. Special Music. This group will learn a song to present during the worship time. You will need "Go, Tell It On the Mountain" from page 186, poster board, markers, construction paper, glue or tape, shelf paper, and several cardboard boxes. Before the session, print the words to the song on poster board. Cover the boxes with shelf paper. Letter one phrase of the song on each side of the boxes.

"Go, tell it on the mountain,
over the hill and everywhere.
Go, tell it on the mountain
that Jesus Christ is born."

"While shepherds kept their
watching o'er wand'ring flocks
by night.
Behold from out of heaven
there shone a holy light."

"The shepherds feared and
trembled and lo above the earth
Rang out the angel chorus
that hailed the Savior's birth."

"Down in a lowly manger
the humble Christ was born
And brought us God's
salvation
that blessed Christmas morn."

Display the poster board for the children. Sing the song for them. Then ask them to sing it with you several times.

The children will make music boxes by illustrating each phrase of the song and taping the pictures to sides of boxes. Assign each child or pair of children one phrase to illustrate. Suggested illustrations follow: Stanza 1—shepherds with sheep, a light in the sky; Stanza 2—a group of angels in the sky; Stanza 3—Jesus in a manger, Mary, Joseph, and Jesus. Provide construction paper or markers. Ask the children to glue or tape their completed pictures to the sides of the boxes.

During *Sharing in Worship*, children will display the pictures as they sing the song.

3. Scripture. This group will make overhead transparencies to illustrate a Scripture. You will need clear transparency sheets, markers, Bibles, a tape recorder, and a blank cassette tape. Before the session, print the following verses on a blank transparency sheet: "And the shepherds saw the baby lying in a feeding box. Then they told what the angels had said about this child. Everyone was amazed when they heard what the shepherds said to them" (Luke 2:17, 18, *ICB*).

Ask the children to find Luke 1:8-20 in their Bibles. Read the verses together. Ask the children to name pictures they could draw to illustrate the story. Write their suggestions on the chalkboard. Assign each child one picture to draw. When the children have completed their pictures, ask them to think of one sentence to say describing their picture. Ask the children to practice saying their sentences in the correct order. Then read Luke 2:17, 18 together at the end. Record the presentation. Pause the tape recorder between each child's sentence to allow children time. Assign children to operate the tape player and overhead projector during the worship time. Practice playing the tape and projecting the transparencies at the appropriate time.

During *Sharing in Worship*, children will play the tape recording and display the transparencies.

4. Devotional. This group will develop a modern-day skit to present to the class during the devotional. You will need a tape recorder and a blank tape, Before the session, make a tape recording of you telling the story from Luke 2:8-20 in your own words. To do so, read the Scripture verses several times, so you are very familiar with the story. Then tell it with enthusiasm, varying the volume and tone of your voice, pausing appropriately, and asking leading questions such as, "And do you know what happened next?"

Ask the children to listen very carefully to the story. Play the tape. Rewind it and play it a second time, stopping halfway through. Have the children finish the story in their own words. Then talk about how the shepherds wanted to tell the good news about Jesus. **When you know something wonderful, you want to share it with everyone. What good news do you know about Jesus that you can share with others at Christmastime?**

Have the group think together about times and ways in which they can share the good news about Jesus. Develop a skit depicting a situation in which someone shares the good news with someone else or invites him or her to come to church.

Suggestions: The setting is a school classroom. The teacher asks the children to draw a picture of what they like best about Christmas. The pictures will be hung on the wall outside the room. When everyone is finished, the teacher asks each child to show and explain his or her drawing.

Nikki: My drawing is a Christmas tree. I love to decorate the tree with ornaments.

Mark: This is Santa Claus. I can't wait for him to come and bring me presents.

Crista: I drew my mom and me baking Christmas cookies. I love to decorate them.

(Add as many other drawings as you have children in your group. End with the child who draws and tells about Jesus' birth.)

Dustin: I drew the manger where Jesus was born. We wouldn't have Christmas without Jesus.

Keep the situation very simple and talk through it so the children are sure of the events of the story. Make a list of the characters in the story. Decide who will play each part. Act out the story, helping the children remember the sequence of actions, as well as what to say, by asking questions that will guide them through the skit. Practice the skit a couple of times so the children are comfortable with it.

During *Sharing in Worship*, the children will present the skit.

5. Devotional. This will prepare gifts to present to Jesus. You will need construction paper, scissors, markers or crayons, and straight pins.

God gave us a great gift when He sent Jesus. What are some gifts we can give to God? Allow responses. Encourage the children to be specific. For example, forgive my little brother for hitting me, sit at lunch with the new boy in my class, and so on.

Distribute the materials. Ask the children to cut badges in any shape they wish out of construction paper. They will write what they will give to Jesus on their badge. When the badges are completed, use straight pins to pin the badges to the children's clothing. Ask the children to cut out enough badges for everyone in the large group to have one.

During *Sharing in Worship*, children will share the gifts they will give to Jesus and distribute the badges.

6. Prayer. This group will write prayers, thanking God for sending Jesus. You will need copies of activity page 16A and pencils or pins.

One gift we can give to Jesus is our thanks. Name some of the different characters found in the Christmas story. (Mary, Joseph, baby Jesus, Caesar Augustus, shepherds, angel Gabriel, other angels, Wise-men.) **Which person will you thank God for? Why will you thank God for that person?** Ask each child to choose one person from the Christmas story to thank God for. For example, "Thank You, God, for the shepherds because they told everyone Jesus was born." Ask the children to write their thank-you prayers on activity page 16A.

During *Sharing in Worship*, children will read their prayers.

Sharing In Worship
(20-25 minutes)

Omit any of the following sections if you did not offer the corresponding activity. The devotional may be completed without the presentation of Groups 4 and 5.

Call to Worship (Group 1): Group 1 will show their sand-pan verse of Psalm 9:1 and recite the verse. Then they will name what they will tell others at Christmastime.

Lord's Supper: God chose a very special way to tell us He loves us: He sent His Son, Jesus. At Communion time, We remember that Jesus came to earth to show us God's love. Let's thank God for His very special gift.

Offering: We give to God when we do right things. We give to God when we tell other people about Him. Now is our time to give to God from our money. Let's thank Him by giving to Him now. Ask four children to collect the offering.

Special Music (Group 2): Group 2 will sing "Go Tell It on the Mountain" and present their illustrations.

Scripture (Group 3): Group 3 will present their overhead transparencies and their recorded Scripture.

Devotional (Groups 4 and 5): **What if someone gave you a birthday party and all of your friends came? But instead of bringing presents for you, they brought presents for each other. You didn't receive any presents. How would you feel?** (Allow response.) **I wonder if God feels that way at Christmastime. We save our money to buy gifts for our families and our friends. And we take time to wrap those gifts so they will be pretty. But what do we give to Jesus at Christmas?**

Jesus doesn't need new toys or new clothes, but there are things we can give to Him. Think about things you can give to Jesus as we watch this skit by Group 4. Ask Group 4 to perform their skit. Then ask the large group to tell what was given to Jesus. If you did not offer this activity, read the skit included in the activity and ask the children to tell what was given to Jesus.

What are some ways you could give to Jesus? Ask children to share. Ask Group 5 to display their badges and tell what they will give to Jesus this week. Then ask them to distribute the badges to the large group. **Write on your badge what you will give to Jesus this week. When you are finished, I will pin your badge to your clothing. Take it home to remind you what you will give to God this week. We will have a special time next week for you to tell the large group what you gave to God this week.**

Prayer (Group 6): Ask Group 6 to read their thank-you prayers to God.

Closing Moments
(10-15 minutes)

You will need copies of activity page 16B and crayons or markers.

Distribute the activity pages. Ask the children to think of ways to thank God for sending Jesus every day this week and write them on the Christmas calendar. Ask them to decorate the calendar and take it home to remind them to thank God for Jesus every day this week.

Option: Children can make crayon-resist secret messages to give to a friend. Instruct the children to think of the persons to whom they would like to give the messages and to decide what to write.

With white crayons and white drawing paper, have the children write a message about Jesus (such as "Christmas is Jesus' birthday"), or letter an invitation for a friend to come to Sunday school and church. Tell the children to give the secret message to a friend and have him or her paint over it with thin paint to discover the message.

For Next Week

Gather the following items for Jesus' birthday party: cupcakes or cookies, icing, and toppings such as sprinkles, candies, and so on; milk or punch; paper cups; napkins; decorations, such as a small nativity set, Christmas cards, bows, ribbons, and so on; white shelf paper; colored markers; and tape. You may wish to make invitations to the party and send them to every child in your group.

Plague Poem for Session 10

The Lord said to Moses, "Go to Pharaoh and say,
'Let my people go to worship God today.'"
Pharaoh heard the message, but in his mind,
He'd never let them go. You see, he wasn't very kind.
So God sent the first plague, all water turned to blood.
Blood was everywhere in Egypt, even in the mud.
Moses said to Pharaoh, "God says, 'Let my people go.'"
Pharaoh's heart was hard, and he still said, "No!"
God's second plague was dreadful, frogs in houses and in beds!
Why some Egyptians may have had green frogs upon their heads!
Moses said to Pharaoh, "God says, 'Let my people go.'"
Pharaoh's heart was hard, and he still said, "No!"
Plagues three and four were buggy, houses full of gnats and flies.
Pharaoh thought he'd had enough, so he told a little lie.
Moses said to Pharaoh, "Will you let God's people go?"
Pharaoh lied and said, "Yes," but he really meant no.
So God sent another plague and all the livestock died.
But all animals of the Israelites God spared and kept alive.
Moses said to Pharaoh, "God says, 'Let my people go.'"
Pharaoh's heart was hard, and he still said "No!"
Then boils and hail and locusts were spread throughout the land.
But God cared for His people with His shielding hand.
Moses said to Pharaoh, "God says, 'Let my people go."
Pharaoh's heart was hard, and he still said, "No!"
Plague nine was total darkness for three long days, but God cared for His people and they had light always.
Moses said to Pharaoh, "God says, 'Let my people go.'"
Pharaoh's heart was hard, and he still said, "No!"
The last plague was the worst, all the firstborn died.
"All right, we've had enough!" Pharaoh cried.
Moses didn't have to ask, "Is your answer still "No!?"
For Pharaoh called him in the night saying, "Go! Go! Go!"
God led His people out with fire in the night.
He led them with a cloud when it was daylight.
God cared for His people all the nights and all the days,
God cares for all His people, you and me, always.

Honor God for Sending Jesus

Worship Focus

We joyfully honor God and His Son, Jesus.

Transition Time
(10-15 minutes)

Allow time for a rest room and drink break. As children arrive, involve them in the following activity.

Review hunt. Prior to worship time, print the following words on index cards and hide them around the room: Mary, Joseph, Jesus, Bethlehem, Herod, star, Wise-men, east, gold, frankincense, and myrrh. You may make several sets of these words, depending upon the size of your group.

When the children return from the rest room, have them hunt for the cards. After several minutes, call the children together.

Launching the Theme
(10 minutes)

The children will act out the story of the Wise-men, as told in Matthew 2:1-12, while a teacher reads from the Bible.

Decide who will play the parts. Use the index cards from *Transition Time* as identification signs to pin on the actors. Help the children take their places. The actors will not deliver any lines, but should listen carefully to the story and do what the narration indicates.

Have the children act out the story twice if there is time. You will need to help the children know when and where to move as the narration is read, as well as help them not get too excited.

After the children have acted out the story, have a brief discussion.

The Wise-men honored Jesus because they knew He was the most special baby ever born. Let's think a little about what it means to honor someone. Honoring someone means to show him or her by what you say and what you do that he or she is special to you. Today we will honor God for sending His Son, Jesus.

Explain the choices of *Building the Theme*. Allow the children to choose in which group to participate. Ask children to gave gifts to Jesus last week to participate in Group 2.

Building the Theme
(30 minutes)

1. Tell others: This group will prepare a Scripture presentation of Psalm 75:1: "God, we thank You. We thank You are near. We tell about the wonderful things You do" (*ICB*). You will need poster board, markers, index cards, and paper. Before the session, prepare a pocket chart to help the children memorize the verse. Staple squares of paper to the poster board to make sixteen pockets. Write the words of Psalm 75:1 on 16 index cards. You will need to write two words on one card. Place the cards in order in the pocket chart. The verse words should be visible when the cards are in the pockets. Print the words to the verse on the chalkboard.

Read Psalm 75:1 from the chalkboard. Read the verse aloud as the children follow along silently. Point to each word as you say it. Have the group read the verse aloud together a time or two. Display the pocket chart. Have the children work together as a group to put the cards in correct order in the pockets. Then remove the cards, one at a time, and encourage the children to fill in the missing words. Have the children practice saying the verse so they can say it confidently.

Remember how we talked in our large group about honoring someone? We said you could honor your grandmother by telling others what a special person she is. The verse we just learned talks about honoring God by telling others the wonderful things He has done, and by thanking Him for those things. The best thing God did for us was to send His Son, Jesus. We can tell other people about Jesus, and we can thank God for Him.

During *Sharing in Worship*, the group will quote Psalm 75:1 together.

2. Offering. This group will present gifts to Jesus. You will need small boxes, wrapping paper, slips of paper, markers, and pencils.

The Wise-men brought their special gifts to give Jesus. They showed by the words they said and the things they did that He was special.

We can't bring gifts to Jesus personally, like the Wise-men

did, but we can bring our offerings. These are gifts to Jesus, given in love. That's not all we can give Him. As we give to others and do kind things for them in the name of Jesus, we are giving to Him. Last week, we promised Jesus that we would give a gift to Him during the week. What gift did each of you give to Jesus this past week? Allow children to share. Distribute materials. Ask each child to write the gift he or she gave to Jesus on a slip of paper and place it in a box. Children may decorate the boxes in any way they wish. If someone did not give a gift to Jesus last week, encourage him or her to name a gift he or she will give to Jesus this week. Suggestions follow: make cookies to share with someone, surprise someone in the family by offering to help with a specific task, write a note or letter to a missionary, do something nice for a friend or family member, tell grandparents you love them.

During *Sharing in Worship*, children will place their gifts beneath the "Praise Tree" (See Group 4) and tell the gift they gave to Jesus. After the session, allow the children to take their gifts home to open on Christmas to remind them of what they gave to Jesus.

3. Special Music. This group will learn new words to the chorus of "Jingle Bells." You will need copies of activity page 17A, "Christmas Song" from page 187, poster board, and markers.

Distribute the activity page to the children. Sing the song for them. Then ask them to sing it with you. Have the children practice this several times. Add bells or rhythm for an extra effect. Ask the children to print the words of the song in large letters on the poster board for the large group.

During *Sharing in Worship*, children will display the poster board and sing their song. Then they will ask the large group to sing the song with them.

4. Devotional. This group will prepare a skit for the worship time. You will need copies of activity page 17B.

Distribute the activity page to the children. Read the skit aloud to them. Then assign parts. Allow the children to practice the skit several times.

How do you think Bobby felt about not receiving any presents? How would you feel? Allow response. **Christmastime is Jesus' birthday. But sometimes we forget about Jesus. We forget to give gifts to Him. God gave us the best gift when He sent Jesus. We can remember to give gifts to God.**

During *Sharing in Worship*, children will present the skit.

5. Praise Party. This group will prepare a party for the worship time. You will need cupcakes or cookies; icing; paper cups; milk or punch; shelf paper; and markers. Before the session, cover the table for the party with shelf paper.

Today we are going to plan a birthday party for our group. Whose birthday party are we going to plan? (Jesus' party.) Ask children to ice cookies and fill cups with milk or punch. Then ask them to use markers to draw praise pictures on the shelf paper covering the table. They may draw pictures from the story of Jesus' birth or pictures of ways they praise Jesus at Christmas.

During *Sharing in Worship*, children will serve the refreshments to the large group.

6. Personal Praise. This group will make a "praise tree" to share with the entire group during the worship time. You will need a long length of butcher paper or a large piece of poster board, a pencil, paper, markers or crayons, and green tempera paint. Before the session, make a pencil sketch outlining an evergreen tree on the butcher paper or poster board.

One way we can honor Jesus is by telling Him "thank You" for the wonderful things He has done, and telling Him how great He is. God is happy when we talk to Him. By thanking Him for things, we show that they are from God in the first place. When we tell God how great He is, we are honoring Him.

Display the tree you sketched before the session. Ask the children to paint the tree with the green tempera paint. When the children have finished painting, hang the tree in the front of the worship area. Distribute the paper and ask the children to prepare enough cards for everyone in the class, including the teachers. To prepare the cards, have the children fold a sheet of paper in half twice and put a design on the outside.

During *Sharing in Worship*, the children will distribute the cards and pens or pencils to the large group.

Sharing In Worship
(20-25 minutes)

Omit any of the following sections if you did not offer the corresponding activities. The offering and devotional may be completed without the presentations of Groups 2 and 4.

Call to Worship (Group 1): Group 1 will present their Scripture chart and say the verse. **This verse reminds us that when we honor someone, we do some of the same things as when we honor God. Our worship service is to honor God. That's what we'll be doing the rest of this time.**

Lord's Supper: At this special time in our worship service we honor Jesus by taking time to thank Him for what He has done for us. The bread and the juice help us remember that Jesus'

body was hurt by bad people when they put Him on the cross. Finally Jesus died. When we take the Lord's Supper, we also remember that Jesus came back to life and He has promised that we can live forever with Him in Heaven someday, if we love an obey Him. Pray and serve the Lord's Supper.

Offering (Group 2)**:** Ask Group 2 to place their gift boxes beneath the "praise tree" and tell what they gave or will give to Jesus. **Christmas is wonderful because we remember that God gave us the gift of his Son. We give our offerings to Him as gifts. by giving our offerings, we say thank You to the Lord and show Him we think He is special.** Choose four children to collect the offering.

Special Music (Group 3)**:** Group 3 will present the song "Christmas Song." Then they will ask the large group to sing with them.

Devotional (Group 4)**:** Ask Group 4 to present their skit. If you did not offer this activity, distribute copies of activity page 17B and read the skit together.

How did Bobby feel when his friends all brought presents for each other, but not for him? Allow response. **Christmas is Jesus' birthday. It is a happy time and a time to give gifts to each other. We take great care choosing and wrapping gifts for our friends and families. And we go to many Christmas parties. But many times, we forget to give gifts to Jesus.**

We learned last week that although Jesus does not need new toys or new clothes, there are many things we can give Him. Can you name some of the things we can give to Jesus? Allow response. **The Wise-men took gifts to Jesus when they went to worship Him. We can't give Jesus gifts personally as the Wise-men did, but we can tell Jesus the gifts we give to Him to show Him we love Him.**

Praise Party (Group 5): **Right now, we are going to have a birthday party for Jesus. But it won't be a party where Jesus doesn't receive any gifts. At the end of our party, we are going to give some gifts to God and Jesus.** Ask children from Group 5 to assist in distributing refreshments. Ask the children to sing "Happy Birthday to Jesus."

Personal Praise (Group 6): **One gift we can give to God and Jesus is our praise. And we are going to have a chance to give Him the gift of praise right now. Group 5 made a praise tree for us. They are going to pass out some praise cards. I want you to write your praise to God on the card. You could thank God for Jesus, or tell Him you love Him, or thank Him for something or someone He has given you.** Allow children time to complete their praise cards. Then ask them to come forward and attach them to the tree.

Prayer: Ask a teacher to offer a prayer of thanks for Jesus, God's greatest gift to us.

Closing Moments
(10-15 minutes)

Ask children to help you clean up the room and put away all supplies. Sing favorite Christmas carols as the children clean up. Or ask children to think of different praise stanzas to the tune "Happy Birthday" to sing together. For example, "Thank You for Your gift," "You are very great," "We love You, Jesus."

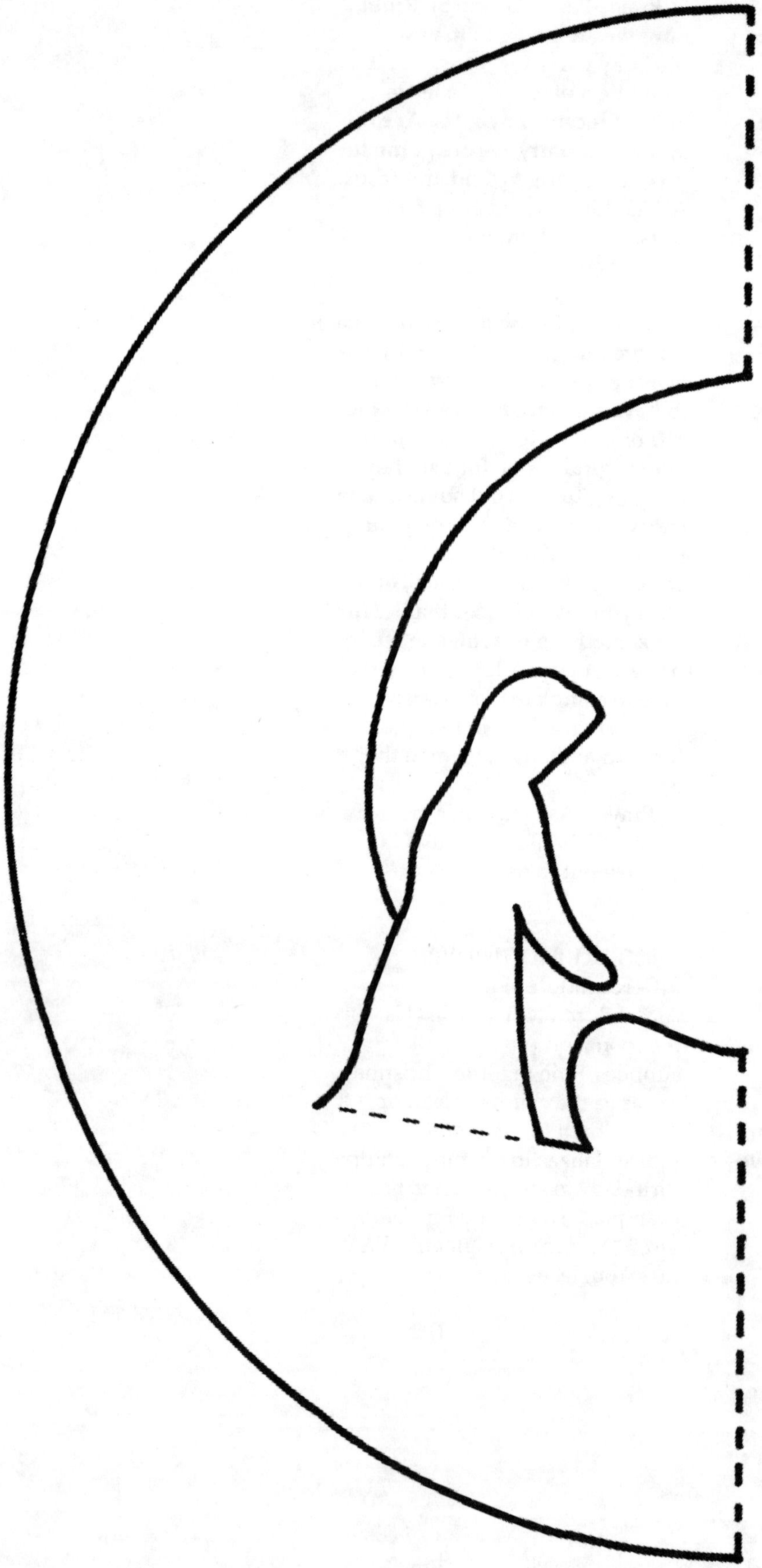

Jesus Was a Special Child

Worship Focus
We worship Jesus because He was a special child.

Transition Time
(10-15 minutes)
Send the children in small groups to the rest room and water fountain. Welcome newcomers and involve them in the following game.

Growing Game. You will need shelf paper, a yard stick, markers, and a portable scale. Before the session, hang a piece of shelf paper that is longer than the tallest child on the wall.

Measure the children and mark their heights on the chart. Allow the children to write their names beside their marks on the chart. Also weigh the children and allow them to write their weight beside their height on the chart.

Launching the Theme
(10 minutes)
You will need pictures from activity page 18B, colored and mounted on construction paper.

We just spent some time finding out how big we are! Are you the same height that you were two years ago? Are you the same weight? Of course not. You are getting bigger. It's easy to see the way we grow physically. But we grow in other ways too. What are some other ways we grow? Allow response. **We grow in how much we learn and how much we know. We grow in our understanding of God and Jesus. We grow in the way we get along with other people. And we make mistakes along the way. We sometimes are mean to other people, or we forget about God, or we don't feel like learning. We aren't perfect.**

But there was one child who grew perfectly. He always chose what was right. And He always obeyed His parents. That child was Jesus. In fact, the Bible tells us how perfectly Jesus grew. Display the pictures from activity page 18B. **This pictures will give you clues to how Jesus grew. What are the ways the Bible tells us He grew?** Allow children to guess by looking at the pictures. Answers follow: Jesus playing with friends—favor with man or in the ability to get along with other people; Jesus sitting with teachers—wisdom or in learning; Jesus praying—favor with God; Jesus eating a meal—stature or physical growth. **Jesus was a perfect child. We can try to be like Him. Today we will worship Jesus because He was a special child.**

Explain the choices of activities for *Building the Theme.* Allow the children to choose in which group to participate.

Building the Theme
(30 minutes)
1. Call to Worship. This group will prepare a choral reading for the worship time. You will need copies of activities page 18A.

Distribute the activity pages to the children. Ask them to listen as you read the choral reading for them. Then read the verses again, allowing the children to practice their parts. Practice the reading many times until the children are comfortable with their part.

During *Sharing in Worship,* children will present the choral reading.

2. Special music. This group will prepare a song for the worship time. You will need "Jesus, I Want to Be Like You" from page 188, poster board, and a marker. Before the session, print the words to the song on the poster board.

We have talked about how Jesus was a perfect and special child. One way we can honor Jesus is by being like Him. We are going to learn a song about being like Jesus. Display the poster board. Sing the song for the children. Then ask them to sing it with you several times. When the children are comfortable singing the song, teach them the accompanying actions and practice the song with the actions.

During *Sharing in Worship,* children will present the song.

3. Scripture. This group will prepare a verse and pictures for the worship time. You will need construction paper, markers, a chalkboard, and chalk. Before the session, print Colossians 3:20 from the *International Children's Bible* on the chalkboard. "Children obey your parents in all things. This please the Lord."

Point to the verse on the chalkboard. Read it aloud to the children, pointing to each word as you say it. Then ask the children to say the verse with you. Discuss with your children ways in which they can obey their parents every day. Print their suggestions on the chalkboard. Then ask the children to draw a picture of one of the suggestions on the board. You may need to assign pictures so each child draws something different.

When the children have completed their pictures, help each child make a sentence about what the or she drew. After each child says his or her sentence, the group will say, "This pleases the Lord." Following is an example:

Group: "Children, obey your parents in all things. This please the Lord."

Child: I can obey when my mom asks me to clean my room.

Group: This pleases the Lord.

Child: I can obey when my dad asks me to sweep the porch.

Group: This pleases the Lord.

During *Sharing in Worship*, children will share the verse and the pictures. Practice the presentation during the small group time.

4. Devotional. This group will prepare skits about ways we can grow like Jesus did.

Jesus was a special child. What are the four ways we said that Jesus grew? (Physically; in wisdom; in knowledge about God; in getting along with other people.) **We can honor Jesus by being like Him. Listen to these stories and think about the ways Jesus grew. Then tell me how these children could be like Jesus.**

- **Gina wants to go to her friend's party tonight, but she has math homework to do.**
- **Brandon has to be Eric's partner for the reading project. Eric is strange, and Brandon doesn't want to be his partner.**
- **Justin is supposed to memorize a verse for Sunday morning. But it's Saturday night, and he's too tired.**
- **Molly chose a candy bar instead of an apple for her after-school snack.**

Ask the children to tell how each child needs to grow like Jesus. Then Divide the children into four groups. Ask each group to act out one situation, showing how the child could grow to be like Jesus.

During *Sharing in Worship*, children will act out their situations.

5. Personal Praise. This group will prepare a poster of ways they will grow to be like Jesus. You will need poster board, old magazines, scissors, markers, construction paper, and glue.

Jesus was a special child. What are the four ways we said that Jesus grew? (Physically; in wisdom; in knowledge about God; in getting along with other people.) **We can honor Jesus by being like Him. What are some ways you can grow physically? In knowledge of God? In getting along with others? In wisdom or learning?** List children's ideas on a chalkboard or paper. Ask them to cut out or draw pictures of ways they will grow like Jesus grew and glue them to the poster board. Children will make a collage of ways they will grow.

During *Sharing in Worship*, children will display the collage and tell the ways they will grow to be like Jesus.

6. Prayer. This group will prepare a guided prayer for the worship time. You will need a poster board and a marker.

What are the four ways we said that Jesus grew? (Physically; in wisdom; in knowledge about God; in getting along with other people.) **We are going to write a prayer to thank God that Jesus was a special child. What are some good ways that you think Jesus grew physically? In knowledge about God? In getting along with other people? In wisdom and learning?** Allow children to share. List their ideas on a chalkboard or poster board. Assign each child or pair of children one of the four areas of Jesus' growth. Ask the children to think of a sentence or two, thanking God for ways Jesus grew in that area. For example, "Thank You, God, that Jesus studied Your Word and listened to teachers to learn about You." "Thank You, God, that Jesus learned how to be kind to others and how to be a friend."

During *Sharing in Worship*, you will introduce each area by saying, "Thank You, God, that Jesus grew physically." Then the children will say their sentences about Jesus growing physically. Continue with the other areas of growth.

Sharing In Worship
(20-25 minutes)

Omit any of the following sections if you did not offer the corresponding activity. The devotional may be completed without the presentation of Group 4.

Call to Worship (Group 1): Ask Group 1 to share their choral reading.

Special Music (Group 2): **One way we can honor Jesus for being a special child is by being like Him. Group 2 learned a song about being like Jesus.** Ask Group 2 to present their song.

Lord's Supper: Each week when Christians take the Lord's Supper, we remember Jesus' death. The cracker reminds us of Jesus' body, and the juice reminds us of His blood. He asked us to remember Him in this way. We worship Him today because He is special. He loved us enough to die for us.

Offering: Before class, ask four children to be ready to collect the offering at this time.

Scripture (Group 3): **Jesus was a very special child because He always obeyed His parents. The**

Bible tells us that obeying our parents pleases God. Group 3 learned a verse about obeying our parents and thought of ways to obey like Jesus did. Ask Group 3 to share their Scripture and ways to obey.

Devotional (Group 4): **Last week, we talked about Jesus as a young child. We don't know very much about what happened to Jesus between the years of two and twelve. But what the Bible tells us is very important. It says that Jesus obeyed His parents, and that He grew in four ways. Do you remember in what four ways Jesus grew?** Allow response.

During those years, Jesus probably lived a pretty normal life in some ways. He learned in the school. He grew taller and heavier, just like we discovered that we do when we weighed and measured ourselves. He may have helped His father, Joseph, in the carpenter's shop. He probably played with other children.

But in another way, Jesus' life was not normal. It was not normal because He was the Son of God. Jesus was perfect. He never disobeyed His parents or lied to them. He never was mean to a friend. He never cheated in school. Jesus did nothing wrong. We should try to follow His example and grow as He did. Group 4 prepared some skits about ways we can grow like Jesus. Ask Group 4 to present their skits. After each skit is presented, ask the large group to tell in which area the child is growing like Jesus did. If you did not offer this activity, read the situations listed in Group 4 and ask the large group to tell how each child could grow like Jesus.

Personal Praise (Group 5): **What are some ways that you can grow like Jesus did? Group 5 thought of some ways that they will grow. They will praise Jesus by telling Him the ways they will grow like He did.** Ask Group 5 to share their poster and ways to grow like Jesus.

Prayer (Group 6): **Let's thank God for sending Jesus so we could see how to grow. Let's thank God that Jesus was such a special child.** Ask Group 6 to share their thank-You prayers now. Close with prayer, thanking God for Jesus.

Closing Moments
(10-15 minutes)

Play a variation of "Simon Says" using the phrases "Mother Says" or "Father says." Give as many children as possible the opportunity to be the leader.

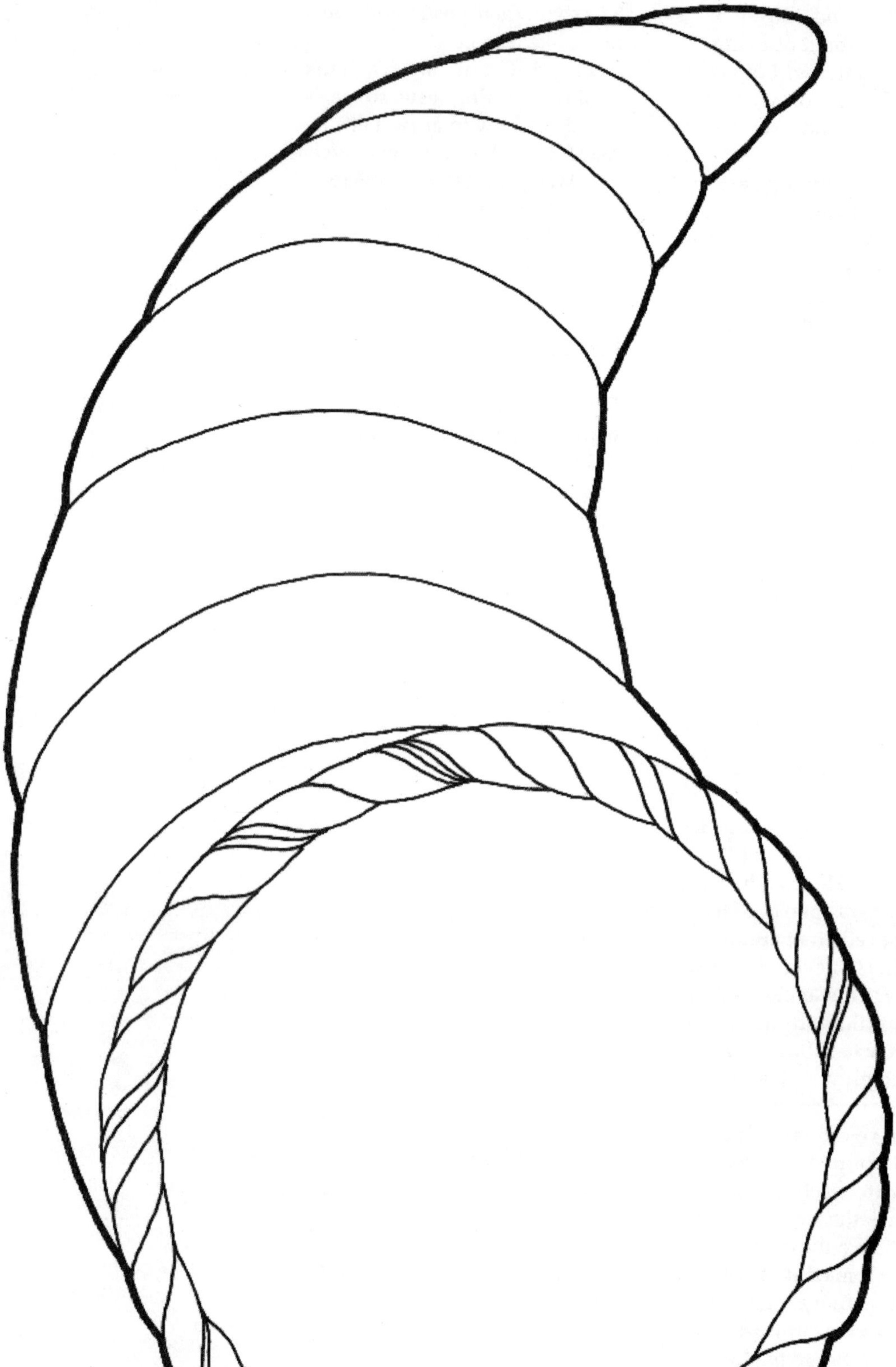

Unit Five
Worship Jesus for Giving Us Friends

Session 19

Jesus Gives Us Friends

Worship Focus

Worship Jesus because He is our friend.

Transition Time
(10-15 minutes)

Direct the pupils to the rest room and allow them time to get a drink at the water fountain.

Follow the leader. Explain the game. "Follow the leader." One child will be the leader. The other children will imitate the leader's actions. The leader may jump up and down, skip, touch his or her toes, smile, and so on. To help the leader with creative movement, try playing background music during the game. After you see that the game is understood, divide the pupils into small groups. Choose one pupil in each group to be the leader until you indicate that he or she should choose a new leader. Change often so that each pupil may have a turn as leader.

Launching the Theme
(10 minutes)

Prepare a fish;ng rod by attaching a string to a short rod or stick. Secure a small magnet to the end of the string. Use the pattern on page 104 to cut a construction paper fish for each student. Attach a small paper clip to each fish. Ask each child to print his or her name on a fish. In a large bowl or bucket place all the fish. Allow each child to come to the front and "fish" for a friend. When they have "caught" a friend they should say, "(Child's name) is my friend."

We went fishing and caught friends! The Bible tells us that one day Jesus watched two men named Simon and Andrew fishing. Jesus called them to be His friends and to follow Him wherever He went. Jesus said "I will make you fishers of men!" What kind of men did Jesus choose to be His special friends and helpers? Were they rich men? Did they have lots of education? Were they handsome and well-dressed? Did they have important positions or were they popular with all the people? Let the pupils discuss this. Stress that Jesus carefully chose men who were willing to give up everything and follow Him.

Use your "fish" to divide the children into the group sessions. Allow group leaders to select the members of their groups by "fishing" a specified number of fish from the bowl.

Building the Theme
(30 minutes)

1. Call to Worship. This group will prepare a poster, thanking God for being our friend. You will need two pieces of poster board, markers, several pie pans, sponges. several bright colors of tempera paints. and potatoes.

Before the session, print "Jesus was a friend to fishermen" at the top of one poster board. Print "Jesus is our friend" at the top of the other poster board.

Peter, Andrew, James, and John were fishermen. When Jesus met them, how was He a friend to them? (He talked to them; He helped them.) **Jesus is our friend too. How is Jesus our friend?** (He loves us; He takes care of us when we are afraid or hungry or sad; He listens when we pray to Him.)

Display the two pieces of poster board. On the first poster board, children will use markers to print how Jesus was a friend to fishermen. On the second poster board, children will print ways Jesus is our friend.

Cut the potatoes in half. On each cut surface, trace a fish, using the pattern on page 90. Carefully cut away about 1/2" of the potato, all around the fish, leaving the fish shape intact. When the pupils are ready to paint, you will pour a small amount of tempera paint into a pie pan and place a sponge in the paint. The pupils will press their potato "stamp" against the sponge and get just enough paint to make a good print. Show the children how to make fish prints on the posters.

During *Sharing in Worship*, children will display the posters and tell how Jesus was a friend to fishermen and how He is our friend. Assign children which part to tell during the small-group time.

2. Special music. The children will learn a new song with motions, to present to the entire group. You will need "A Round" from page 188, poster board, and a marker.

Before the session, print the words to "A Round" on the poster board.

Jesus wants us to follow Him. What does this mean? Does He expect us to leave home, family, school, and friends now? Give the pupils time to talk this over. Then explain that Jesus wants us to follow His example, trying to live as He lived, to be the kind of person He was.

Display the poster board for the children. Sing the song for them once. Then ask them to sing the song with you. After you have practiced it several times, ask the children to develop motions to be used while singing the song. If you know someone who is familiar with sign language, ask him or her to teach it to the children.

During *Sharing in Worship*, the children will sing the song with motions for the large group.

3. Scripture. This group will tell a Bible story to the large group. You will need activity page 19A, construction paper, scissors, and glue.

Who were the four fishermen that Jesus called to be His followers? (Peter, Andrew, James, and John.) **What did Jesus tell them they would fish for?** (Men.) Distribute the materials. Ask the children to color the pictures, cut them out, and place them in the correct order on the construction paper. When the pictures are placed in order, they will make a fish shape. Ask the children to glue the pictures to the construction paper. Assign each pupil or pair of pupils a picture to describe.

During *Sharing in Worship*, the children will display their pictures and tell the Bible story.

4. Offering. The pupils will learn a poem and recite it during offering time. You will need poster board and a red, blue, and black marker.

Before the session, print the following poem on the poster board. Print the first line of each stanza in blue, the second line in red, and the rest in black.

"What can we give to Jesus?
What can we give our Lord
There aren't too many nice things
Small children can afford."

"I'd give Him my new bicycle
Or any of my toys
But Jesus said that what He wants
Is loving girls and boys."

Every Sunday we take up an offering for God. But you don't have to have money in order to give a gift for God. In the Bible story about the Wise-men we learn that God wants us to give Him our time. Doing good things for others is also a gift for God.

Divide the children into two groups. The first group will say the blue lines. The second group will say the red lines. All the children will say the black lines. Practice reading the poem several times. If you have time, children may illustrate the poem with pictures of ways they can be friends to God.

During *Sharing in Worship*, the children will read the poem for the large group.

5. Devotional. This group will present role plays about friends.

When Jesus chose His friends, He chose men who wanted to follow Him and to learn about God's love. We can learn from Jesus' example how we can choose friends. What kind of friends would Jesus want us to have? Allow pupils to discuss this. **We are going to act out stories about friends and try to make good decisions about friends just as Jesus did. I'll read the story to you and then ask some of you to act it out. After we have watched the story being acted out we'll try and decide who was a good friend.**

A. Carmen, Eva, and Amy are walking home from school. Carmen wants to stop at the game and video center, but Eva is not allowed to go to the game center without an adult. Carmen tells Eva to go anyway. Amy tells Eva she should obey her parents.

B. Andy, Tyler, and Adam ride their bikes down to the store. Tyler dares Andy to steal a pack of gum. Adam tells Tyler to forget about stealing and come play ball.

C. Christina is a new girl at school. Aaron and a group of other kids tell Christina they won't be her friend until she rides her bike down a steep drop-off behind the school. Jesse tells Christina the drop-off is too dangerous. Forget about it.

Ask the children to act out the role plays. After each situation is acted out, ask **Who was a good friend? How was he or she a friend?**

During *Sharing in Worship*, the children will present their role plays and ask the large group who was a good friend.

6. Prayer. This group will prepare a section of a bulletin board about friends. Each week for the next four weeks the pupils in this group will complete one of the four sections of the bulletin board entitled "We're Jesus' Friends." This week's section is entitled "Our Special Friends." You will need a large area for a bulletin board (wall or door would work); letters cut from poster board or construction paper to form the title "We're Jesus' Friends"; pictures of church leaders/workers (ask permission to use pictures from an extra church pictorial directory or have children draw their own); Plasti-Tak; construction paper; tape.

Before the session, use the cut-out letters to form the title "We're Jesus Friends" at the top of the bulletin board. Divide the bulletin board into four equal parts. Divide these parts either with tape or strips of construction paper. In one section, place the title "Our Special Friends."

When Jesus began to travel and tell people about God, He chose some very special men to be His friends. Today Jesus gives us some very special friends who tell us about God and the wonderful things Jesus did for us. Many of these are the people we see in God's house every Sunday. Can you tell me who some of these people might be? Give your children time to suggest several names. Encourage them to talk about the different ways these people serve God. Don't forget to mention that everybody has a special job in God's family.

At this time, pass out pictorial directory pages and ask the pupils to search for a "special friend." When they have chosen a picture, instruct them to carefully cut it out. Once this has been done, provide them with a piece of construction paper and tape. Use the construction paper to "frame" the picture and to write the name and job of their "special friend." When this has been completed, they may tape their picture to the section of the bulletin board labeled "Our Special Friends." If pictorial directories are not available, ask the children to draw and label their own pictures.

During *Sharing In Worship,* each child will point to the picture he or she chose and say a short thank-You prayer to God for that person.

Sharing in Worship

(20-25 minutes)

Omit any of the following sections if you did not offer the corresponding activity. The offering and devotional may be completed without the presentations of Groups 4 and 5.

Call to Worship (Group 1): **Jesus was a friend to Peter, Andrew, James, and John, and Jesus is our friend.** Ask Group 1 to display and tell about their posters.

Special Music (Group 2): **Our group is going to share a song with you called "A Round." We will sing it through twice with motions and the third time we would like everyone to help us sing.** Group 2 sings their song.

Scripture (Group 3): Group 3 presents their story about Jesus calling four fishermen.

Lord's Supper: Read Matthew 26:42 from the *International Children's Bible.* **The night before Jesus died on the cross, He spent time talking to His Father. Jesus did not want to be nailed to the cross, but Jesus knew that this was God's plan to help people who did wrong. He agreed to do what God wanted Him to do, even though He knew how much He would have to suffer. He obeyed God and went to the cross.**

Offering (Group 4): **Many of us don't have lots of money we can give to God, but there are things that we have to give that God wants very much. Our group is going to share with us about that now.** Group 4 will recite their poem before the ushers pass the offering plates.

Song: Sing "Come, Follow Jesus Wherever He Leads Us" from page 190.

Devotional (Group 5): **We have learned today that not only did Jesus chose His friends very carefully, but Jesus Himself was a very good friend to others. And we still have another special truth to learn! If we follow Jesus' example, He can help us choose good friends. Choosing good friends is sometimes hard to do.** Ask Group 5 to come forward and present their role plays, asking the large group to tell who was a good friend in each situation. If you did not offer this activity, read the situations listed in the activity and ask the large group to tell who was a good friend.

What things made the children we talked about good friends? (Helped other children do right; stood up for them when no one else did; helped them obey their parents.) **We can choose good friends who will help us do right. But Jesus is the best friend. He is always with us. He helps us do right. He always cares about us. He always listens to us. Jesus is our best friend.**

Prayer (Group 6): **We have made a bulletin board called "We're Jesus' Friends!" Every week we will add a new group of friends. This week's friends were the people that we meet at church. Our teachers, helpers, minister, and other workers. In our prayer time today our group will be saying sentence prayers**

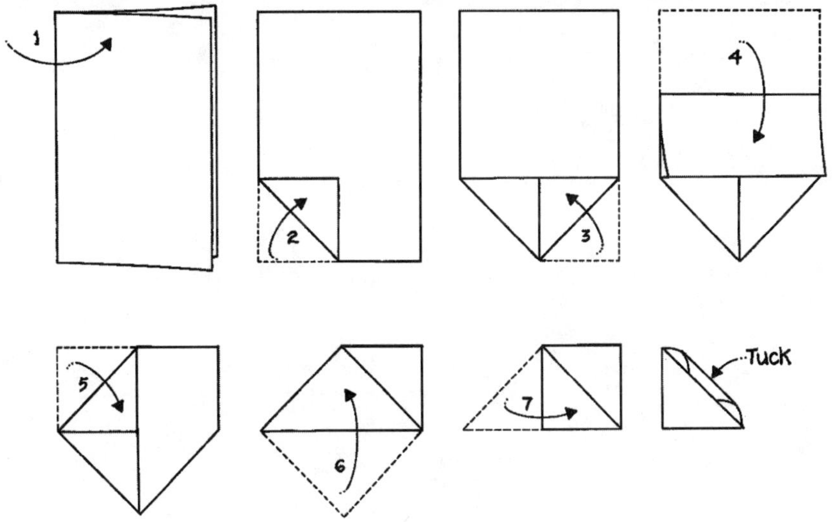

to thank God for these special friends. Ask Group 6 to say their thank-You prayers. Then close with prayer asking God to help us be kind and helpful friends.

Closing Moments
(10-15 minutes)

You will need copies of activity page 19B, scissors, and crayons or markers. See the illustration on this page showing how to fold the friend letter. Make a sample letter before the session to show the children.

Distribute the materials. Ask the children to color, cut out, and fold their friend letter. They may send the letter to a special friend or keep it to remind them of special friends.

Jesus Shows Us How to Be a Friend

Worship Focus

Worship Jesus because He is a friend to children.

Transition Time
(10-15 minutes)

Allow time for the children to use the rest room and to get a drink of water. Involve everyone in the following game.

Friendship Musical Chairs. Use recorded music or ask a piano player to play during the game. If you have a large group, you may want to have two games going at the same time. Arrange the chairs in a circle so there is one chair for each child. On one chair, tape a paper that reads "I can be a friend." As the music plays, the children walk around the chairs. When the music stops, the person sitting in the designated chair will share with the group one way in which he or she could be a friend. ("I can be a good friend by telling Amy about Jesus.") When it is time for the worship session to begin, rearrange the chairs accordingly.

Launching the Theme
(10 minutes)

You will need unlined paper and dark-colored crayons.

Distribute the paper and crayons. Ask the children to fold the paper so that it is divided into four sections.

Who is your favorite person to spend time with? Draw that person's face in the upper left-hand section of your paper. (Allow children time to do so. Allow several children to tell about their person.) **How do you feel when you are with this person? Print how you feel in the upper right-hand corner of your paper.** (Allow time to do so.)

Some children in the Bible got to spend time with Jesus. Jesus' followers wanted to keep the children away. They thought Jesus had more important things to do. But Jesus said, "No. Let the little children come to me." How would you feel if you got to sit on Jesus' lap? Draw how you would feel in the lower left-hand corner of your paper. (Allow children to do so.) **How do you think the children in the Bible felt when the disciples tried to make them go away? Draw how you think the children felt in the lower right-hand corner of your paper.** (Allow time to do so.)

Jesus was a friend to the children in Bible times. Jesus is a friend to children today. We will worship Jesus because He is a friend to children.

Explain the choices of *Building the Theme* activities. Allow the children to choose in which group to participate.

Building the Theme
(30 minutes)

1. Call to Worship. This group will read and illustrate a Bible story about Jesus being a friend for the worship time. You will need white construction paper, Bibles, and markers or crayons.

Let me tell you a story from the Bible. I think this story will help you to know how special Jesus thinks you are. Read Mark 10:13-16, *ICB*. **Now that I've told you the story, I'd like to hear one or two of you tell the rest of us the same story in your own words.** Allow one or two children to do this. **I think Jesus thought children were very special because He took time to show them He cared about them.**

Distribute to each child one piece of white construction paper, markers and/or crayons. Assign a small section of the story to each child. For instance, one child may simply draw the words "Mark 10:13-16." One child could draw pictures of Bible parents with their children. Another child might draw pictures of Jesus' followers discouraging the children from getting Jesus' attention. Another child might portray Jesus' displeasure at His followers for keeping the children away. Another child would draw Jesus with the children on His knees taking time for them. Select one person from the group to tell the story audibly while the rest of the group holds up their pictures in mural-like fashion. Practice the presentation during the small-group time.

During *Sharing in Worship*, children will share their story and pictures.

2. Special Music. This group will present a Scripture and a song during the worship time. You will need "I Will Be a Friend to You" from page 189, poster board, and a marker. Before the session, print the words to the song on poster board.

Jesus tells us that we are His friends when we do what He asks us to do. Let me read to you what Jesus said about this in the Bible. John 15 verse 14 says, "You are my friends if you do what I command you." Try saying this verse with me. Repeat this verse with your class until they are comfortable with it. **To be good friends of Jesus, we better remember what it is He asks us to do! Can you think of some of the things Jesus wants us to do?** Allow the children to share their ideas. Remind them that Jesus wants us to love each other and be good friends to the people around us.

Display the poster board with the words of the song written on it. Sing the song once for the children. Then ask them to sing it with you.

During *Sharing in Worship*, children will recite John 15:14 and sing the song.

3. Offering. This group will share ways to be a friend to introduce the offering. You will need activity page 20A, pencils, poster board, and crayons or markers.

In the first part of our worship time we shared how each of us has a special friend. We like to have friends and we like to be liked! There are many things we can do to be friends with other people. Did you know there is actually a rule to help us be a good friend?

Distribute activity page 20A and pencils to each child. Instruct your group to cross out each 0, C and Q. When this has been completed, they are to write the remaining letters on the space provided. When all the children have completed the puzzle, ask a reading student to read the secret message. (ALWAYS BE KIND.)

What are some ways you can be a good friend? (Allow children to respond.) **Choose a way you can be a good friend. Print or draw a picture of that way to be a friend in the box provided on your activity page.**

Ask the children to copy the secret message from their activity page in large letters on the poster board.

During *Sharing in Worship*, the children will ask the large group to decode the message. Then they will tell the ways they drew to be a friend. Practice the presentation during the small group time.

4. Scripture. This group will learn a verse about being a friend and tell times to be a friend. You will need construction paper, poster board, and markers. Before the session, copy **"A friend loves at all times." Proverbs 17:17** in large letters on the poster board.

We've been talking about friends today. In the Bible we read that Jesus had friends who were just your age. He thought that the children who were His friends were very important people. Maybe there have been times when it wasn't easy for you to be a good friend. I know that the Bible says there were times when Jesus was very tired and very busy, but He always had time to be a good friend. The Bible says in Proverbs that "a friend loves at all times." Display the poster board. **I think that's a good verse for us to remember. God wants us to learn how to be good friends.** Ask the children to repeat the verse with you several times. **When are some times to be a friend?** Allow children to share. Write their ideas on the poster board.

Distribute materials. Ask the children to copy the verse onto a piece of construction paper. Then ask them to turn the paper over and draw a time to be a friend. They may choose a time from the list the group made or choose their own time.

During *Sharing in Worship*, each child will show his or her picture and share the time to be a friend. Then the group will turn their papers over and recite Proverbs 17:17 together.

5. Devotional. This group will prepare a game telling ways to be a friend. You will need copies of activity page 20B, scissors, markers, and paper fasteners.

There are many places in the Bible where we are told that Jesus wants us to be His friends. John 15:14 says that we are His friends when we do what He asks us to do. Proverbs 17:17 says, "A friend loves you all the time." John 15: 17 says "This is my command: Love each other." In order to be friends of Jesus, we must love each other. Have any of you ever had a hard time loving or being a good friend? Allow them to discuss this briefly. **Let's share times when it is fun to love or easy to be a good friend**. Allow children to discuss this.

Distribute materials. Ask children to color and cut out the spinner and arrow. Ask them to use a paper fastener to attach the arrow to the spinner. Divide the children into groups of two or three. Ask each group to take turns spinning the spinner and telling how they could be a friend to the person in the picture. Suggestions follow: boy with first place ribbon—be happy for him, tell him he did a great job; girl whose dog was hit by a car—tell her you are sorry, pray for her, give her a hug; boy who broke a car—forgive him, tell him it's OK; girl who is swinging alone—go swing with her, invite her to play with you. Allow the children to play for several minutes. Then ask them to share the ways they told to be a friend to each person. Record their ideas on a poster board. Assign four children to tell about the children in each of the pictures on the spinner during the worship time. Assign four children to tell how to be a friend to each of the children.

During *Sharing in Worship*, children will share the ways to be a friend.

Option: Enlarge the spinner onto a poster board. During *Sharing in Worship*, ask for volunteers from the large group to come forward and spin the spinner. Then ask children from the small group to tell how to be a friend to each person.

6. Prayer. This group will prepare a section of a bulletin board to introduce the prayer time. You will need white and colored construction paper, children's magazines, pictures of children of missionaries your church supports, scissors, Plasti-Tak, and markers or crayons. Before the session, cut out the letters "Our Friends to Grow With" and place it on a section of the bulletin board begun last week. If you did not prepare a bulletin board last week, place the letters on a blank wall or bulletin board.

Read Mark 10:13-16. **The Bible tells us that Jesus was a good friend to children. We can follow Jesus' example by being a good friend to the children we know! Let's each share one way that we can be a good friend this week.** Allow children to share their ideas at this time. **It makes us feel good to know that Jesus really loves and cares about us, no matter how old we are! We are going to work on a bulletin board. Our bulletin board will be covered with pictures of children. This will help to remind us that Jesus loves us!**

Pass out magazines and/or construction paper. Tell your children they may either look for pictures of children in the magazines or they may choose to draw a picture of their own friend. If you have pictures of missionary children available, be sure and introduce this child or children to your group. Explain to them where they live and how they are being good friends by telling others about Jesus. When the children have completed cutting or drawing, assist them in attaching the pictures to the bulletin board.

Ask each child to think of a sentence prayer, thanking God for a friend. Decide in what order the children will say their prayers.

During *Sharing in Worship*, the children will say their prayers, thanking God for friends.

Sharing in Worship
(20-25 minutes)

Omit any of the following sections if you did not offer the corresponding activities. The offering and devotional may be completed without the presentations of groups 3 and 5.

You may wish to have the basic order of worship displayed on a poster in your classroom. Children feel comfortable when they know the routine and what's expected of them. This is also a good time to utilize the talents of your students who may be learning to play musical instruments. Choose two children to be offering helpers and one child to give the offering prayer.

Call to Worship (Group 1): **Listen to this story of how Jesus was a good friend to children.** Group 1 presents their pictured Bible story.

Special Music (Group 2): **Our group has learned a special song about being a good friend. We are going to share it with you. After we have sung it twice, we want you to be good friends and help us sing it again!** Ask Group 2 to present their song.

Lord's Supper: Jesus wants us to be friends with others and love others just as He did. He loved each of us so much that He went to the cross to suffer and die for all the bad things we have done. We remember Jesus at this time by drinking the juice and eating the bread. This reminds us of His death, burial, and resurrection. Let's remember Jesus, our Best friend, by thinking about Him right now. Pray and serve the Lord's Supper.

Offering (Group 3): Ask Group 3 to come forward at this time. **Some of the money we give will be used by the church to spread the Good News about Jesus. One of the best ways we can be a friend to someone is to tell them about Jesus, our Best Friend. Group 3 has decoded a special message about being a friend.** Ask Group 3 to display the coded message and ask the large group to decode the message by leaving out all O's, C's, and Q's. Then ask Group 3 to tell ways to be a friend.

Scripture (Group 4): **The Bible gives us good advice about being a friend. Group 4 learned a verse about being a friend. See if you can learn it too.** Ask Group 4 to share their verse and pictures. Then ask the large group to repeat the verse with them.

Devotional (Group 5): **I want to share with you something Jesus said in the Bible. He said, "You are my friends if you do what I command you." One of the things Jesus commands us to do is to love each other. I think that one of the very best stories about being a friend and showing love is found in the Bible. Do you remember the story about the Good Samaritan?** Allow children to share. Discuss the story. Ask questions to encourage them to share. The story is found in Luke 10:26-37. **The Samaritan was a good friend to the man who was hurt. Jesus tells us at the end of that story that we should do the same thing the Samaritan man did. We may not find very many hurt people by the side of the road, but there**

are many ways in which we can be good friends to the people around us. Group 5 discovered some of those ways. Ask Group 5 to come forward and share ways to be a friend now. If you did not offer this activity, describe the children pictured on activity page 20B and ask the children to tell you how they could be a friend to those children.

What are some other ways to be friends to other children? Allow children to share. **Friends aren't always people who are the same age we are. Sometimes friends might be older, or younger. No matter who they are or how old they are, if you can find a way to be kind or helpful or show them Jesus loves them, you are doing what Jesus asked you to do. You are one of Jesus' friends. I want Jesus to think of me as His friend. Don't you? I will be praying for you this week that you will find ways to be good friends to everyone around you.**

Prayer (Group 6): Ask Group 6 to assemble beside the unit bulletin board. **Today in our prayer time, we are going to pray for our friends. Group 6 has made a bulletin board of different kinds of friends we can pray for.** Ask Group 6 to share who they have included on their bulletin board and pray for their friends. **Let's all stand and make a prayer circle. As we go around the circle pray for a friend of yours and ask Jesus to make you a better friend.** When the children have prayed, close with prayer. **Dear Father, thank You for sending Your Son Jesus, who is our Best Friend. Please help us to show love and concern to others as You showed to us. In Jesus' name, amen.**

Closing Moments
(10-15 minutes)

Care and share bag. Give each child a piece of paper and tell him or her to write his or her name on the paper. Place the names in a bag and shake well. Allow each child one at a time to draw a name from the bag. When they have done this,ask them to tell the rest of the group what name they selected and share one good thing that they know about this person. For instance, "Jane is a good reader." Or "Bobby can draw very well." When each person in the group has had an opportunity to do this, explain to the group that being a good friend sometimes means helping others to feel good. You and the assistant teachers might want to include your names in the bag also.

Jesus Is a Friend to Leaders

Worship Focus

Worship Jesus because He helps us be a friend to leaders.

Transition Time

(10-15 minutes)

Send the children in small groups to the rest room and drinking fountain. When everyone has returned, ask the children to sit in a circle. Arrange the chairs in one or two circles, depending on the size of your group.

Leader pantomime. Before the session, print on cards or construction paper the titles of several leaders. Include police, fireman, President, minister, teacher, and so on. Put the titles in a sack or basket.

Ask a child to begin the game by asking who is wearing red socks (or something similar). Ask that child to choose a paper from the sack. He or she will pantomime to the rest of the class something that leader does. The child who guesses correctly may have the next turn. Continue the game until all children have had a turn.

Launching the Theme

(10 minutes)

I am going to read to you several job descriptions! As I am reading these, I want you to listen and try to decide who I am describing. When you think you have the right answer, raise your hand.

Note: you may want to make some descriptions of your own based on personalities in your own community.

I have a very important job. I am at least 35 years of age. I live in a very busy city in the United States. I talk to people all over the world. I make decisions about laws for our country. I have my job for four years and sometimes as many as eight years if I am re-elected. I live in a big white house. The first person to have my job was named George. Who am I? (The President of the United States.)

I wear a uniform while I am working. I often drive or walk around the same part of the city every day. I help people in many different ways. I wear something shiny on my shirt. Sometimes I ask drivers to stop their cars and give them a piece of paper they don't want. Sometimes my job is scary. Sometimes I blow a whistle or turn on a siren. Who am I? (A police officer.)

On the one day many other people don't work, I do! I love to work with people. I have been called at all hours of the day and night to talk with people. I go to lots of weddings. There is a special book I study and read every day. It is very important to my job. When people want help, I must go to the book I study. Often I must talk to the person who wrote the book. Who am I? (Minister.)

After the children have guessed the leaders you have described, ask them to list ways to help those leaders. As you begin dividing them into groups for *Building the Theme*, ask children who have not yet worked on the unit bulletin board to be in group #1.

Building the Theme

(30 minutes)

1. Call to Worship. This group will make a bulletin board of leaders. You will need magazines, newspapers, construction paper, glue, scissors, markers, crayons and Plasti-tak. Before this session, prepare the title words "Our Friends Who Help Us" and attach them to one section of the bulletin board begun in Session 19. If you did not make the bulletin board in Session 19, use a section of the wall or an empty bulletin board.

Let's make a list of all the people you can think of who are leaders. (This list could include teachers, policemen, librarian, doctor, minister, parents, and so on.) **Today we are going to make a bulletin board about our leaders.**

Distribute magazines, newspapers and construction paper. Instruct the children to look through the magazines and newspapers for examples of leaders that we should be praying for. Some children may prefer to draw their own. When the children have located the pictures or drawn them, instruct them to cut them out, mount them on a piece of construction paper, and use Plasti-Tak to attach them to the bulletin board.

Romans 13: lb Says, "No one rules unless God has given him the power to rule." That means that the leaders in your life were

put their by God! That also tells us that we should do our very best to obey and help our leaders. Help your group practice saying Romans 13:lb.

During *Sharing in Worship*, the children will say Romans 13:1b. Then each child will point to a leader on the bulletin board and say, "God has given (name of leader) power to rule."

2. Scripture. This group will make Scripture cards. You will need eight sheets of poster board or card-stock paper. Before the session, print in pencil each word of the phrase "Love each other as I have loved you" on separate pieces of poster board. Use a paper hole punch or a sharp pointed object of punch holes along the outline of each letter. Cut yarn for sewing the cards. For easier handling, dip one end of each yarn strand into glue and let dry.

Give each child a card or cards and pieces of yarn. Help each child sew his or her words with the yarn. When the children finish instruct them to practice putting the words of the phrase into correct order.

Who are we to love? (Allow students to answer.) **Today we are talking about leaders that we know. Leaders are very special people who have very important jobs. I want each of you to think of a leader you know. As we go around the group, I want you to tell us the name of the leader you're thinking about and a way you think you can help that leader or show that leader you love them.**

During *Sharing in Worship* the children will display the Scripture cards in order and recite the verse. Then they will name ways to show the leaders they love them.. Practice the presentation during the small-group time.

3. Special Music. This group will learn a song for the worship time. You will need "Come Follow Jesus Wherever He leads Us" from page 190, poster board, and markers. Before the session, print the words to, "Come, Follow Jesus Wherever He Leads Us" on the poster board.

Today we are thinking of ways to be good friends to leaders. There are many great leaders that we could name. But Jesus is the greatest leader. And he is also our best friend! Jesus is a leader; He is also our friend. When we think of ways to please our leaders, pleasing Jesus should be first on our list! Following Jesus is one sure way of pleasing Him. How can we be good friends with Jesus! (Let the children share their ideas at this time.)

Display the poster board for the children, Sing the song through once with the children, Then ask them to sing it with you. Practice the song until the children are comfortable singing it. If time allows, ask the children to write ways they can be a friend to Jesus on the poster board.

During *Sharing in Worship*, children will display the poster board and sing the song.

4. Devotional. This group will pantomime a Bible story. You will need Bibles. This activity is for older or gifted children.

Let me tell you a story about a leader who came to Jesus for help. (Read John 3:1-21, ICB.) **Nicodemus was a very important man. Most of the time people came to Nicodemus when they needed help. But in our story we see that Jesus was the one who helped Nicodemus. How do you think Jesus was a friend to Nicodemus?** (He listened; He answered his questions.) **Sometimes just listening to our friends can be a wonderful way to help them. Jesus knows how to be a good friend.**

Select two of your students to act as Jesus and Nicodemus. The rest of your group will be readers. Assign each reader a portion of John 3:1-21 to read aloud. Instruct the two actors to silently act out the scene which the readers are reading. Although the actors will not say anything, they must pay attention to what is being said and act accordingly. Their facial expressions and their body movements should accurately reflect what is being read. For example: John 3:14 says, "Moses lifted up the snake in the desert." Perhaps the actor portraying Jesus would lift his arm up to indicate this while it is being read. Rehearse this as time allows.

During *Sharing in Worship*, children will present the pantomime.

5. Prayer. This group will be making prayer cards and writing simple sentence prayers to be presented during the prayer time in *Sharing in worship*. You will need construction paper, scissors, and markers for this activity.

I would like for each one of you to tell me a leader you know and one way in which you could help that leader. (Allow children to answer.) **Who is able to help all our leaders the most?** (God!) **Although there are many ways that we can and should help our leaders, one of the best things that we can do for them is to ask God to help them. This is something every one of us can do!**

Give each child a piece of construction paper and a pair of scissors. Ask each child to fold his or her paper in half and lay his or her hand on the paper next to the fold. Trace around the hand and cut it out, being careful not to cut the fold. The hand can now be opened like a card, and each child can write a sentence prayer on the card. Ask each child to think of a leader he or she knows. Then ask them to fill in the following sentence: "Thank You, Jesus, for helping me be a friend. I will be a friend to (leader) by________." Model the prayer for the children;

then print the sentences on the chalk board for them to copy. When each child has written a prayer, help them practice saying their prayers.

During *Sharing in Worship*, the children will read their prayers.

6. Personal Praise. This group will name ways to help leaders for which they are thankful. You will need activity page 21A and pencils or crayons. This activity may be completed with out adult guidance. Print or tape record the instructions.

Distribute the activity page. **During our busy week, we see many leaders. Look at the leaders on this page. Draw a line from the leader to a way you could help that leader.** (Allow children time to do so.) **Name a leader for which you are thankful. How could you help that leader?** Ask children to print or draw a picture of the way they will help the leader.

During *Sharing in Worship*, children will name ways to help the leaders for which they are thankful.

Sharing in worship

(20-25 minutes)

Omit any of the following sections if you did not offer the corresponding activity. The Devotional may be completed without the presentation of Group 4.

Call to Worship (Group 1): **Leaders are important people who have a lot of power. But God has all power. He gives leaders their power.** Ask Group 1 to present.

Lord's Supper: Read 1 Corinthians 11:23-26, *ICB*. **During the Lord's Supper today, let's remember that Jesus died for His friends. Jesus died for us.**

Offering: Before the worship session, appoint children to collect the offering for your group. This is also an excellent time to make use of the various talents found within your group for an offertory. The children may can recite appropriate poetry or play a simple piece of music. Be sure that you have contacted the young people early enough in the week to give them a chance to prepare themselves for worship.

Scripture (Group 2): The leader of group 2 should help the students to assemble in proper order at the front of the group. **It is important to help our leaders. It is important to treat them in the same way we would like to be treated.**

Special music (Group 3): **Our group has prepared a song called "Come, Follow Jesus Wherever He Leads Us." We are going to sing this through for you twice. After we have sung it, we're going to ask you to help us sing it again!** Group 3 sings.

Devotional (Group 4): Group 4 presents their pantomime. When the presentation is over, ask the children to tell how Jesus was a friend to Nicodemus. If you did not offer this activity, read or tell the story of Jesus and Nicodemus from John 3:1-21, and ask the children to tell you how Jesus was a friend.

Jesus shows us how to be a friend to leaders. Listen to this story about a boy your age who followed Jesus' example of being a friend.

During the war with Iraq in January of 1991, there was a boy who wanted to do something for his country. He knew that there were men and women in the United States armed forces who had very dangerous jobs. He was grateful that these men and women were brave enough to protect his country. This young man wished very hard for something he could do to help too. In school one day he received an address where he could write to one of the men stationed in Saudi Arabia. This boy and the marine began to write back and forth, sharing what was happening in their lives. In one letter the boy wrote, "I wish I could do more to help you. I pray for you every night and ask God to keep you safe whatever you may be doing." The marine answered by saying, "I don't know of any more important thing you could be doing for me than to pray. I know God is watching over me!"

One day each one of you young boys and girls may grow up to be a leader. But right now you can be doing something very important for today's leaders. Just like the young man in our story, you can pray for the leaders that you know. They need prayer to make good decisions, to keep them safe, to know right from wrong and to keep them strong. As we close our worship time together we are going to pray for our leaders.

Prayer (Group 5): **Each member of our group has written a prayer for a leader they know. At this time, we would like to share those prayers with you. As we are praying these prayers please bow your heads and pray along with us.** Group 5 prays.

Personal Praise (Group 6): **We can be a friend to leaders by praying for them. But there are other ways we can be a friend to leaders. Group 6 found ways to be a friend to leaders for whom they are thankful.** Group 6 shares. Close with prayer, thanking God for leaders.

Closing Moments

(10-15 minutes)

Writing a letter. You will need a manila envelope, activity page 21B, and pencils. **Have you ever received a card or letter from your grandma or grandpa or maybe a friend who moved far away? It is exciting to get mail from people who care. How did you feel when there was some mail for you?**

Today we have been talking about being a friend to leaders. The President of the United States is a very important, powerful leader. He has a difficult job to do. What are some of the things the President must do? (Allow children to answer.) **He has many people to look after. He must get very tired and discouraged by all the problems in our country. Show the pupils a manila envelope. We are going to send pictures and letters to the President to let him know we are praying for him!**

Distribute out activity page 21B and pencils. If you have younger children, ask them to dictate a group letter rather than writing individual letters. Read aloud as many letters as time allows. Before mailing the envelope, write a letter of explanation. Assure the President that these children have been praying for him. If possible, include a picture of the class. Follow through by consciously including church and government leaders during your weekly prayer time. Of course, if you receive a response from the White House, bring in the letter and read it to the children!

Jesus Is a Friend to Those Who Are Happy or Sad

Worship Focus

Worship Jesus because He helps us when we are happy and when we are sad.

Transition Time

(10-15 minutes)

Send the children in small groups to the rest room and drinking fountain. Welcome newcomers and involve them in the following activity.

Montage. You will need modern-day pictures from magazines or old Sunday school materials that show people having happy and sad experiences (birthdays, playing, a new baby, and so on), half sheets of white paper, crayons or markers, pencils, scissors, and glue. Hang a large piece of butcher paper or poster board on the wall. **How do you feel when it's your birthday?** (Allow children to answer.) **How do you feel when you accidentally break a favorite toy?** (Allow pupils to share their ideas.) **This morning we're going to talk about happy and sad feelings. I've brought with me magazines and drawing paper. Let's spend a few minutes finding picture of people who are either happy or sad or if you'd rather you may draw your own happy/sad picture.**

Instruct the pupils to glue the pictures to the large paper to make the montage.

Launching the Theme

(10 minutes)

You will need the montage made during *Transition time.*

This montage shows times when we are happy and times when we are sad. Who wants to tell about a happy time? Ask several of the children to tell about their happy experiences. List the happy times on the chalkboard. Include the happy times from the montage. **Who would like to tell about a sad time?** Ask several children to tell about a sad experience. List these sad times in another column on the chalkboard. Include the sad times from the montage.

In today's Bible story we will learn how Jesus was a friend to a family during a sad time. The family's names were Mary, Martha and Lazarus. Jesus is our friend when we are happy and when we are sad. Look at the happy times and sad times listed on the chalkboard. How is Jesus a friend to us when we are happy and when we are sad? (Jesus is a friend by giving us friends, parents, and other people to help us, talk with us, play with us, celebrate with us; Jesus is always there to hear us when we pray to Him.) **We want to worship Jesus today because He helps us when we are happy and when we are sad.**

To divide the pupils into the six *Building the Theme* groups, ask them to draw from a paper bag containing six different colored happy/sad faces. Like colors will be in the same group.

Building the Theme

(30 minutes)

1. **Call to worship.** The children in this group will write a call to worship based on Psalm 71:6 and the different places where Jesus helps them. Before the session, print Psalm 71:6 on the chalkboard or poster board. Use the International Children's Bible.

Read the verse twice to the children, pointing to each word as you say it. Ask them to read the verse with you the third time. Display the poster board.

This Bible verse tells us something important about Jesus. He is our friend all the time. He is our friend every where. What are some of the different places you go? Print the children's answers on a chalkboard along with the name of the child who suggested it. **Now let's start at the beginning of this list. When we come to your suggestion, I want you to say, "Jesus, You have been my help at (fill in with their suggestion)."**

The following is an example of the call to worship.

Leader: I have depended on you since I was born. You have been my help from the day I was born. I will always praise you. Psalm 71:6 *(ICB)*

Child: Jesus, You have been my

help at school.

Group: We will always praise You.

Child: Jesus, You have been my help at home.

Group: We will always praise You.

Child: Jesus, You have been my help at church.

Group: We will always praise You.

Practice the presentation until the group is comfortable.

During *Sharing in Worship*, you will read the verse and children will name places where Jesus has been their help.

2. Special Music. This group will present a song during the worship time. You will need "Jesus Is My Special Friend" from p. 189, poster board, marker, pen, and paper. Before the session, print the words to the song on the poster board.

How do you know when somebody loves you? What kind of things do you do for somebody you love? We know Jesus loves us - let's list some ways He shows us His love. Examples: He stays through good and bad; He is God's Son; He answers our prayers; He helps us; He will forgive us; He loves us.

Display the poster board. **We will sing a song about ways Jesus shows us He loves us.** Sing the song once for the children. Then ask them to sing it with you. Ask the children to write a new stanza to the song, using the ways Jesus loves us that they named. Stress the meaning of the lines more than the rhyme. Print the new stanza on the poster board. Practice singing both stanzas several times.

During *Sharing in Worship*, the children will sing both stanzas of the song.

3. Scripture. This group will recite a verse and use sign language. You will need activity page 22A, a poster board, and markers. Before the session, print Psalm 105:4 (*ICB*) on the poster board.

Display the poster board for the children. Read the verse for them. Then ask them to read it with you several times. Distribute the activity page and practice the signs. Practice saying the verse with the signs many times.

During *Sharing in Worship*, children will recite the verse with the signs.

4. Personal Praise. This group will prepare thank-You books for God. You will need activity page 22B, scissors pencils, and crayons or markers. To prepare for this group's activity, the leader may want to make a thank-you card before the session. Be prepared to share with your group a time when God helped you.

Let's look the montage we made at the beginning of our worship time. Let's talk about good times and bad times when Jesus is our friend. Distribute the activity page. Ask the children to cut out and fold the book. Then ask them to write or draw a picture of a happy time and a sad time on the pages. On the last page, ask them to write or draw a time they are thankful God helps them.

During *Sharing the Worship*, the children will name the times God helps them.

5 Prayer. This group will prepare a bulletin board of happy and sad times to lead the prayer thoughts. You will need construction paper, scissors, crayons or markers, and tape or Plasti-Tak. Before the session, cut out letters for the title "Our Friend at All Times." Place the title in the fourth section of the bulletin board begun in Session 19. If you did not make the other sections of the bulletin board, attach the title to a blank wall or bulletin board. Distribute the materials to the children. Ask them to draw pictures of happy and sad times and attach them to the bulletin board. Then ask them to think how God helps us at those times.

During *Sharing in Worship*, each child will point out a happy or sad time he or she drew and say a sentence prayer, thanking god for helping us at that time. Practice the presentation during the small-group time.

6. Devotional. This group will present a pantomime of a Bible story. You will need Bibles. **I want to read to you a story from the Bible. Listen!** Read John 11:1-44. After reading the Bible story discuss the following questions: **Why was Jesus sad? What did Jesus do when He was sad?** (He cried, He asked God for help.) **What happened after Jesus prayed?**

Select children from your group to portray Lazarus, Jesus, Mary and Martha. The rest of the group may be divided into mourners and Jesus' followers. Read the story aloud and have the characters mime the events.

During *Sharing in Worship*, children will present the pantomime as you read the story.

Sharing in worship
(20-25 minutes)

Omit any of the following sections if you did not offer the corresponding activity. The devotional may be completed without the presentation of Group 5.

Call to worship (Group 1): Read Psalm 71:6; then ask Group 1 to present the places God is our help.

Special music (Group 2):. **How can we know that Jesus loves us?** (Children respond.) **Group 2 learned a song about ways we can know Jesus loves us and is our friend.** Ask Group 2 to display the poster board and sing. Then ask the large group to join them.

Scripture (Group 3): **When is God able to help us? Group 3 will share a verse that tells when God helps us.** Group 3 presents. If you have time, teach the signs to the large group.

Lord's Supper: Jesus loved Mary, Martha, and Lazarus. He even cried when Lazarus died. Jesus loved all of us so much that He died for the wrong things we have done and will do. Let's remember our friend, Jesus during this special time. Pray and serve the Lord's Supper.

Offering: Before the worship session, ask four children to be ready to collect the offering. Ask one child to say the offering prayer.

Personal Praise (Group 4): **When are you thankful God helps you? Group 4 thought of times they are thankful for God's help.** Ask Group 4 to share their books.

Devotional (Group 5): **We all like to have good days. We like to have good friends, good grades, nice clothes, warm, sunny weather and food that tastes great! But sometimes our days aren't always full of good things. Sometimes our friends hurt our feelings, and sometimes our bodies don't feel good. Sometimes what we have for supper is not our favorite food! Our days are made up of good things and bad things, happy times and sad times. But even though we may not always feel the same, Jesus is always our friend. He is a good friend when we feel good, but also when we feel bad. He had bad days too, and He understands what is feels like to be unhappy or hurt. Listen as Group 5 presents a story about a sad and happy time in Jesus' life.** Group 5 presents their pantomime. If you did not offer this activity, review the story of Mary, Martha and Lazarus from John 11:1-44.

Jesus understands how we feel because He has been happy and sad too. When we need His help, all we need to do is talk to Him and tell Him why we are sad or why we are happy. When we're sad, He'll help us know how to feel better. When we're happy, we should remember to tell Him thank you for the good things He sends us!

Prayer (Group 6): Ask Group 6 to share their thank-You prayers. Then close with prayer, thanking God for being our friend at all times.

Closing Moments
(10-15 minutes)

Ask your group to stand in a large circle. Provide one student with a bouncing ball. **Sometimes we are Jesus' helpers when we help sad people be happy. When the ball is bounced to you think of a way you could make someone happy and share it with the rest of the group.** Instruct the student holding the ball to share with the group first and then bounce it to another student.

Jesus Is a Friend to Those No One Likes

Worship Focus

Worship Jesus because He is a friend to those no one likes.

Transition time
(10-15 minutes)

Divide the children into several small teams to play "A Cup of Water Relay." Each team will need a small pan of water containing about 2 cups of water, a sponge and an empty cup sitting in a pie pan. The object of the game is for each team to transfer one cup of water from the bowl to their cup, one sponge full at a time. The first team to accomplish this and sit down behind the starting line wins. The containers may be placed directly on the floor to make team lanes. (You may wish to put a trash bag under each station.)

Launching the theme
(10 minutes)

You will need to draw a large colorful water jar on the side of a grocery sack before the session. Ask two leaders to serve as a narrator and Samaritan women in the following script. Provide copies of the script for them.

Allow the children to stand and demonstrate their ability to balance something on their heads. Then ask the children to listen to the drama by the leaders. The woman leader should stand with the sack on her head.

Narrator: I would like to tell you about the day this woman met Jesus. She had gone to the well to get water. There was a man at the well. He was tired and thirsty from a long journey. He asked if she might get a drink of water for Him. She was very surprised! You see, she was a Samaritan and He was a Jew. The Jewish people hated Samaritans! They did not even talk to Samaritans. This man was different. He talked to her, and she had never met Him before. Jesus told her to call her husband. She had done many wrong things. Jesus knew all that She had done. He knew she had many husbands. She thought He was a prophet a special man of God, but He told her that He was God's Son. Let's have the woman tell us what happened next.

Samaritan Woman: I ran into town and told everyone that I had met Jesus. I told how He had known all about my life. Everyone wanted to meet Jesus. All the people followed me to where Jesus was. They listened to Him teach for two days. After hearing Jesus for themselves, they also believed that He is God's Son. I am glad I met Jesus. He taught me about His Father in Heaven. Now I am happy. I tell everyone about my Savior.

Briefly explain the activities available to the children. Allow them to choose in which group to participate.

Building the theme
(30 minutes)

1. Call to Worship. This group will prepare a poster of ways to show and not to show love. You will need a large piece of poster board, felt-tip markers, construction paper (red and green), and tape. Before the session, draw a line down the middle of the board, vertically. At the top of the left-hand column, glue a large green happy face. At the top of the right hand column, glue a red sad face.

We have been talking about how Jesus talked to and loved all the people, no matter who they were, no matter what they had done. He wants us to care for and be kind to all people too.

The Bible tells us, in 1 John 4:19 and 21, "We love because God first loved us . . . . Whoever loves God must also love his brother" (ICB). God loves us and expects us to love other people. We are going to think of some times when we can show love and concern for those others do not like. We are also going think of some things we do that do not show love.

Let the children suggest things, either good or bad, and then have everyone decide whether you should print them on a green circle for good or a red circle for bad. Suggestions follow: Things that show love–eating lunch with someone who is alone, choosing someone to be in your group or team, inviting someone to a party at home or church; Things that do not show love–calling someone names, laughing at the way someone looks or what they are wearing, refusing to let someone play on your team.

Discuss and sort out the situations but do not attach them to the chart. Return the ideas to children and have them put a tape roll on the back of each. They may wear them to group worship time and at the appropriate time share them in front of the group and place them on the chart correctly.

During *Sharing in Worship*, ask a child a child to read 1 John 4:19, 21. Then ask each child to tell a way to show or not show love and attach it to the appropriate column on the poster.

2. Special Music. This group will sing a song about the woman Jesus met at the well. You will need "There Was a Woman at a Well" from page 191, poster board, markers, and 15 pieces of construction paper. Before the session, write the words to the song on poster board.

"There was a woman at a well
Who met a man named Jesus.
J-E-S-U-S, J-E-S-U-S, J-E-S-U-S.
Yes, Jesus was His name."

"The woman was not liked by some,
But Jesus showed He cared.
C-A-R-E-D, C-A-R-E-D, C-A-R-E-D.
Yes, Jesus showed He Cared."

"Jesus is our friend today.
Yes, Jesus loves us too.
L-O-V-E-S, L-O-V-E-S, L-O-V-E-S.
Yes, Jesus loves us too!"

We just talked about a woman no one liked that Jesus met. How was Jesus a friend to the woman? (Talked to her; helped her.) **Jesus is a friend to everyone, even those no one likes.** Display the poster board and sing the song for the children. Then ask the children to sing the song with you.

You may wish to have the letters J-E-S-U-S, C-A-R-E-D and L-O-V-E-S on individual pieces of construction paper. Have the children hold these letters up as the are sung in the song. The children may decorate around the edge of each letter card.

If the children are older, ask them to write new verses for the song naming ways Jesus shows His love. The ways must be five-letter words. An example follows:

"Jesus is our friend today.
He hears us when we pray.
H-E-A-R-S, H-E-A-R-S, H-E-A-R-S.
He hears us when we pray."

Other suggestions follow: Italicized words are to be spelled out in the song. He is our best *friend*; Jesus *gives* us food; He died on the *cross*.

Practice the song until the children are comfortable singing it.

During *Sharing in Worship*, children will present the song as special music.

3. Lord's Supper. This group will create sentences about God's love to introduce the Lord's Supper. You will need copies of activity page 23B, a poster board, markers and pencils. This activity may be completed without adult guidance. Print or tape record the instructions. Before the session, print the code from the activity page at the top of the poster board.

We just heard about how Jesus was a friend to a woman no one like. Jesus is a friend to everyone, no matter who they are or what they have done. What is the greatest way that Jesus showed He is our friend? Allow children to respond. Distribute activity page 23B. **The words on this page are about the greatest way that Jesus is our friend. What do these words have to do with Jesus being our friend?** Allow pupils to respond. **God gave us the gift of Jesus because He loved us. Jesus came to die for all the world. Because Jesus came back alive, He is our Savior.** (He can forgive all the wrong things we do.) **If we believe that Jesus died and came back alive, we will have eternal life.** Assign each child or pair of children a word to write in code on the activity page. Then ask the children to write the coded word on the poster board. Leave room beside each coded word to write the decoded word during *Sharing in Worship*.

During *Sharing in Worship*, the large group will decode the words. After each word is decoded, a child from the small group will say a sentence, telling what that word has to do with Jesus being our friend. Practice the sentences during the small-group time.

4. Scripture. This group will prepare a banner of a Bible verse. You will need a 6 foot piece of shelf paper, a white crayon, and broad-tipped markers or watercolors. Before the session, print 1 Corinthians 11:1 with a white crayon on the shelf paper. "Follow me as I follow Christ."

Display the shelf paper for the children. **There is a Bible verse hidden on this paper. This verse is part of a letter Paul wrote to the Christians in Corinth. They were not getting along with each other. Do you always get along well with your friends? Let's see what advice Paul gave the people at Corinth.**

The children may use broad tipped markers or watercolor to expose the prepared verse by marking over the crayoned verse.

They should leave as much margin area white as possible for later drawings. While the banner is drying, help the children find 1 Corinthians 11:1 in the Bible and read aloud together.

Paul was telling the people to be like Jesus. We should always try to be like Jesus and follow His example. Earlier today we learned that Jesus was kind to a woman who others didn't like. Let's think of some ways we can be a friend like Jesus. Allow time for ideas and discussion. **I'd like for us to write or draw our ideas around the edge of our banner. Then we can each share our idea during worship time when we show our banner.** Pictures and ideas could be done on separate paper and attached to the banner.

During *Sharing in Worship*, children will display the banner and say the verse together. Then they will tell the ways they can be friends like Jesus.

5. Devotion. This group will prepare a story strip to present a Bible story. You will need one copy of activity page 23A, seven copies of activity page 23A with a piece of white paper taped over the title in the middle part of the page, markers, and clear tape. You will need to obtain a large cardboard box and transform it into a television set. In the bottom of the box cut two parallel slits, the distance of one activity page apart. Each slit should be wide enough to allow the children's finished filmstrip to roll easily through during their presentation.

Today we receive news almost instantly by phone, radio, and television. How is this different from communication in Jesus' time? Allow children's responses. **The good news that the Samaritan woman had to share spread quickly even without modern inventions.**

Our group is going to be a news team. Guess what big event we've been assigned to film today? Our assignment is to report the meeting of Jesus and the Samaritan woman. The news of it has already spread. To make our news story we need to show and tell our viewers what happened. The Bible gives us the facts we need in John 4:4-41. Let's review the event. Distribute the seven blank activity pages. On each page, print one of the following events of the story for children to illustrate.

1. Jesus sitting at the well.
2. The Samaritan woman coming to the well.
3. Jesus tells her He is the Son of God.
4. She was so excited that she leaves her water jar at the well.
5. She goes to town the share the news.
6. She invites the people to meet Jesus.
7. Many Samaritans went to see Jesus.

Assign individuals or teams of children to illustrate the frames of the film. As the children complete their work help them connect the frames in the correct order. Include the title frame and a blank frame at the beginning and the end. Cover each seam, front and back, with clear tape.

Bring in the TV you prepared. Help the group tread the film through the viewer. Each end of the film strip may be attached to cardboard tubes to make displaying the film easier.

During *Sharing in Worship*, two children will operate the TV. Other children will say a sentence describing each frame. Practice the presentation during the small-group time.

6. Prayer. This group will prepare a prayer, thanking Jesus for being our friend. You will need paper and pencils.

We just heard how Jesus was a friend to a woman no one liked. Can you think of someone you know who has no friends? How would Jesus treat that person! (Allow response.) **How could you be kind to that person?**

Distribute paper and pencils. Ask the children to write a short prayer. thanking Jesus for being a friend to that person and telling him how they will be kind to that person. Ask the children not to use the name of the person. For example, "Dear Jesus, thank You for being a friend to the new boy in my class. I will sit next to him at lunch." "Dear Jesus, thank You for being a friend to the girl who plays alone at recess. I will swing with her this week."

During *Sharing in Worship*, the children will read their prayers.

Sharing In Worship
(20-25 minutes)

Omit any of the following sections if you did not offer the corresponding activity. The devotional and Lord's Supper may be completed without the presentations of Groups 3 and 5.

Call to Worship (Group 1)**: In 1 John 4:19 and 21 we read these words. "We love because God first loved us...Whoever loves God must also love his brother." (ICB)** Group 1 will share the decisions they have made about how to show and not show love.

Songs: Allow the children to choose and sing several of their favorite songs.

Special Music (Group 2): Group 2 will present the song they learned today, "There Was a Woman at a Well."

Lord's Supper (Group 3)**: What is the greatest way Jesus showed He is our friend? Group 3 found some words that tell about the greatest way Jesus is our friend.** Ask the large group to decode the words. Then ask the children from Group 3 to share their sentences. **Jesus came to die for those who did wrong things. The Samaritan**

woman had done many bad things. The people in the town did not love her, by Jesus loved her. As we take the Lord's Supper, let us remember that we also do things that are wrong. We need a Savior too. Jesus died that we might be saved.

Offering: Listen as I read Romans 6:23. In this verse, what is God's gift to us? (Eternal life.) **How did He give it?** (Through Jesus' death.) **We bring our offerings as a gift to God to say thank you for His gift and for all the others He gives to us.**

Scripture (Group 4): **Group 4 made an exciting discovery during their activity. Listen carefully as they share it with us.** Group 4 presents their banner.

Devotional (Group 5): **We're going to interrupt our program at this time for a special report from our Group 5 News Team!** Group 5 should present their filmstrip and narration. If you did not offer this activity, briefly review the Bible story from John 4:4-41.

Some people might have made fun of Jesus or been mad at Him for talking to a woman no one like. But Jesus was kind to the woman anyway. He was her friend. Who is your best friend? (Allow response.) **Why is that person your best friend?** (Allow response.) **We choose people that we like to be with to be our friends. We choose friends who like and dislike the same things we do. But Jesus chooses us to be His friend no matter what we do. He will be our friend no matter how many people like or don't like us. Jesus is our friend all the time.**

Let's look up John 3:16 and read it together. Jesus told the woman at the well what we just read. God tells us over and over again that He loves us, He wants us to believe that Jesus is His Son and by excepting Jesus as our Savior we can each enjoy the gift of eternal life. This is exciting news. . . just as the Samaritan woman shared it, God expects you and I to share it with others.

Prayer (Group 6): Group 6 reads their prayers. Close with prayer, thanking God for being a friend to everyone, even those no one likes.

Closing Moments
(10-15 minutes)

You will need poster board, old magazines, markers, scissors, and glue. Title the poster board "Jesus' Friends." Ask the children to cut out pictures of many different kinds of people and glue them on the poster board. **These people are all very different, but Jesus knows them and loves them. He is their friend, and He is our friend.**

Jesus Is Our Friend When We Do Wrong

Worship Focus

Worship Jesus because He is our friend even when we do wrong.

Transition Time

(10-15 minutes)

This activity will require a small step ladder and adult supervision. Place the ladder in an open area of the room. Choose six colors, one for each activity group. Prepare an equal number of two inch squares in each color and put them in a small basket. Place the basket on the top of the ladder. The children should stand in a group around the ladder.

When you are in a crowd of people, do you find it hard to see? The Bible tells us about a small man who wanted to see Jesus but knew he wouldn't be able to see him if he stood in the crowd. Zacchaeus climbed a sycamore tree to see Jesus. I want each of you to get to climb out above our crowd today. Everyone will get a turn to climb our tree (point to the ladder) **and get a piece of paper out of the basket at the top. Keep your paper with you and stand in the crowd after your climb.**

Send the children in small groups to the rest room and water fountain after they have had their turn.

Launching the Theme

(10 minutes)

Close your eyes and imagine that you are the in the story I'm going to tell you.

Jon couldn't believe it! So many people had gathered to see the parade. "We are early," he said to his sister.

Amy looked at him. "I know. I guess we should have been earlier. I can't see a thing!"

Jon said, "Maybe we can take turns lifting each other up."

"I don't think so," said Amy. She reminded Jon, "The parade lasts for at least thirty minutes. There has to be some way for us to get a better view!"

Open your eyes. You are there. You want to see the parade. How could you solve the problem? Allow the children to suggest solutions.

We know Zacchaeus wanted to see Jesus. Why do you think he wanted to see Him? Perhaps Zacchaeus wanted Jesus to forgive him for the wrong things he had done.

Jesus wanted to see Zacchaeus. I'm sure no one was more surprised than Zacchaeus, when Jesus told him to come down from the tree because he planned to go to his house that day. Jesus was Zacchaeus' friend even though Zacchaeus had done many wrong things. Today we will worship Jesus because He is our friend even when we do wrong.

Divide the children into activity groups using the colored squares they drew from the basket earlier. Children will go to the activity whose color corresponds with their squares. Explain briefly what each group will be preparing for worship time and dismiss them to their groups.

Building the Theme

(30 minutes)

1. Call to Worship. This group will develop a choral reading to be presented as the call to worship. You will need pencils, crayons, and paper.

When are some times that Jesus is our friend? List children's ideas on chalkboard or poster board. Ask each child to choose one situation to illustrate. When the children have completed their pictures, ask them to create a choral reading praising Jesus for being our friend. An example follows.

Child 1: When I obey my parents,
Chorus: Jesus is my friend.
Child 2: When I help a friend
Chorus: Jesus is my friend.
Child 3: When I tell a lie I ask His forgiveness,
Chorus: Jesus is my friend.

During *Sharing in Worship*, the children will present their pictures and the choral reading.

2. Devotional. This group will create a Bible-story game. You will need clip clothes pins, fine point markers, a small note pad, and a quart jar.

Before the session print each of the following questions on a clothes pin. Do not print answers.

What is the name of the tax collector? (Zacchaeus)

Why couldn't Zacchaeus see Jesus? (He was too short to see through the crowd.)

How did Zacchaeus see Jesus over the crowd? (He climbed the sycamore tree.)

What did Jesus tell Zacchaeus? (To come down so he could go to his house.)

What did people say about Jesus when He went to Zacchaeus' house? (He has gone to be the guest of a sinner.)

How do you think the people felt about Jesus going to Zacchaeus' house? (Angry, jealous.)

Why do you think the people were upset? (They didn't understand why Jesus was a friend to Zacchaeus because Zacchaeus had done so many wrong things.)

What did Zacchaeus tell Jesus he would give to the poor? (Half of his possessions.)

What did Zacchaeus tell Jesus he would give tot he people he cheated? (Four times the amount he cheated.)

Ask the children to find Luke 19:1-10. Read the verses together. Then ask each child to choose a clothespin and read the question. When each child has answered a question, he or she may stand over the quart jar and try to drop the clothespin in the jar.

During *Sharing in Worship*, each child will read his or her question and ask the large group to answer. The first person to answer correctly will come forward, stand over the jar, and try to drop the clothes pin in the quart jar.

3. Scripture. This activity will require a piece of poster board, old newspapers with lots of headlines for large letters, glue, scissors, and Bibles.

Help the children find 1 Thessalonians 5:15 in their Bibles. Print the verse on a chalk board, Assign each child letters to find and cut out of the newspaper headlines. **When you find your letter put it on the poster board and when the verse is complete we'll glue it on. If we can't find a letter, we can make our own.** Allow the children to work together to complete the verse. **If someone does something to hurt you, should you try to get even?** (Allow responses.) **Jesus is our friend when we do wrong. We should be friends to others even when they do wrong to us. When are some times we could be a friend when others do wrong to us?**

If you have time, ask the children to write or draw on the poster board times they will be a friend when others do wrong. Examples follow: When a friend tells a secret I told her not to tell; when a friend doesn't invite me to a party; when a friend gets mad at me or is mean to me.

During *Sharing in Worship*, the group will read the verse together. Then they will each share a time to be a friend when others do wrong.

4. Special Music. This group will write words to a song. You will need copies of activity page 24A, yarn, a paper hole punch, "Jesus Is my Friend" from page 191, poster board, and markers. Before the session, write words to the song on posters board. Leave room for children to write additional stanzas.

"When I obey,
When I do wrong,
Jesus loves me.
Jesus is my friend."

What wrong things had Zacchaeus done? (Cheated people; probably lied to people and taken too much of their money.) **How do you think other people felt about Zacchaeus?** (Probably mad; didn't like him; stayed away from him.) **How did Jesus treat Zacchaeus?** (Jesus was his friend; He spoke to Zacchaeus; He visited Zacchaeus' house; He forgave the wrong things Zacchaeus had done.)

What are some wrong things we do? (Lie; get mad and say mean things; don't share; and so on.) **How does Jesus treat us?** (He loves us; He forgives the wrong things we do; He is always our friend.)

Today we are going to make a sign and write a song telling how Jesus is our friend even when we do wrong things. Display the poster board for the children. Sing the song for the children, then ask them to sing it with you. Ask the children to write new stanzas for the song, listing times they obey or disobey. An example follows:

"When I am kind,
When I don't share,
Jesus loves me,
Jesus is my friend."

Write the new stanzas on the poster board. Practice singing the song together. Distribute the activity page. Ask children to write on the page a time Jesus is their friend. Punch holes where indicated and string yarn through the holes to make hangers of the signs. Encourage children to take their signs home and hang them up to remind them that Jesus is their friend.

During *Sharing the Worship*, children will display the activity pages and sing the song. Then they will ask the large group to sing with them.

5. Personal Praise. This group will make birds' nests to remind them of ways God helps us do right. This activity requires a small brown sandwich bag for each child, scissors, markers and white paper.

Jesus told people how important they were to God in

Luke 12:6, 7. Let's find this Scripture and read it together. Jesus said that God doesn't forget about a sparrow and that we are of more value than many sparrows. He said that God knows how many hairs are on each of our heads! Today we are going to make a bird's nest to remind us that Jesus is our friend. Distribute brown bags and other material. To make the nests follow these steps:

1. Fringe the top of the folded bag about 5 inches down.
2. Open the bag and curl the fringed strips.

God loves us very much. With our white paper let's cut out some egg shapes and write down times we are thankful that Jesus is our friend.

During *Sharing in Worship*, children will tell the times they are thankful that Jesus is their friend.

6. **Prayer.** This group will discover times and places Jesus is our friend when we do wrong. You will need activity page 24B, markers, writing paper, and glue.

Zacchaeus was a tax collector. What bad things had he done? (Lied; cheated people.) **Do you think Zacchaeus felt good or bad about himself?** (Bad.) **Did the people who knew Zacchaeus like him? Were they his friends?** (No.) **Because Jesus was good to Zacchaeus and taught him, what did Zacchaeus want to do?** (Pay back the people he hurt.) **Do you think Zacchaeus liked himself after meeting Jesus?** (Yes.)

We are going to make a block out of paper. **Distribute the activity sheet. On the sides of your block you should draw pictures to go along with the words.** Allow the students to decorate and assemble their blocks. **Jesus didn't record the story of Zacchaeus in the Bible so Zacchaeus could read about it. He wanted us to know that He loves us and that if we ask He will forgive for the wrong things we do.**

Roll your block on the table. Read the place that lands on top. When is Jesus your friend at that place? Say a prayer, thanking God for being a friend at that place. As time permits, allow children to continue rolling their blocks and naming times Jesus is their friend.

During *Sharing in Worship*, children will say their prayers, thanking God for being a friend at the place they rolled.

Sharing in Worship
(20-25 minutes)

Omit any of the following sections if you did not offer the corresonding activity. The devotional may be completed without the presentaion of Group 2.

Call to Worship (Group 1): Group 1 will present the choral reading they have prepared. Ask the large group to join them in saying, "Jesus is my friend" after each picture is described.

Lord's Supper: We can trust Jesus. He showed His love for us when He died on the cross for our sins. He died so that we could be God's friends. When we share the Lord's Supper, we remember that Jesus is our special friend.

Devotional (Group 2): **Let's see how much you know about how Jesus was a friend to Zacchaeus.** Ask Group 2 to present their questions and allow those who answer correctly to try to drop the clothespins in the jar. If you did not offer this activity, read the questions from that activity to the children. They may look in Luke 19:1-10 to find the answers.

Zacchaeus was not a nice person before he met Jesus. In fact, sometimes he was probably mean and dishonest. Very few people wanted to be Zacchaeus' friend. But Jesus did! He not only was kind to Zacchaeus, He also forgave all the wrong things Zacchaeus did.

Jesus will be our friend even when we do wrong things, too. And he will forgive us again and again. If Zacchaeus had cheated someone after he met Jesus, would Jesus have forgiven him? (Yes. Jesus would still be his friend.)**No matter how many bad things we do, Jesus loves us. Nothing we do is so awful that He won't forgive us! Jesus is always our friend.**

Scripture (Group 3): **Jesus is our friend when we do wrong. We should be friends to others even when they do wrong.** Ask Group 3 to share their Scripture verse and times to be friends.

Offering: One way to thank God is to give Him back part of what He has given us. Choose two children to collect the offering.

Special Music (Group 4): **Group 4 wrote new words to a song about times Jesus is our friend. See how many times you can hear.** Group 4 sings song.

Personal Praise (Group 5): Read Luke 12:6, 7. **We are very important to God. He loves us very much. He knows more aobut us than anyone. I am thankful He is my friend.** Ask Group 5 to share times they are thankful that Jesus is their friend.

Prayer (Group 6): **Let's pray to thank God for being our friend anytime and any place.** Ask Group 6 to share their prayers with the large group.

Closing Moments
(10-15 minutes)

Tell the children that you will need the friend blocks made by Group 6.

Divide the children into groups of 3-4 children. Ask them to take turns rolling their friend blocks and telling a time Jesus is their triend in the place that lands on top.

Unit Six

Worship Jesus for Being Our Friend

Session 25

Jesus Forgives Us When We Do Wrong

Worship Focus

Worship Jesus because He forgives us when we are sorry for doing wrong.

Transition Time

(10-15 minutes)

Pupils may allowed to get drinks and use the rest room during this time but should not be dismissed until after directions for the activity have been explained.

Scavenger Hunt. You will need copies of activity page 25A (one copy for every four children), scissors, construction paper, and glue. Cut out the pictures in the activity page and glue each picture to a piece of construction paper. Use a different color of construction paper for each set of pictures. Hide the pictures around the room. Make copies of the following list of clues.

1. I asked Jesus to eat at my house.
2. I went to Simon's house to eat.
3. Jesus sat at me while He ate.
4. The woman poured me on Jesus' feet.
5. The woman poured perfume on me.
6. This is what the woman did because she loved Jesus.
7. The woman dried Jesus' feet with me.
8. The woman kissed Jesus' feet with me.

Divide the children into groups of four. Each team will get a list of clues and a color. Hidden in the room are pictures that answer the clues. Each team will read the clues and find the pictures mounted on their team color. The groups should return to the worship area when they have completed the scavenger hunt or when time is called. The team who finds all the pictures first, wins.

Remind the children that teams that get carried away during the activity will be required to take a time out, which will add a lot of time to their team's score.

You may wish to read through the clues together before signaling the start of the hunt.

Launching the Theme

(10 minutes)

When the pupils have gathered in the worship area, compliment them on their fine job of answering the clues.

Review the story of Jesus visiting Simon's house found in Luke 7:36-50. Display the pictures from activity page 25A at the appropriate times as the story is told.

Jesus forgave the woman who had done many wrong things because she was sorry. Jesus also will forgive the wrong things we do if we are sorry for doing wrong. Today we will worship Jesus for forgiving us.

Briefly describe the activities available for *Building the Theme.* Allow the teams to select their group in the order of their placement in the scavenger hunt.

Building the Theme

(30 minutes)

1. Call to Worship. This group will prepare books of times God forgives. You will need activity page 25B, scissors, pencils, and markers or crayons.

What does it mean to forgive someone? (To act as if it never happened.) **When does God forgive us?** (When we do something wrong and are sorry.) **When are some times we need God to forgive us?** List children's answers on chalkboard or poster board.

Distribute the activity pages. Ask children to cut out and fold the books using the following instructions. Demonstrate each step for the children as you explain it.

1. Fold the paper in half vertically.
2. Unfold.
3. Fold the paper in half horizontally.
4. Fold the paper in half horizontally again.
5. Unfold, leaving only the fold from step 3.
6. Cut on the solid line which should from the folded edge to the fold from Step 4.
7. Unfold paper. The cut should be in the center.
8. Refold the paper long ways.

9. Pinch the ends and push them together to allow the center cut to form a diamond.

10. Push together and crease folds to make a book.

Then ask them to write times God will forgive us on the pages of the books.

During *Sharing in Worship*, children will name the times God will for give as when we are sorry. After each time is named, the group will say," God will forgive us."

2. Lord's Supper. This group will present a skit to show what we should do when we have done wrong. You will need paper, pencils, a chalkboard, and chalk.

Listen to this story. How should Joshua act to show he is sorry?

While doing his math paper, Joshua left several of the answers blank. After the test, the teacher wrote the right answers on the board so the pupils could grade their own papers. Before checking his paper, Joshua filled in all his empty spaces with the correct answers from the board. Then he checked his answers and got a perfect score. No one saw him cheat!

How should Joshua feel? (He should feel guilty about cheating.) **What should he do?** (He should ask Jesus to forgive him and help him have the courage to tell the teacher what he did.) **What will Jesus do if Joshua is sorry and asks His forgiveness?** (He will forgive and help Joshua do what is right.)

We are going to act out this story and show what Joshua could to do to show he is sorry. Assign parts for the skit and help children decide how to act it out. Encourage them to act as if they are taking the test, checking their answers by looking up at the teacher's answers and turning their papers into the teacher.

During *Sharing in Worship*, children will present the first part of the skit. The leader will ask the large group what Joshua could do to show he is sorry. Then they will present the last part of the skit.

3. Special Music. This group will be presenting the special music portion of the worship time. You will need shelf paper, and markers. "I Will Sing of the Mercies of the Lord" from page 192. Before the session, print the words to the song on shelf paper.

What is mercy? (Allow response.) **Mercy is being kind to someone even when they don't deserve it. God shows mercy to us when we do wrong. He forgives the wrong things we do. Today we will sing a song about God's mercy.**

Display the words to the song. Read the words for the children. Then ask them to read with you. Sing the song for the children. Then ask them to sing with you.

When are some times that God forgives us? Make a list of times children name. Ask the children to write new words about times God forgives us for the words, "With my mouth will I make known They faithfulness to all generations." An example follows.

"God forgives when we do wrong,
When we are mean, or when we lie.
God forgives when do wrong.
He is kind when we say we are sorry."

Practice the song many times, using the new words.

During *Sharing in Worship*, children will sing the song with the new words.

Option: If you have younger children, use the word kindness instead of mercies in the song. Rather than asking children to write new words. Bring the words above on shelf paper before the session.

4. Scripture. This group will prepare a Scripture and bookmarks. You will need Bibles, construction paper or card stock, markers, glue, toothpicks, and butter tubs with enough salt or sugar to cover the bottom 1/4" of the tub.

Ask children to find Luke 7:48 in their Bibles. Read the verse. **"Then Jesus said to her, 'Your sins are forgiven.'" What does it mean to forgive someone?** (To act as if it never happened.)

Ask each child to print the word forgive vertically on paper in fairly large letters (one or two inches) with a black marker. Give him or her a small butter tub with sugar or salt. Tell him or her to put a small bit of glue on a toothpick and trace one letter at a time. As he or she traces, tell him or her to carefully shake the sugar/salt onto the glue, then pour the rest of the substance back in the tub. Continue this with each letter until the letters are covered with sugar/salt.

When the bookmarks are completed, ask the children to use them to mark Luke 7:48 in their Bibles.

During *Sharing in Worship*, the group will read Luke 7:48 together. Practice reading the verse during the small-group time.

5. Devotional. This group will make a puzzle poster about God's forgiveness. You will need a sheet a of poster board, markers or crayons, scissors, cellophane tape, pencil, and paper.

Guide the children in deciding what they should do after they have done something wrong. (Some suggestions follow: Feel sorry inside; say, "I'm sorry"; pray to ask God's forgiveness; show you are sorry by what you do; quit doing wrong.) You may need to guide the children toward similar answers by asking questions. Be ready to explain the word *forgive*. (Forgive means to act as if it never happened.) Condense the children's responses to no more than six phrases. Write these on your paper.

Ask the children to write "Jesus forgives us," in large letters on the poster board.

Help the children cut the poster board into the same number of pieces as they had responses. Cut the board into puzzle pieces. The pupils will now write on the blank side of each poster piece. They will copy onto a piece of the puzzle one of their responses that you recorded earlier. When the pieces are put together one side of the poster will list the things we should do when we have done wrong. On the other side it will read, "Jesus forgives us."

During *Sharing in Worship*, the children will read the puzzle pieces and tape them together to make a complete poster.

6. Prayer. This group will be interviewing each other and recording the information on the designed activity sheet. They will compose a directed prayer which includes the special needs and concerns discovered though the interviewing process. You will need paper and pencils.

Pass out an activity sheet to each student. Allow them to cut out the forms. (They may need additional sheets if time permits.)

Choose two people in the room to interview. Ask them their name, age, and what prayer request they have this week.

Sometimes people close to Jesus couldn't understand why He made friends with people who they considered sinners. The woman in today's lesson is an example of this. Did Jesus forgive her many sins? Read Luke 7:48.

Allow children time to do so. Then ask them to share their information. **It's nice to talk to friends. Friends always listen to us. Jesus is our friend, and He always listens to us. Let's write a short prayer, thanking Jesus for listening to us.**

During *Sharing in Worship*, ask children to pray for the requests of the person they interviewed. Close by reading the prayer, thanking God for listening to us.

Sharing in Worship
(20-25 minutes)

Omit any of the following sections if you did not offer the corresponding activity. The Lord's Supper and devotional may be completed without Groups 2 and 5.

Call to Worship (Group 1): Ask Group 1 to share their forgiveness books.

Lord's Supper (Group 2): **How do we show we are sorry when we have done wrong? When we do wrong things, Jesus is ready to help us. He is the way our wrong things are forgiven, or taken away. Because Jesus died, the wrong things we have done are forgiven. Because Jesus lives now, we can know He'll always be our friend. As we think about Jesus' death, let's thank Him for forgetting what we have done wrong.** Pray and serve the Lord's Supper.

Special Music (Group 3): Group 3 presents song.

Scripture (Group 4): Group 4 reads their verse together.

Offering: Our offering is what we give to Jesus. The woman we talked about today gave to Jesus. What did she give? (Perfume) **You have much to give too. You can give your money, your time by helping others, your praise in song, and your prayers.** Choose two children to help collect the offering.

Devotional (Group 5): **Let's read Luke 6:37. Tell me some of the things Jesus says we should not do.** (Allow the children to respond.) **If we don't do these things, what will not happen to us?** (Allow the children to respond.) **This verse reminds us to forgive and be kind to others just as Jesus is kind to us.**

When the woman who was a sinner washed Jesus' feet at Simon's house, Simon didn't think she should be there because of the wrong things she had done. But Jesus was the woman's friend. We don't need to be like Simon. We need to be like the woman and like Jesus. We need to be kind to others when they do wrong. And we need to be sorry when we do wrong.

What are some ways we can show we are sorry when we do wrong? Ask Group 5 to come forward and share their puzzle poster. If you did not offer this activity, ask children to share ways we show we are sorry or make your own puzzle poster before the session.

God loves us very much He knows there is no way we can make up for all the bad things we do. So He sent Jesus to die to make up for those bad things. When we say we are sorry, God forgives all those wrong things.

Prayer (Group 6): **Our good friends like to listen to us. God always listens to us because He is our friend.** Ask Group 6 to share their prayers.

Closing Moments
(10-15 minutes)

Write the following scrambled words on the chalk board or on separate sheets of paper: drienf, yorrs, eirgovf, sesuJ, eovl, shankt, torgef.

Ask the pupils to unscramble the words. (If necessary, give this hint: The last letter should be first and the first letter, last.)

After the pupils have unscrambled the words, ask them to use each word in a sentence, telling something about themselves and Jesus. (For example, Jesus is my best friend.)

Unit Six
Worship Jesus for Being Our Friend

Session 26

Jesus Is Our Friend

Worship Focus

Worship Jesus because He is a friend.

Transition Time

(10-15 minutes)

Allow the children to use the rest rooms and get drinks during this portion of the session. You will need three large shirts with buttons, three pairs of socks, three blindfolds, and three sets of ear muffs.

Divide the children into three groups. There should be an adult stationed with each group to assist and guide discussions. These are groups, not teams. The children will experience, to some degree, the feeling that a handicapped individual might experience in accomplishing even simple tasks.

One person in each group should wear the large shirt unbuttoned and put the socks on their hands. Another person should wear the blindfold and stand beside the group. A third person should wear the earmuffs and sit with the group.

The leader of the group should then softly whisper to the group that the child with the shirt and socks on should button their shirt. (The person that is blindfold can not see what is happening and the person with the earmuff won t be able to hear what is said very well.) After allowing the student to try and button the shirt, have all the children take off their props and give them to someone else in the group. Repeat as time allows, but make sure everyone experiences at least one of the simulations.

The worship leader should observe the groups as they work and be able to incorporate these observations into *Launching the Theme* portion of the lesson.

Launching the Theme

(10 minutes)

The groups should assemble in the worship area.

Jesus was a friend to many people. He was a friend to the Samaritan Woman, to Zacchaeus, and to the sinful woman. Do you think any of these people thought Jesus would be their friend? (Allow response.) **These people encountered Jesus in different ways. Jesus was at the well when the Samaritan woman came to get water. Zacchaeus ran ahead of the crowd and climbed the tree to see Jesus. The sinful woman interrupted a dinner to worship Jesus. And the man who couldn't walk interrupted Jesus teaching. How did the paralyzed man's four friends get him in to see Jesus?** (Let him down through a hole in the roof.) **What did Jesus do for the man?** (Made him able to walk again; forgave his sins.)

Jesus was a friend to the paralyzed man. He is a friend to people with handicaps. How did you feel when you couldn't use your hands or hear very well or see? (Allow children to share.) **It is hard for handicapped people to do some things we do very easily. And sometimes it is hard for them to find friends. Many people ignore handicapped people or make fun of them. But Jesus is a friend to handicapped people. Today we will worship Jesus for being a friend.**

Describe briefly the activities available for *Building the Theme* and allow the children to choose the group they wish. (Know how many should be in each group and have the children take their second choice if a desired group is filled.)

Building the Theme

(30 minutes)

1. Call to Worship. This group will say a Scripture verse about friends. You will need twenty-five colored note cards and markers. Before the session, write one word from 1 Thessalonians 5:15 on each note card.

Ask each pupil to open his of her Bible and find 1 Thessalonians 5:15. **Let's read the verse aloud together as a group. Is it easier to do right when someone is being kind or mean to you? Is it hard to help someone who can't do anything for you? What can you do if someone doesn't want your help?**

Distribute the note cards. **Put your cards in the correct order as I read through the verse. Then we will read it together.** Read the verse along with the children. **Now mix up the memory verse cards. When I say go, put them in the correct order on the table.** Repeat the activity until children can say the verse from memory. The children should then mix up the cards and leave them ready to put in the correct order during the call to worship. **Can you name some times when friends do wrong things?** Allow response. Ask each child to choose a wrong thing a friend might do to share during the worship time.

During *Sharing in Worship*, each child will tell a wrong thing a friend might do. After each child shares, the group will say the verse. For example, "My friend may get mad and yell at me. But God says, 'Make sure that nobody pays back wrong for wrong, but always try to be kind to each other and to everyone else.'"

2. Special Music. This group will prepare a song and mural for the worship time. You will need shelf paper, markers, and "I will Be a Friend" from page 191. Before the session, print the words to the song on shelf paper.

Jesus was a friend to a tax collector, a sinful woman, and a paralyzed man. Who are some different types of people to whom we can be friends? List children's ideas on scratch paper. **Today we will sing a song about being a friend.** Display the shelf paper. Sing the song for the children. Then ask them to sing with you. Practice the song until the children are comfortable singing it.

Ask children to illustrate people to whom we can be friends on the shelf paper. They may use people from the list you made earlier.

During *Sharing in Worship*, children will display the shelf paper and sing the song.

3. Offering. This group will make place mats reminding them to give to friends. You will need copies of activity pages 26A and 26B, scissors, tape, and markers.

Jesus was a friend to everyone. One way we can give to Jesus is by being a friend to everyone. Distribute materials. Ask children to assemble place mats using the following instructions.

1. Cut out the rectangle and heart on your activity pages.
2. Fold the rectangle on the dotted line. Then cut on the solid lines to make slits.
3. Weave the heart through the slits.
4. Tape the heart to the paper on the back.

What are ways to worship Jesus for being our friend? (Allow response.) **One way we can worship Jesus is by being a friend to other people. Jesus was a friend to those no one liked and to those who had done wrong things. Jesus was a friend to those who were sad and alone and to handicapped people. Can you think of some people to whom you can be a friend? How will you be their friend?** Ask the children to write the ways they will be a friend on the blank parts of the heart on the front of their placemats. They may color and decorate their place mats.

During *Sharing in Worship,* children will display their placemats and tell the ways they will be friends.

4. Scripture. This group will prepare a mobile of a Scripture. You will need crayons or markers 9″ x 24″ white paper strips, a stapler, and string.

Ask the children to find Mark 2:1-12 in their Bibles. Ask the children to volunteer to read the verses. **We are going to make a mobile to illustrate these verse. What pictures should we include on our mobiles?** Allow response. List children's suggestions on the chalkboard. Suggested pictures follow: four men carrying paralyzed man on mat; four men making a hole in roof of house; paralyzed man lying in front of Jesus; Paralyzed man standing, holding his mat and smiling. Pass out the materials. **Sketch the scenes of our lesson in the proper order from left to right on the paper and color it in. When the picture is finished, bend it around into a large cylinder, and staple it at the top and bottom.** Allow the children time to complete this much of the project. **Now take 3 pieces of string that have been cut in equal lengths and attach the string in 3 evenly divided spots at the top of the cylinder. Tie the strings together at the top.** Assign children verses from Mark 2:1-12 and allow them to practice reading them aloud.

During *Sharing in Worship*, children will display their mobiles and read Mark 2:1-12.

5. Devotional. This group will be prepare puppet scripts about friends.

This activity is for older or gifted children. You will need several small to medium boxes cut in the middle of the front side and down both sides. (The back should remain in one piece.) You will also need construction paper, scissors, glue, file cards, pencils, and markers. Use a table turned on its side for a puppet stage.

I want you each to take a few minutes to think about your friends. Think of how you would describe a friend. In other words, what is your definition of a friend? Give them a minute to think and then allow them to share their ideas. **Each of you may choose a box to make a puppet out of.** Allow them to choose a box. **Put your thumb in the bottom part of the box and your fingers in the top. Show me that you can open and close the puppet's mouth.** Praise the children for their demonstration. **You may glue colored paper onto the box. Then you can add the tongue, eyes, and ears. As you work on your puppet, I'll help you write down the puppet's script. That script will be your description of a friend. Keep the scripts simple.**

We will share our puppets and ideas of a friend during group worship time today. Allow the children to practice working their puppet and saying their scripts.

During *Sharing in Worship*, children will use their puppets to describe friends.

6. Prayer. This group will make prayer chains. You will need colored 2″x9″ strips of construction paper, markers, stapler (or glue), and a coat hanger.

Jesus tells us how to pray in Matthew 6:9-13. Listen to His example: (Read Matthew 6:9-13.) **This prayer has a title. It is known as the Lord's Prayer. Let's look at each verse, and see what we should include in our prayers.**

Discuss the verses and list the things the children find. Suggestions follow: praise, thanksgiving, needs, forgiveness, and help in difficult situations. Assign a color to each category the children suggest. Write the title of the category on the corresponding color and attach it as a ring on the hanger.

Let's each write something that we praise or thank God for on yellow. Let's each write something that we need (not just want) on a strip of red. Let's each write something that we need forgiveness for on purple. Let's each write something that we need God's help with on a strip of green. Add orange and then blue for additional categories.

Ask children to attach their strips to the matching color of ring to make a chain.

During *Sharing in Worship*, ask each child to share one portion of the chain.

Sharing in Worship
(20-25 minutes)

Omit any of the following sections if you did not offer the corresponding activity. The offering and devotional may be completed without the presentation of Groups 3 and 5.

Call to Worship (Group 1): Ask Group 1 to share their Scripture.

Special Music (Group 2): Ask Group 2 to sing their song for the group. Then ask the large group to join them as they sign the song a second time.

Lord's Supper: It's hard to understand why people do the things they do, or have to endure handicaps, and sadness. Jesus loves us for who we are, not for what we look like or what we can or cannot do. He is our very best friend. Let's think about this wonderful love as we have the Lord's Supper.

Offering (Group 3): **When we are friends to others, we are being a friend to Jesus. One way we can give to Jesus is by being a friend. Group 3 will tell us how they will give to Jesus by being a friend.As you listen to them, think of ways you can be a friend.** Ask Group 3 to share.Then ask four children to collect the offering.

Scripture (Group 5): Ask Group 4 to share their dioramas and their Scripture.

Devotional (Group 5): **What is a friend?** Allow response. **Group 5 made some puppets to tell us what they think a friend is.** Allow Group 5 to share.

We have shared some good ideas about friendship. But the best definition of a friend is Jesus. When we want to know how to be a friend, we can read about how Jesus acted and what He said! And when we need a friend, we can know that Jesus is always our friend.

Who are the people we've talked about to whom Jesus was a friend? (Woman by the well; Zacchaeus; sinful woman; paralyzed man.) **How was Jesus a friend to these people?** (He was kind; He talked to them.) **When we have done wrong, or when we feel like no one likes us, or when we are sad, Jesus is our friend just like He was to these people.**

Personal Praise: What is one time you are glad Jesus is your friend? Allow volunteers to share.

Prayer (Group 6): **Jesus showed us how to pray. Group 6 found the different ways Jesus told us to pray. Let's pray with them now.** Ask Group 6 to share their prayer chains.

Closing Moments
(10-15 minutes)

Write the following note on a poster and provide lined paper for the children to copy it:

"Jesus was a friend to all people. I want to be a true friend this week by _______ . I will pray that I have the chance to a friend to _______."

The children can fill in a way to be a friend and fill in a name of a person that they chose for a friend. Encourage them to make a new friend. This note will be a reminder to the child this week.

ACTIVITY

PAGES

11 12 1 2 3 4 5 6 7 8 9 10

Creation Code

Name each picture. Write the first letter of each picture name on the lines.

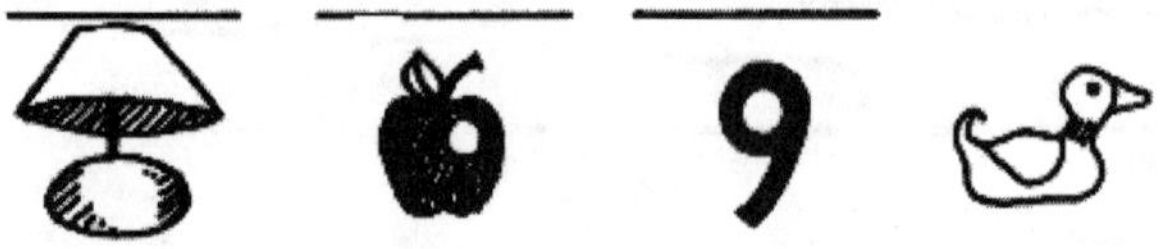

1. What is a lynx?

a large dog

a large bird

a large cat

2. When does a lynx hunt?

in the winter

at night

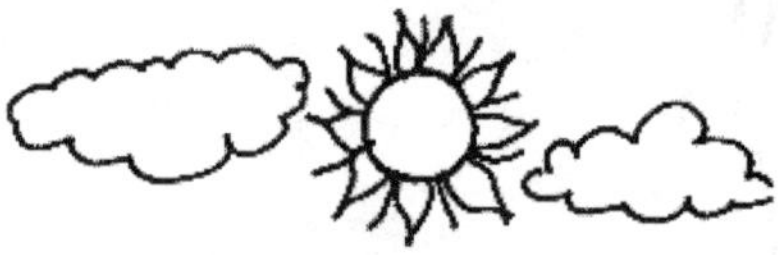

during the day

3. What helps the lynx walk in snow?

his yellow eyes

his stumpy tail

his furry feet

4. Where are salmon born?

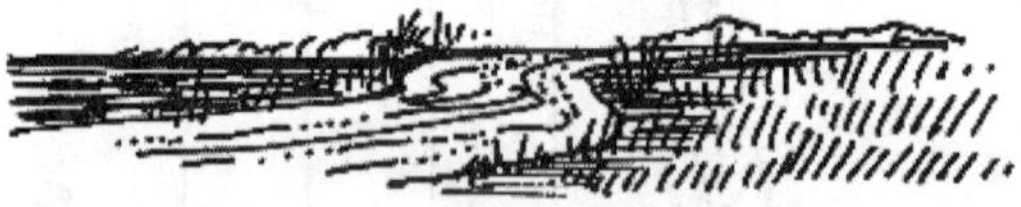

rivers

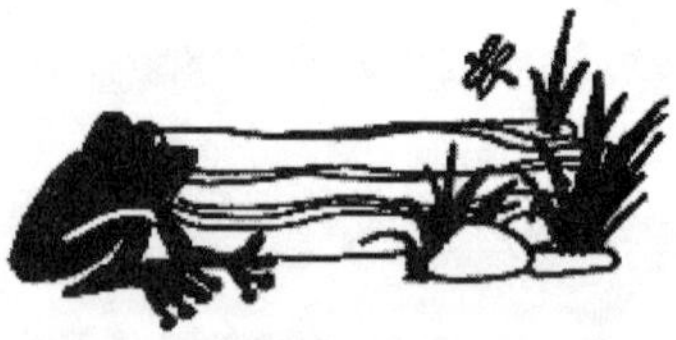

ponds

oceans

5. How long does it take salmon to get to the ocean?

2 or 3 weeks

2 or 3 days

2 or 3 years

6. Where do salmon go when they leave the ocean?

on vacation

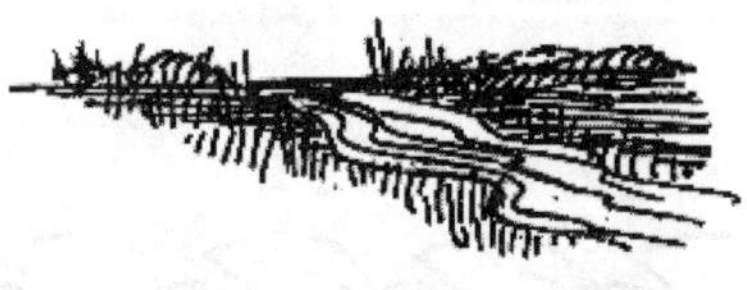

back to the river

they never leave the ocean

I praise you because you made me in an amazing and wonderful way. What you have done is wonderful. I know this very well.

Psalm 139:14

Draw a picture of yourself.

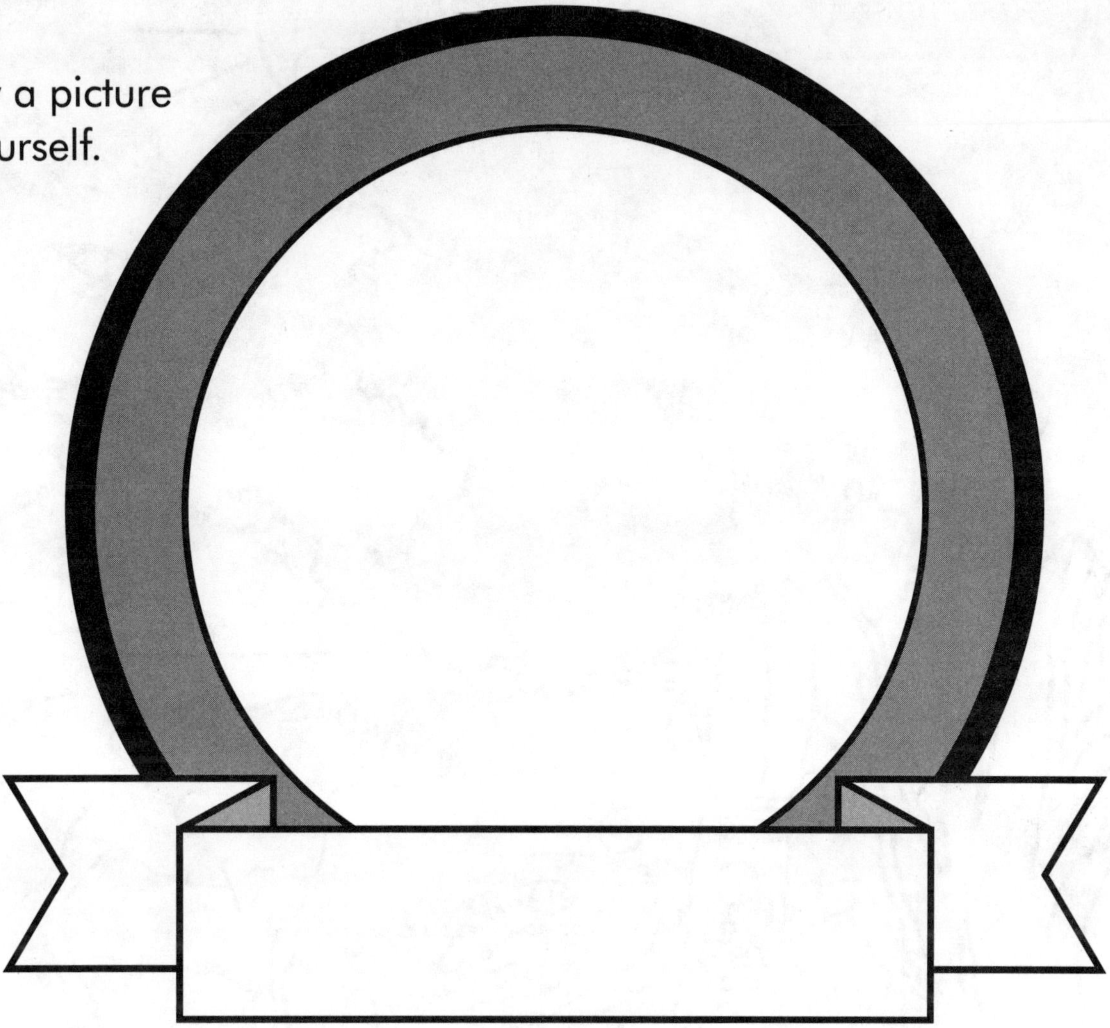

What is one thing you like about yourself?

Write a thank-you prayer to God for making you.

We are the animals two by two;
The lions, the bears, and the kangaroo.
We all were kept safe in Noah's boat.
The cow, the pig, and the billy goat.

We are Noah and his family;
Father, Mother, and sons all three.
We all were kept safe in Noah's boat.
We didn't sink. We stayed afloat.

God kept His promise to all of us.
We did not whine or did not fuss.
And He will keep His promises to you.
Let's worship God because it's true!

I will protect those who know me.

I will never leave you.

MY
Mouth
WILL SPEAK
IN PRAISE OF
THE LORD
MY
Mouth
WILL SPEAK
IN PRAISE OF
THE LORD

Thank You, God.

I worship God.

I praise You, God.

When I am sad,

When I am alone,

When I am afraid,

When I am happy,

You are with me.

You never leave me.

You guide me.

MOV
341-

Draw a picture of a time God kept a promise to you.

God kept His promise, because the Lord will do what He says.

God's Promise

Read about Abraham. Choose the right words to tell the story. Cross out the wrong words.

God made a promise to Abraham Adam. God said, "You will have

100 50

a daughter son." Abraham laughed, "I am 100 50 years old.

15 90

My wife is 15 90 years old. We are too old to have children. But

God said, "I promise. Susan Sarah will have a son. You will name

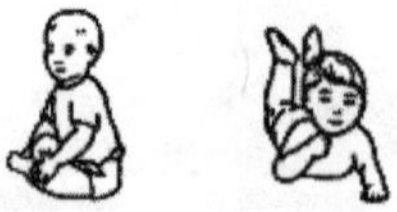

him John Isaac.

When Sarah heard the news, she laughed cried. But God

kept His promise. Sarah gave birth to a baby girl boy. They

named the baby Isaac Anna. Abraham and Sarah were very

happy sad to have a baby.

I will be with you.

Carrie's winter coat is too small. Her family doesn't have money to buy a new coat.

David's family is moving to a new house. He is sad to leave his friends and his big backyard.

Draw a picture of a time you needed something.

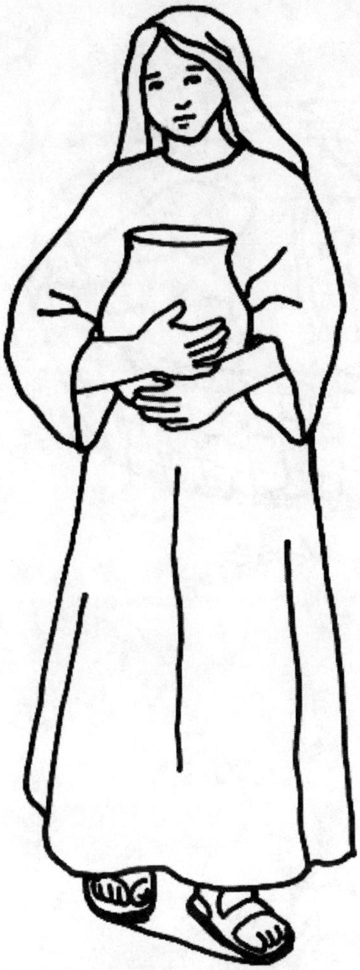

Moses' sister

Moses' mother

Moses

Baby Moses

Pharaoh's daughter

Baby Moses

The Camping Trip

Characters: Narrator, Dad, Mom, Mike, Amy

Narrator: The Clark family was going on a camping trip for the weekend. They had just arrived and were setting up camp.

Dad: Mike and Amy, please go get some sticks so we can start our campfire.

Mom: Be back before dark.

Mike *(to Amy)*: I know where we can find a lot of sticks.

Narrator: Mike and Amy gathered a big pile of sticks. Then Amy had an idea.

Amy: Let's go over by those trees.

Mike: OK. I'll race you.

Narrator: Mike and Amy ran over to the trees. It started to get dark. Mike and Amy could not find their parents. They were lost!

Amy: I'm scared.

Mike: Let's pray. God will take care of us.

Narrator: Mike and Amy prayed to God. They asked God to help them find Mom and Dad. They thanked God for taking care of them.

Dad: Mike! Amy! Where are you?

Mike: We're over here, Dad.

Mom: We're so glad you're safe.

Narrator: God cared for Mike and Amy when they were in the woods. God cares for us wherever we go.

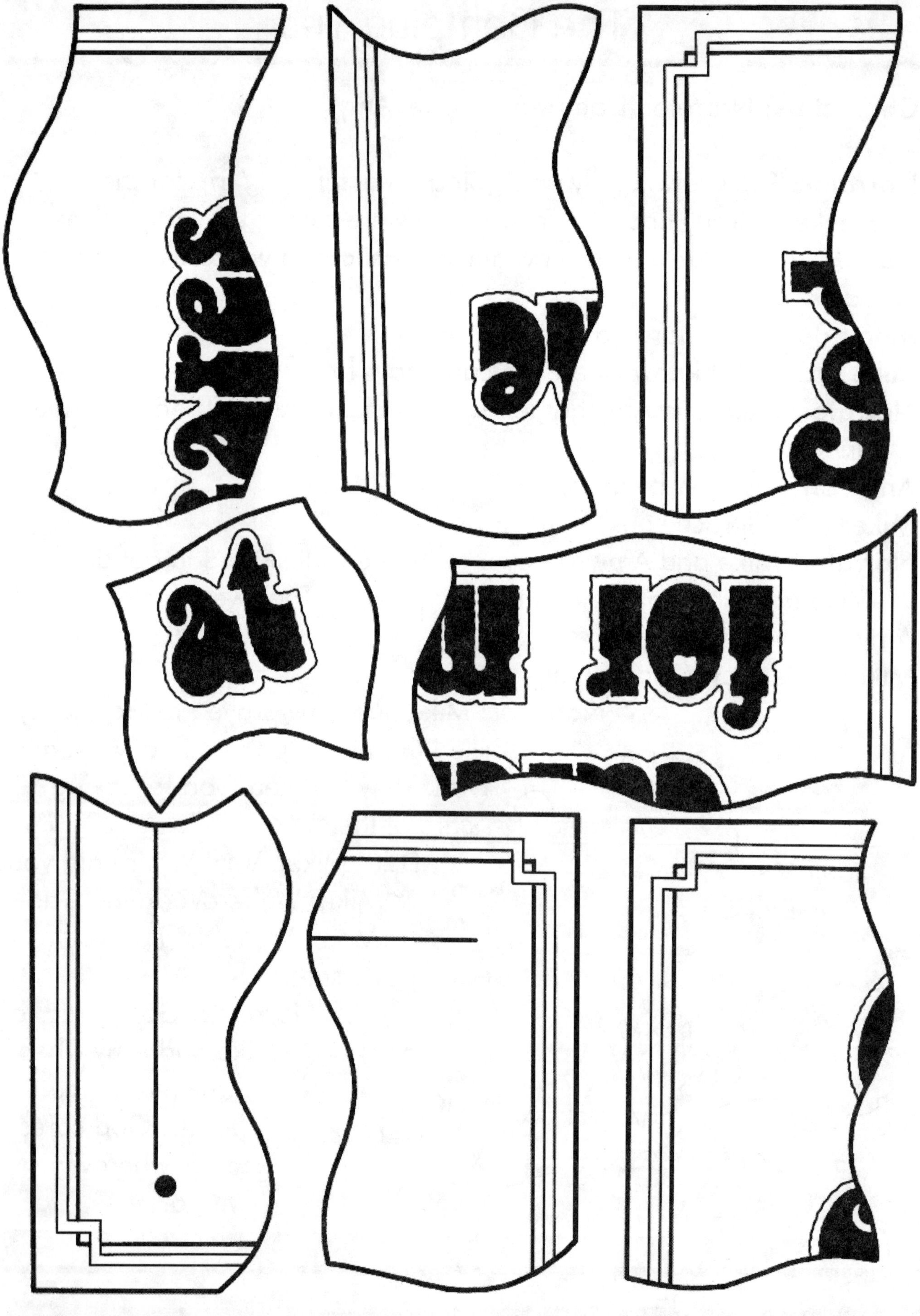
at

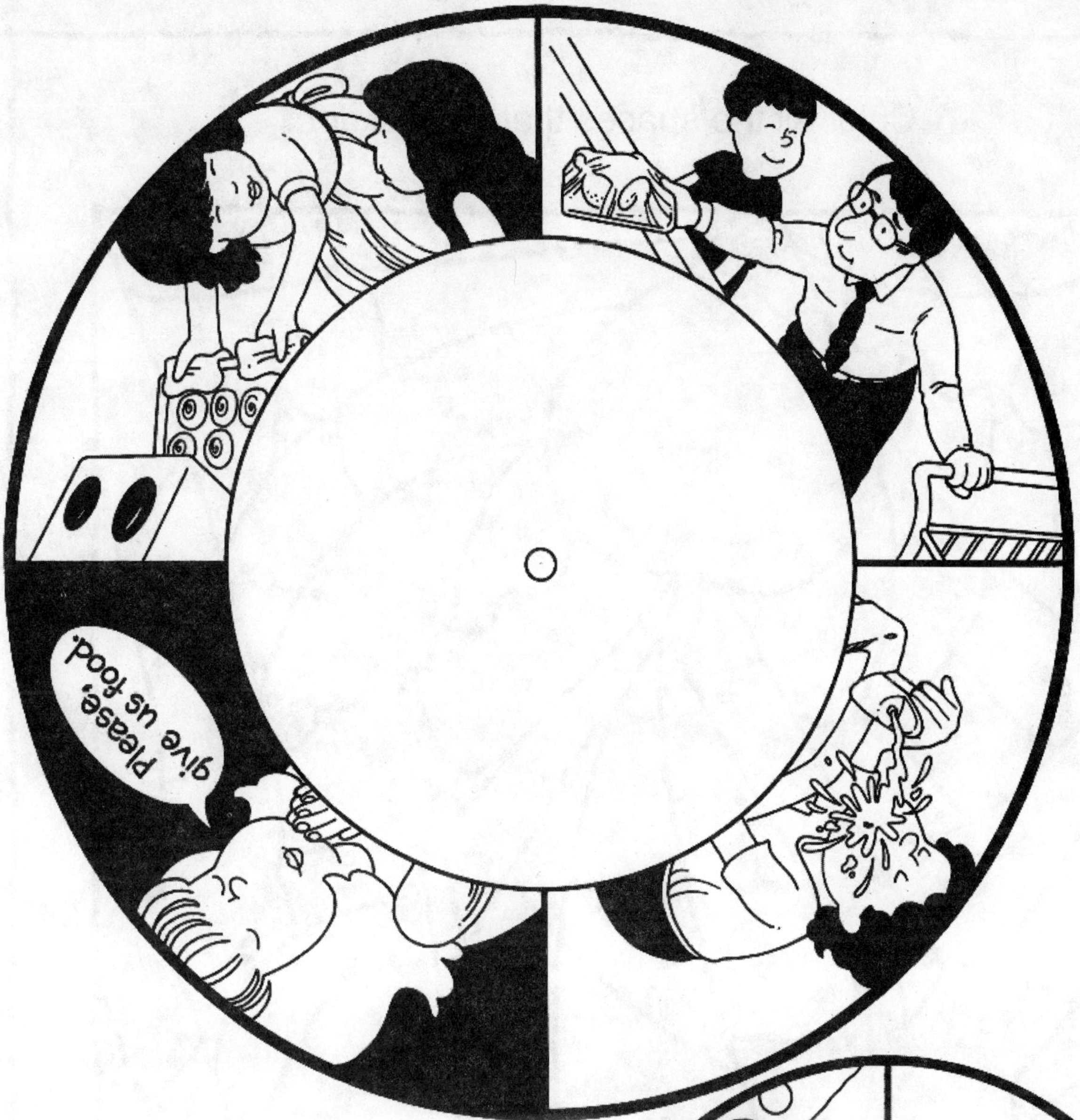
Please, give us food.

We need food

Color all the spaces that have a dot.

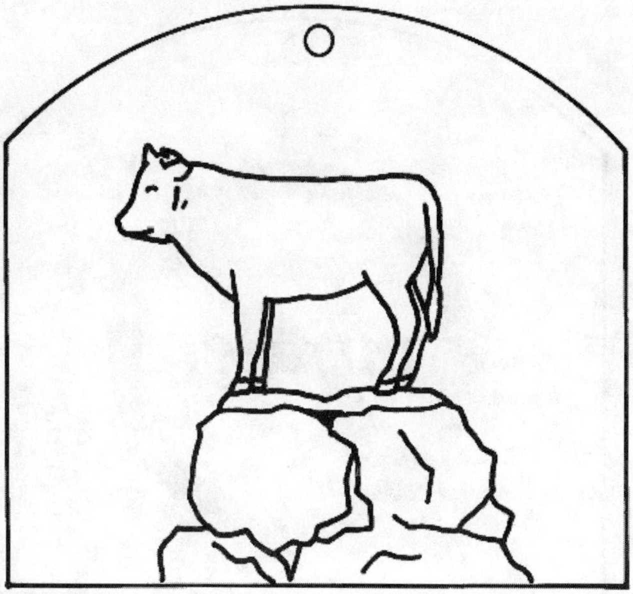

GOD

murder

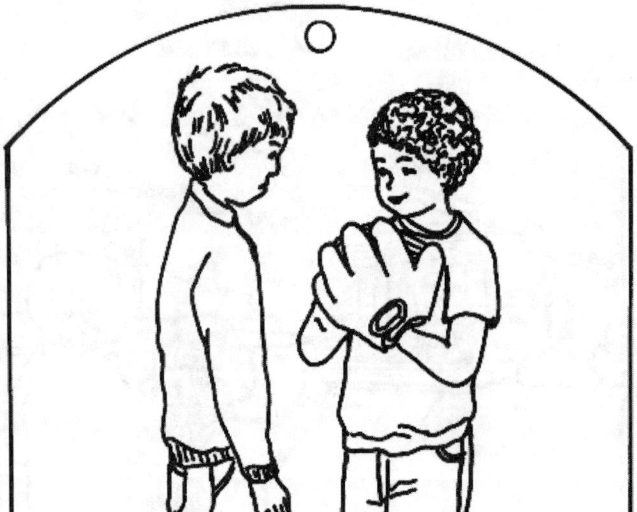

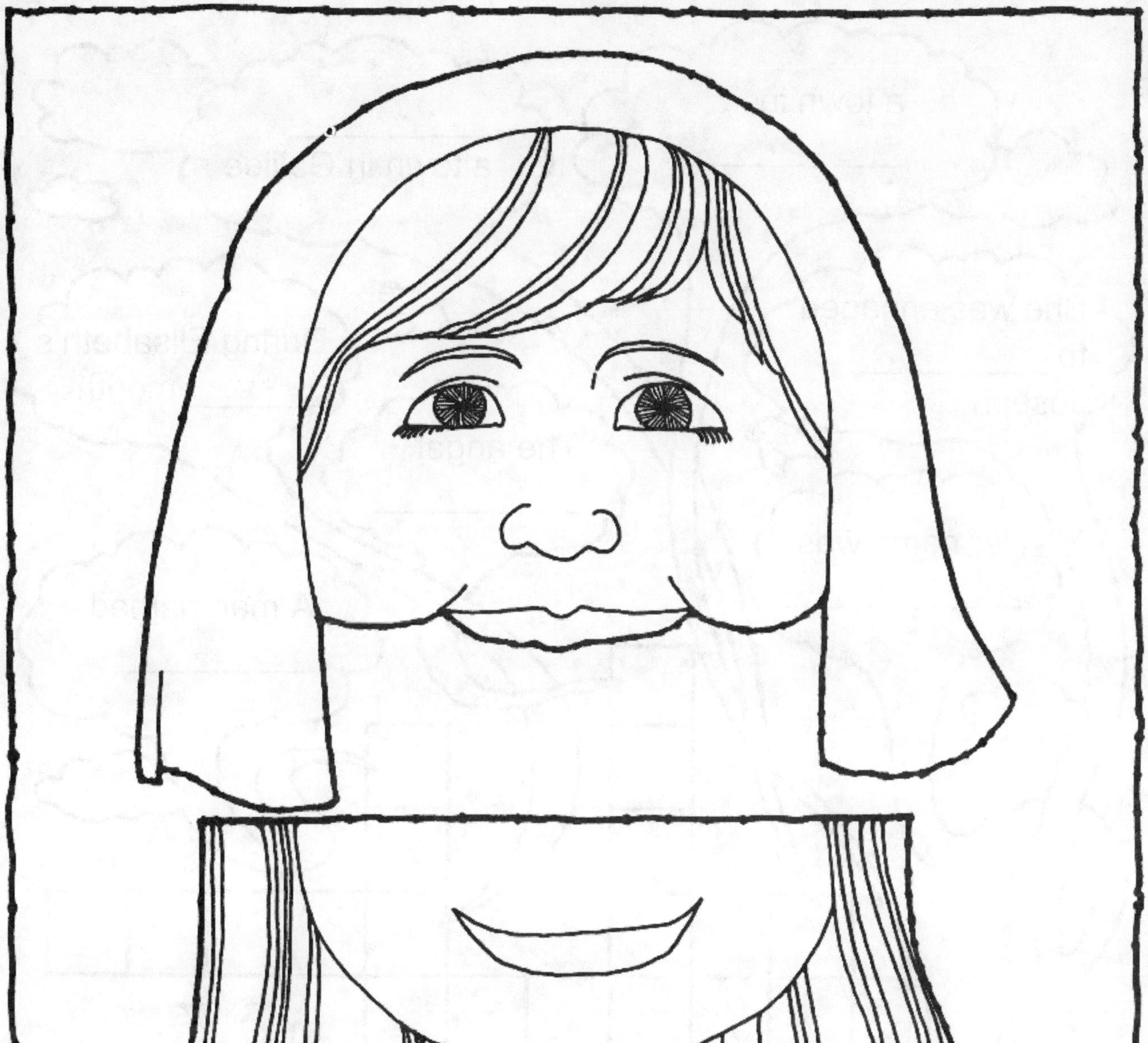

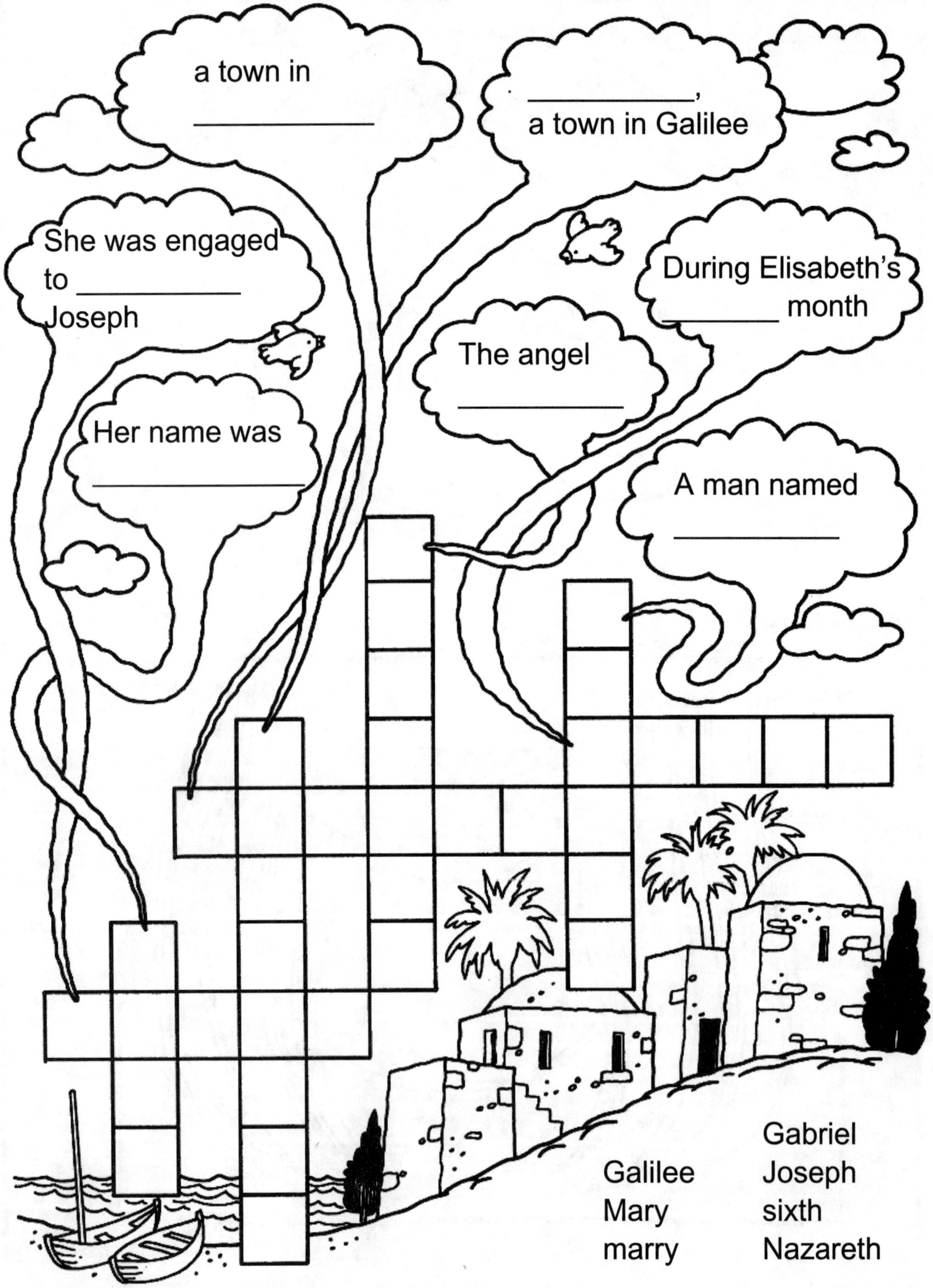
a town in ___________
__________, a town in Galilee
She was engaged to __________ Joseph
Her name was ____________
The angel ___________
During Elisabeth's _______ month
A man named __________
Galilee
Mary
marry
Gabriel
Joseph
sixth
Nazareth

Break the Code

Use the code to to find out something about God's love.

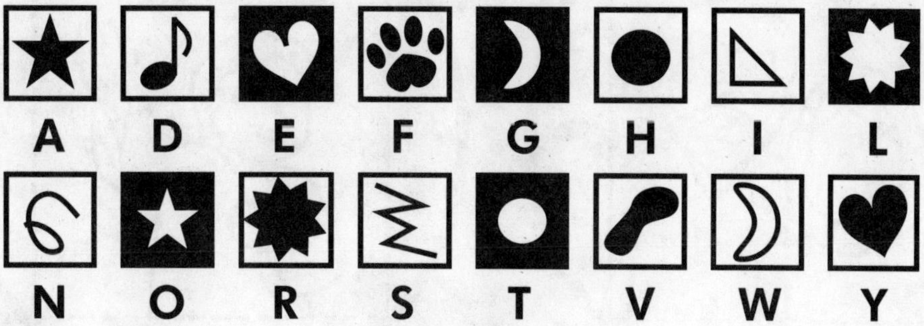

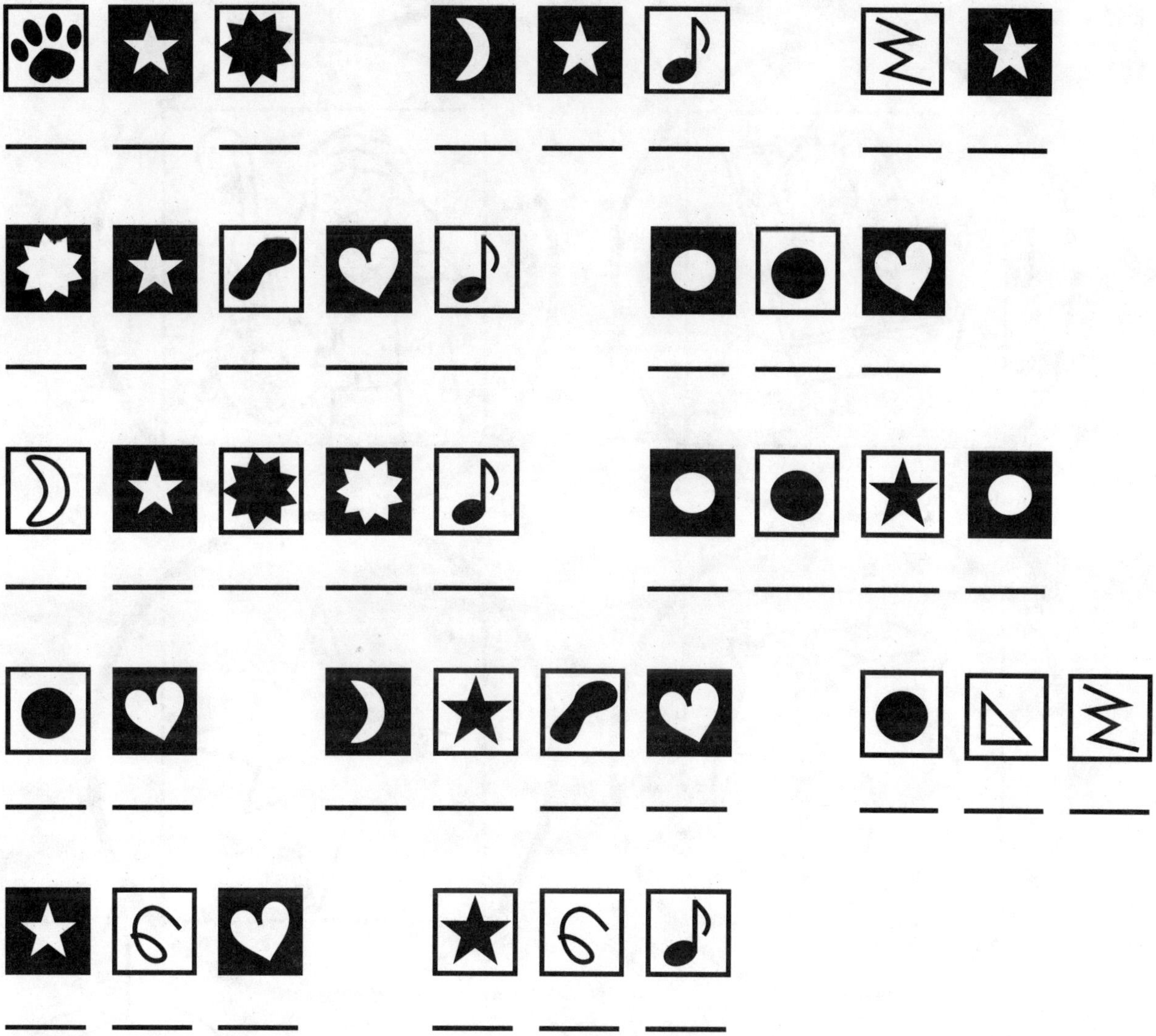

John 3:16a

Dear Jesus,

Love,

Christmas

Worship Calendar

Sunday

Monday

Tuesday

Wednesday

Thursday

Friday

Saturday

The Birthday Party

(Jeff is alone, talking aloud.)

Jeff: I can't wait until my my friends get here for my birthday party. Nine of my friends are coming. That means nine presents! Wow!

(There is a knock at the door. Jeff opens the door. His friend, Sarah, walks in.)

Jeff: Hi, Sarah. That's a pretty package you brought. I can't wait to open it.

Sarah: Oh, sorry, Jeff. This isn't for you. We decided to change things this year. The other kids and I are giving gifts to each other, instead of to you.

Jeff: What? You're coming to my birthday party, but I don't get any gifts. What kind of a party is this?

(Jeff's other friends arrive, one or two at a time. They all begin talking about the gifts they brought for each other. Jeff stands off to one side alone, looking sad.)

Christmas Song

(Tune: "Jingle Bells")

Herod heard;
Prophets told;
Wise men traveled far;
All to see the Baby
That was welcomed with a star!
Angels sang;
Shepherds shook;
Cattle softly mooed.
That is why at Christmas
We say, "Jesus, I love You!"

Praise the Lord!

Leader: Shout with joy to the Lord, all the earth.

Children: *(Children shout.)* Hallelujah!

Leader: Burst into songs and praise.

Children: *(Children sing.)* Praise Him, praise Him, all ye little children. God is love. God is love.

Leader: Make music to the Lord with harps, with harps and the sound of singing.

Children: *(Hum a favorite praise song. Pretend to play a harp.)*

Leader: Blow the trumpets and the sheep's horn.

Children: *(Pretend to blow a trumpet. Make a trumpet sound.)*

Leader: Shout for joy to the Lord, the King.

Children: *(Children shout.)* Hallelujah! Praise the Lord!

Leader: Let everything praise the name of the Lord, the sea, the world, and all who live in it.

Leader and children: Let everything praise the name of the Lord!

Cut out the puzzle pieces. Put the pieces together to make a fish shape. Use the pictures to tell the Bible story.

A friend loves you all the time.

Proverbs 17:17

Jesus is my friend

__________ will be a friend to others.

7

__________ is my church friend.

Dear Jesus

You are my friend

____

____

Love.

____

__________ is my school friend.

How to Be a Friend

Cross out all O's, C's, and Q's. Write the other letters in order in the blanks below.

A	C	O	Q	L	O	O	W	Q	C
A	C	Y	C	Q	C	O	O	O	Q
C	O	Q	S	O	Q	C	C	C	Q
O	Q	C	B	Q	C	C	C	O	Q
Q	C	O	Q	C	C	Q	O	E	Q
K	O	O	O	O	O	Q	C	Q	C
O	O	O	O	Q	C	Q	C	I	C
N	Q	C	O	O	O	Q	D	C	Q

___ ___ ___ ___ ___ ___   ___ ___   ___ ___ ___ ___

Draw a picture to show what you will do to be a friend.

A friend loves at all times
Proverbs 17:17
You can't play with us.
FIRST PLACE
Boots got a hit by a car.
I broke your car. I'm sorry.

Who Are Helpers?

Draw a line from the picture to the helper.

President of the United States
1600 Pennsylvania Avenue
Washington, D.C. 20500

Dear Mr. President,

Jesus Meets a Woman at a Well

Look at the code. Read the words below.
Write the words in the code.

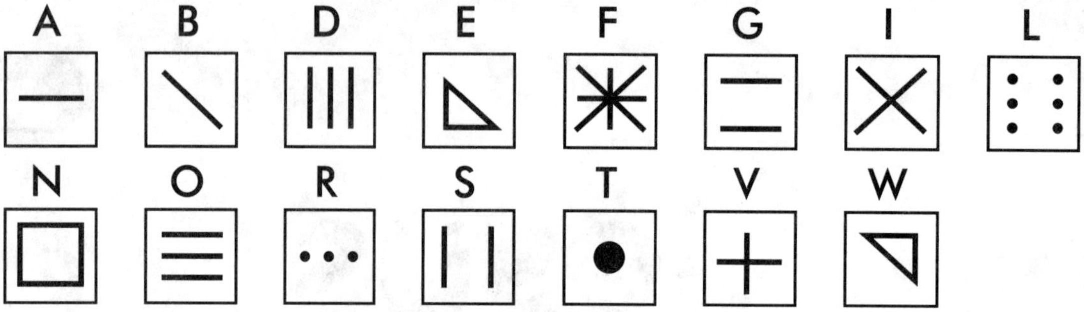

gift

believe

savior

world

eternal
life

When I

Jesus is my friend.

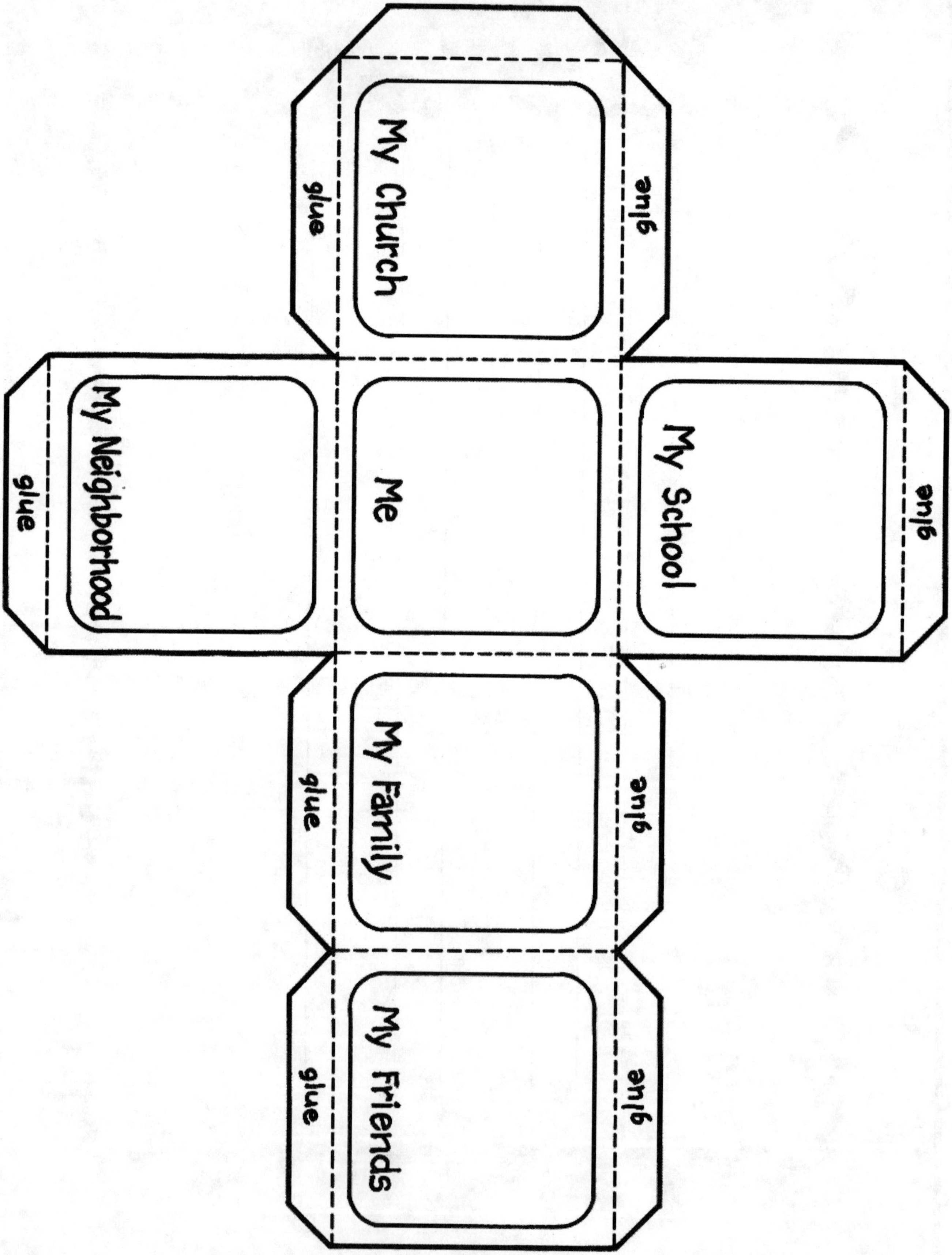
My Church
My Neighborhood
Me
My School
My Family
My Friends
glue

SIMON

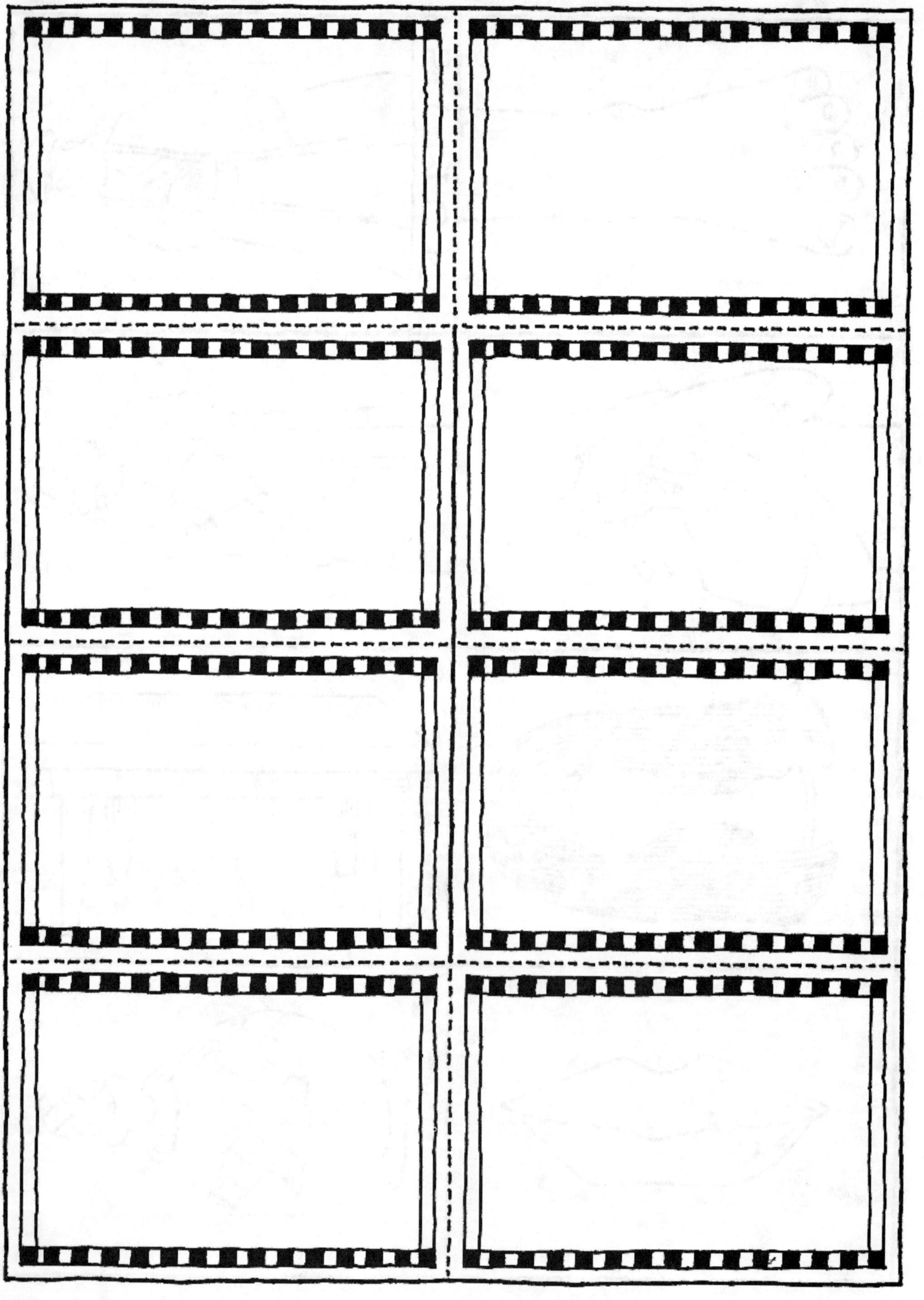

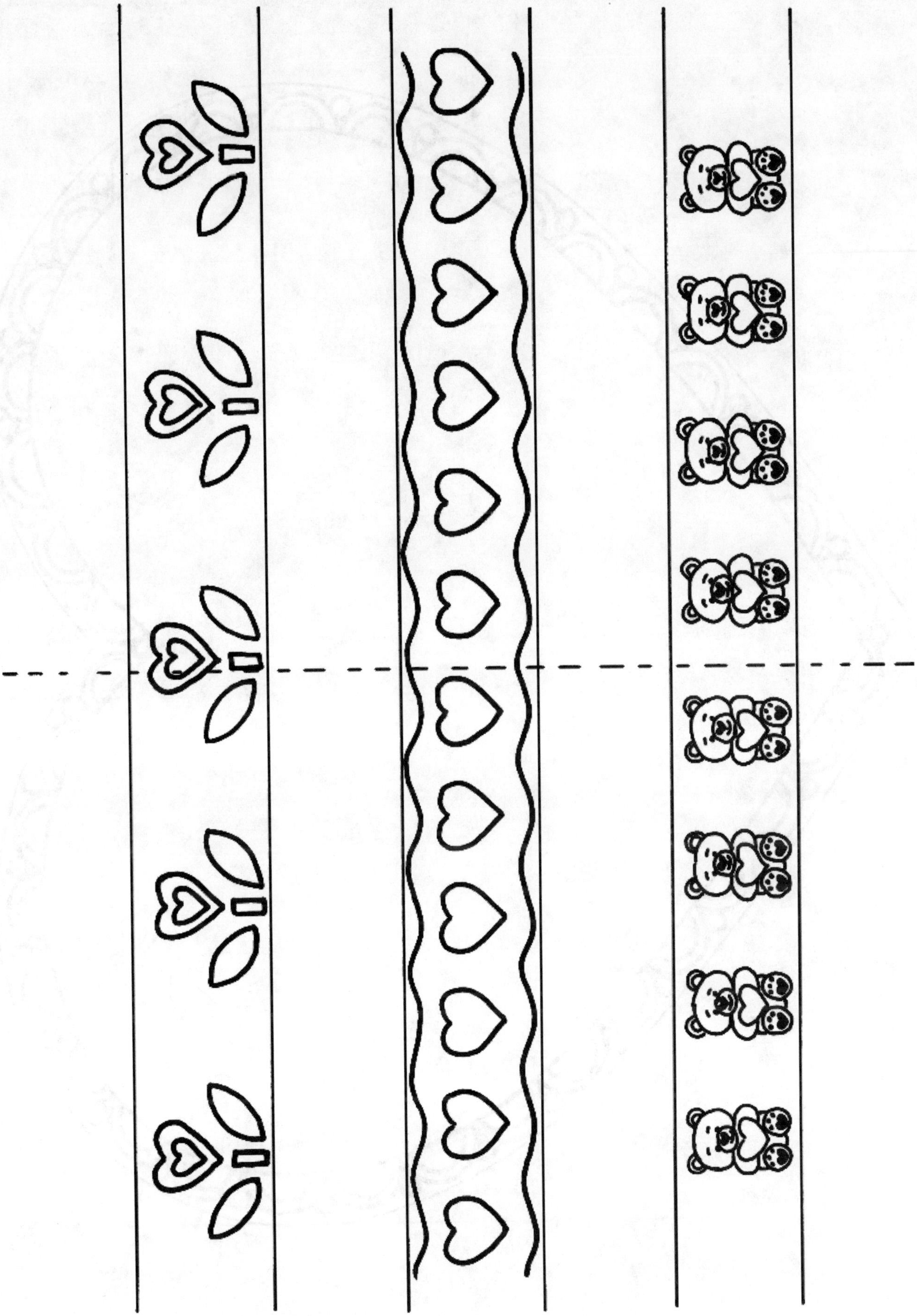

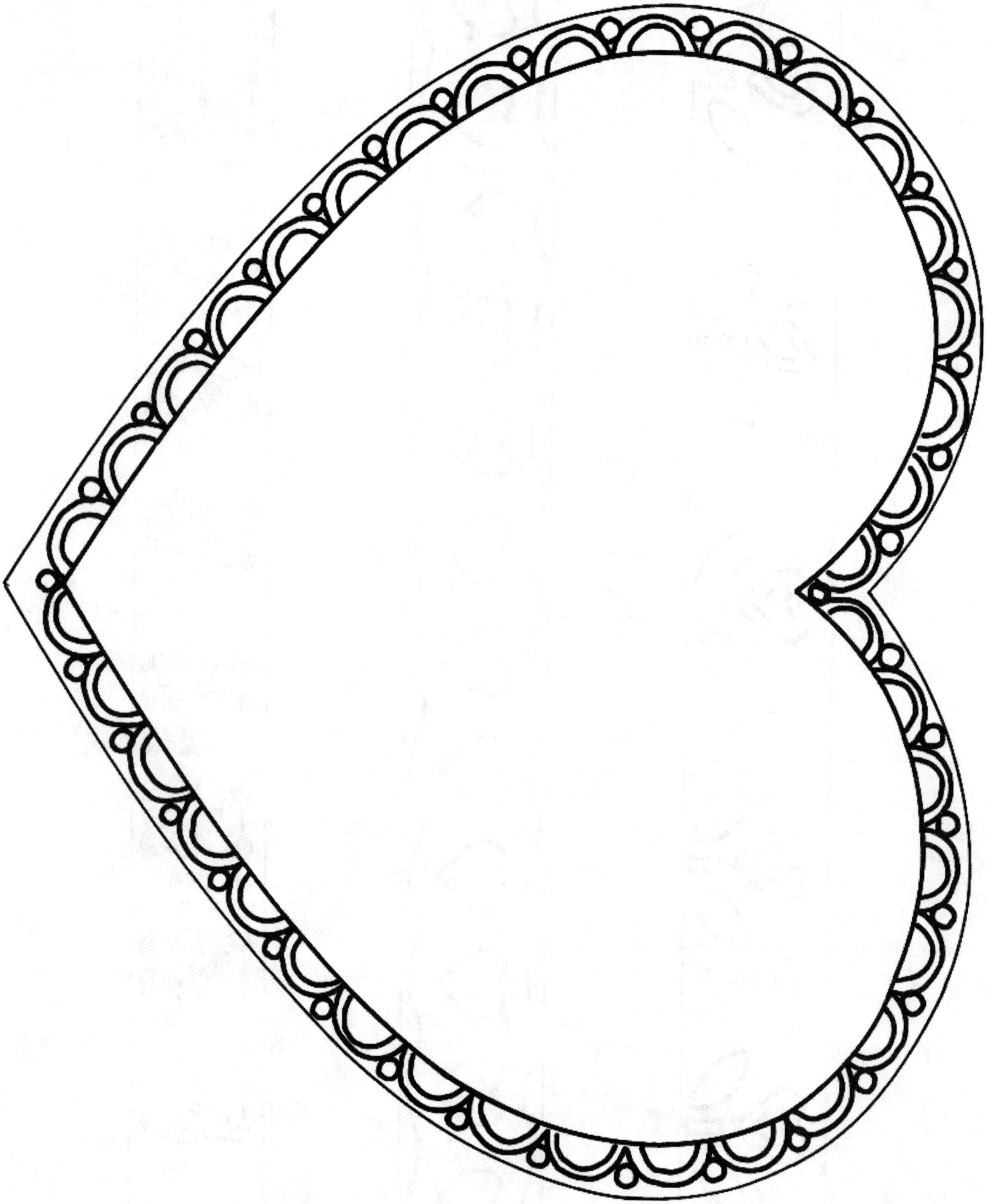

WORSHIP SONGS

God Made the World

Traditional "Farmer in the Dell"
Arr. by Todd Tyler

God Made Me

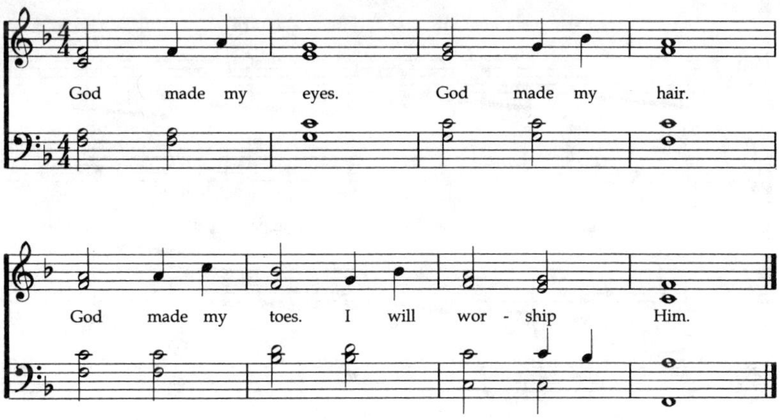

God's Promise Is a Promise

M.K.B. Gently Mary Kay Bottens

God Cared for Moses

Rebecca S. Mahoney

Traditional-Turkey In The Straw

Oh, How We Love God's Rules

Jesus Came

M.K.B. | Mary Kay Bottens

Away in a Manger

V. 1, 2 Anonymous
V. 3 John T. McFarland

James R. Murray

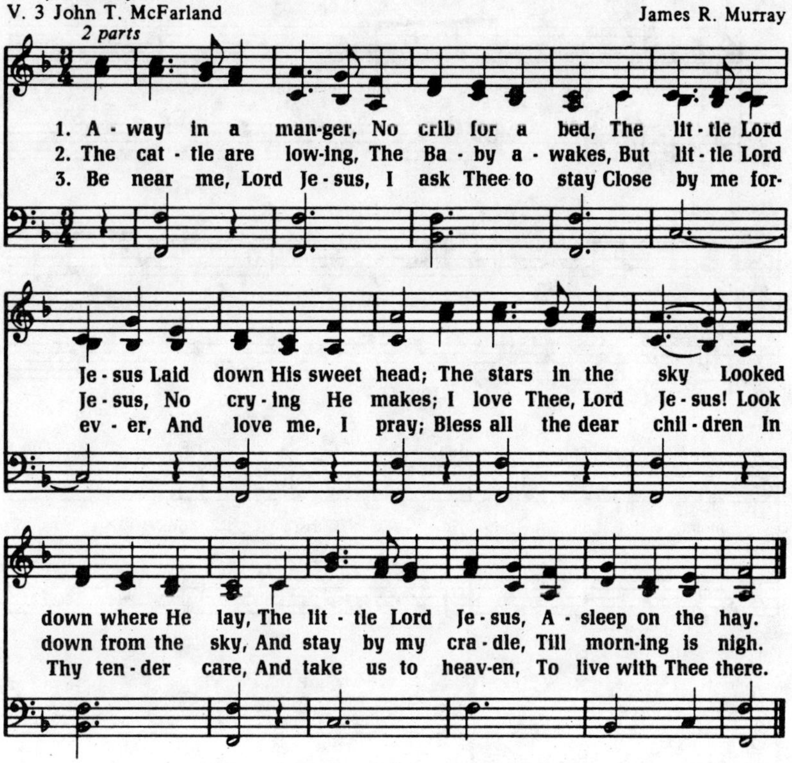

Go, Tell It on the Mountain

Traditional
Arr. by Todd Tyler

Christmas Song

Carla Crane

Traditional "Jingle Bells"
Arr. by Todd Tyler

Jesus, I Want to Be Like You

C.W.P. Cynthia Wagner Pratt

1. Point up.
2. Point to self.
3. Cup hand over ear.
4. Walk in place.
5. Smile.
6. Spoken.
7. Bow head; fold hands.

A Round

J.G. JANET GALLUP

*optional

I Will Be a Friend to You

Carla Crane

Traditional "London Bridge Is Falling Down"
Arr. by Todd Tyler

Jesus Is My Special Friend

Come Follow Jesus Wherever He Leads Us

Mary Kay Bottens

Traditional "Chopsticks"

There Was a Woman at a Well

Carla Crane

Traditional "Bingo"
Arr. by Todd Tyler

Jesus Is my Friend

I Will Be a Friend

Diana Brettschneider

Traditional "Row, Row, Row Your Boat"
Arr. by Todd Tyler

I Will Sing of the Mercies of the Lord Forever

PSALM 89:1 J. H. FULLMORE

Joyfully